T0339757

WAR FOR PROFIT

WAR FOR PROFIT:

ARMY CONTRACTING
VS.
SUPPORTING THE TROOPS

CHARLES M. SMITH

Algora Publishing
New York

Library of Congress Cataloging-in-Publication Data —

Smith, Charles M., CPCM.
 War for profit: Army contracting vs. supporting the troops / Charles M. Smith.
  p. cm.
 Includes bibliographical references and index.
 ISBN 978-0-87586-927-8 (trade paper: alk. paper) — ISBN 978-0-87586-928-5 (hbk.:
alk. paper) — ISBN 978-0-87586-929-2 (ebook) 1. Logistics—Contracting out—United
States—Management—Evaluation. 2. Iraq War, 2003-2011—Logistics—Management.
3. Iraq War, 2003-2011—Personal narratives. 4. United States. Army—Procurement—
Evaluation. 5. KBR (Firm)—Corrupt practices. 6. Defense contracts—United States—
Management—Evaluation. 7. Letting of contracts—United States—Management. I. Title.
 UC263.S54 2012
 355.6'2120973—dc23

                    2012031416

Printed in the United States

To my wife, Jan

TABLE OF CONTENTS

DO WE REALLY SUPPORT THE TROOPS?

The slogan "Support the Troops" becomes a reality when LOGCAP works. When it doesn't work, the troops and the taxpayers both lose.

Most of the housing, meals, laundry, morale boosters, recreation and welfare for US troops in Kuwait, Iraq and Afghanistan, along with a few other countries, were provided the "Logistics Civil Augmentation Program," or LOGCAP. These contracts have spent over $70 billion in taxpayer dollars.

At times this support has been less than adequate. It has certainly been expensive. Over $32 billion was spent on the LOGCAP III contract alone, in Iraq, Afghanistan, Kuwait, Djibouti, the Republic of Georgia and Uzbekistan. Do we know where that money went? Congressional inquiries have found a large amount of waste.

When contracts are mishandled, U.S. strategic goals and servicemen's lives are put at risk, while private pockets are lined and millionaires are made. Congressional oversight bodies need to know where to direct future investigations; and the public needs to know what is being done with precious taxpayer money as well as to take care of our troops. In the meantime, by telling this tale I present a unique angle on the story of US operations in Afghanistan and Iraq.

What Is At Risk?

The United States engages in military operations for reasons deemed to be of utmost national security. If the conduct of such operations could in even a small way be tainted or sabotaged by private pecuniary interests is perilous.

Besides that minor consideration, several hundred thousand American troops have served in Kuwait, Afghanistan, and Iraq since the initiation of conflict following the events of September 11, 2001. A substantial number of US troops are still stationed in Afghanistan, with others stationed in Kuwait and Qatar. These soldiers, sailors, airmen and marines are willing, and often eager, to go in harm's way to perform their duty. They display loyalty to their country and fellow troops in a manner which sacrifices personal safety, the comforts of family life, and the opportunity to advance a more lucrative career. Their loyalty merits the most effective and efficient logistics support which the Army can provide through the LOGCAP program. They will be deployed again and should expect better support than troops received under the LOGCAP III contract.

Whether one agrees with the wars being fought or has opposed them from the beginning, when U.S. troops set out on a mission they need to have every possibility of success. Soldiers perform better when they are well fed, as Napoleon pointed out long ago. They also perform better when they are well rested and have their morale needs cared for. They perform better when they are healthy because base camps have proper sanitation and pure water. They perform better when equipment and supplies arrive at their bases when needed. In Iraq especially, they perform better when a plentiful supply of ice is available. The LOGCAP program is the main source for all of these soldier support requirements.

In addition to the conditions which allow better performance, we owe our troops the greatest degree of safety which can be afforded them, on base as well as in the field. Their bases should have clean water and healthy food. The electrical systems in the base should be safe and not pose a hazard of fatal accidents. We will see that in some cases the soldiers received support which was hazardous to their health and lives.

During Operations Enduring Freedom and Iraqi Freedom, soldiers generally received good support. They received it in a timely manner under difficult circumstances. Thousands of dedicated KBR employees made this happen, and I would never suggest otherwise. Unfortunately, much of this was done at too high a cost. As a student of economics I am very familiar with the concept of opportunity cost. Basically, an excess dollar spent on LOGCAP eliminated the opportunity to provide soldiers with other needed support. During my service on LOCAP through 2005, there was an urgent need for additional body armor, for additional armor for HUMVEEs and for the development of better vehicles to survive IEDs, such as the MRAP. I viewed my job as providing support in both an effective and efficient manner. Effective meant the right support at the right place at the right time. Efficient meant at a cost that did not deprive soldiers of other, more important support.

Evidently this problem was not limited to the United States. During this period KBR was also providing support to British troops operating in the South of Iraq, around the port of Basra. Many of the same problems which we have had under the LOGCAP contract surfaced on KBR's British contract. A good description of these problems is contained in David Scholes' memoir of his time in Iraq as a soldier and a KBR employee.[1]

The Army has an acronym (one of thousands), BLUF, Bottom Line Up Front. When you brief, this is often the first chart. For this book the BLUF is that we spent too much on LOGCAP support. We paid KBR unsupported and unreasonable costs and unearned award fee. We did not provide the proper oversight of LOGCAP III to ensure our troops received effective and efficient support. By wasting this money we deprived the troops of other needed support. In the future we can and must do better.

In this book I cite a large number of sources. These writers have provided invaluable insight and information on the contracting issues which face the military. In addition I want to provide a sense of the amount of information which is available to pursue interest in these issues.

QUESTIONS OF LOYALTY AND RESPONSIBILITY

From 2000 to late 2004, I was the Chief of Field Support contracting for the Army. I managed the $5 billion per year Logistics Civilian Augmentation Program (LOGCAP) contract which provided support to all troops in Iraq and Afghanistan. I was also responsible for the management of pre-positioned stocks program and various other logistics contracts. I was eventually removed from this position due to a disagreement with senior Army leaders over the treatment of the LOGCAP contractor, KBR.

After leaving government service I have testified before Congress, spoken with the Commission on Wartime Contracting, written several

---

1 (Scholes 2008)

articles based upon my experiences with the LOGCAP contract, and cooperated on several newspaper articles concerning that experience. Many civilian and military employees of the US Army consider me to be disloyal, as much of the above is critical of the Army's management of the LOGCAP program.

Of course, loyalty is a complex social virtue. Amid all of one's relationships of being a family member, a citizen, a member of a religion and a professional employed by an organization, there is a web of loyalties; some of which are more important than others. As a professional contracts manager for the US Army I had loyalties to the troops, to the US citizens who paid my salary, to the Army and to my coworkers.

Along with loyalties one also may have certain distinguishable responsibilities. When I studied public administration at the John F. Kennedy School of Government, Harvard University, I had an opportunity to think in some depth on those responsibilities. I felt that my role as a public manager was to create value for the public and to enhance the ability of my organization to create value in the future. In his book *Responsibility*, Oxford philosopher J. R. Lucas writes, "A loyal public servant does not discharge his duty simply by doing what he is told, but must tell the truth, even to his own disadvantage."[2] I have taken this precept to heart and continue to tell the truth about the LOCAP program, even after I have left public employment. When I worked for the Army I always told the truth to leadership, even when I knew the disagreed in advance. This has never been a popular way to advance your career. Many other public servants have followed this same course. The story of Ms. Bunnatine Greenhouse, who objected to the way the Army Corps of engineers handled the Restore Iraqi Oil program is another example. (More later on this story.)

I have written this book on LOGCAP, the Army, Halliburton/KBR and my experience with them with this stance in mind.

BACKGROUND

There are other books which discuss the LOGCAP[3] contract. Some provide useful and interesting information, while others can be a bit misleading. A number of former KBR employees have written memoirs of their service in Iraq and Afghanistan. I have learned something from each

---

2 (Lukas 1993) p. 231

3 In chapter 3 I will explain the LOGCAP program and contract in some (perhaps too much) detail.

of these books and have enjoyed most of the narratives. In addition the New York Times, Washington Post, Los Angeles Times and others have provided helpful coverage of specific issues such as poor water, faulty electrical services and transportation failures.

Since I managed the LOGCAP contracting process from 2000 to late 2004, I can offer a firsthand perspective on this troubled government contract. In August 2004 I was abruptly relieved of that position for reasons which I will explain later. From August 2004 until August 2005, I developed the Army strategy for the LOGCAP IV contract. Upon completing that task, I moved to other duties. During my critical last year on the LOGCAP program, I participated in program briefings to higher authorities along with local program meetings, and I observed the increasingly odd decisions made by the Army on this contract. Since then I have had access to Congressional documentation and testimony, independent research, and discussions with former military, civilian and contractor personnel.

I reached the conclusion that Army decisions were extremely beneficial to the contractor, KBR (Kellogg Brown & Root Services), but these decisions were made at the expense of soldier support and the taxpayer. As Senator Carl Levin said in 2007, "KBR received very favorable treatment from the Army."[4]

While I worked for the Government, I made my views known within my organization, but found myself quite marginalized. After leaving Government, through an earlier than planned retirement, I began to speak to experts in the field, hoping to transfer some of my contracting experience into lessons learned for future support contracting. This led to an article by James Risen in *The New York Times* and my subsequent testimony for the Democratic Policy Committee on two occasions.

In 2003, I had noticed some interest in Congress in oversight of the LOGCAP contract. Representative Henry Waxman, then the minority leader of the House Committee on Government Reform and Investigations, persuaded Representative Davis, the Republican Chairman, to hold several hearings on LOGCAP. When Representative Waxman became Chairman, this committee developed more information about the operation of LOGCAP, especially regarding the problems with electrical wiring in Iraq. In April 2007, the Senate Armed Services Committee held a hearing which elicited testimony from several Army Senior leaders, some of which has turned out to be quite misleading.

---

4   (Senate Armed Services Committee) p. 1

Congress also authorized the Commission on Wartime Contracting, modeled on the Truman Commission of World War II, to investigate several contracting issues, including LOGCAP. This commission has held hearings, taken testimony, interviewed many experts (including me) and issued two interim reports and a final report. While these reports are extremely valuable, I believe the Commission work still does not get to the heart of the problems with LOGCAP.

In fact, as I have reviewed congressional testimony, reports, documentation, newspaper articles and the various books about contracting in Iraq, none of these provide all of the crucial information and perspectives about some of the key points at which the LOGCAP contract went off the rails. While I certainly do not have all of the answers, I can provide additional information and a unique viewpoint for this story.

My Relationship to the Army

For someone like myself, working in Army contracting there are two kinds of professional loyalty, as I noted above, which you can display. One is loyalty towards the troops and the American citizens, who expect you to do your contracting work in an efficient and effective manner. Doing so ensures that taxpayer funds are well spent and that the troops receive the maximum benefit from your work. The other loyalty is to the Army and your leaders. In most cases this is not a problem. Both of these loyalties can center on the same actions. When I worked for GEN Paul Kern, the Commander of Army Materiel Command and Major General Wade Hampton McManus Jr., the Commander of the Army Field Support Command, these two loyalties completely coincided. My leadership in the Army demanded the most effective and efficient support to the troops and taxpayers.

Some people will describe me as another disgruntled employee who had career problems and is taking them out on the Army. I had a wonderful career with the Army and have a deep affection for this agency. I have worked for some of the best leaders I have ever met and with some great soldiers and civilians. I was able to obtain the basic American dream, own a house, cars, raise a family and sent my kids to good colleges and retire with dignity. I accomplished all of this as a public servant, performing valuable and interesting work supporting soldiers.

Army leaders with whom I worked were almost always smart, dedicated men and women of high integrity. The aforementioned GEN Paul Kern, MG Wade Hampton McManus Jr., GEN George Casey, MG Anthony Taguba and MG Vincent Boles are some of those great leaders I will mention in this book. Unfortunately, what I will occasionally refer to as the institutional Army does not always support the ideals of its leaders. The institutional Army occasionally is too defensive to admit problems, too close to contractors and not willing to support soldiers and civilians who challenge the conventional wisdom. These are characteristic of many large bureaucracies and can be found in both government and business.

For example, the Army is a proponent of a lessons learned approach to operations. At the end of an action you review what went right and what went wrong with an eye to future actions. You want to retain what went right and avoid what went wrong. To do this you must be very honest about what went wrong. This will, of course conflict with human nature, which does not like to admit that very much, ever went wrong. The Army did recognize some of the major flaws of the LOGCAP III contract. I was part of the team which corrected those in LOGCAP IV. Some of the problems associated with the old LOGCAP III contract have not been officially recognized and are not corrected under the new LOGCAP IV contract. If I appear extremely critical of the Army, it is mainly due to the need to expand the "what went wrong" analysis.

I am proud to have worked for the Army for 31 years. I have always felt part of a team that was performing a critical service to the United States. I have formed personal relationships which I will treasure for the rest of my life. I have constantly learned from everyone with whom I have worked. My main goal in writing this book is to provide information which can help the Army do a better job of providing soldiers with combat service support.

SERVICE CONTRACTS

This book may also serve as a case study in military service contracts. Most of the military acquisition literature deals with the acquisition of hardware, especially major systems. It used to be the case that most of the money was there. In 1989 defense expert William H. Gregory published a book with the title, *The Defense Procurement Mess*.[5] In this book he discussed systems and spare parts. He had little need to discuss services. Now, however, services account for half of the Defense procurement budget. Paul Light noticed the start of this trend in 1999, mainly in

---

5 (Gregory 1989)

the area of information technology support.[6] Since that time, the increase in military combat support and combat service support contracting has been staggering.

As we shall see with LOGCAP, service contracts present a set of new administration and oversight challenges. To give one example, the Defense Contract Management Agency (DCMA) is responsible for administration of the contracts in the field, especially quality control. Most of the DCMA personnel sent to Iraq and Afghanistan had only experience with production contracts. They came from a Defense contractor's plant, where they oversaw a production line and inspected the quality of parts and systems. They went to Iraq and oversaw a base camp operation, with quality of meals, water, electrical work as their responsibility (along with the contractor, of course). As we shall see, there were significant failures of quality control in all of these areas.

By 2007 military service contracting expenditures reached $152 billion, while hardware procurement was $142 billion.[7] This was the first time the Pentagon spent more on services than on hardware.[8] This trend is steadily increasing. With this amount of money at stake, we need much more analysis of service contracting.

A NOTE ON CONTRACTUAL INTERPRETATION

Throughout this book I will explain the meaning of many of the LOGCAP III and Task Order clauses, scopes of work, referenced regulations and other parts of the contract. The clauses set forth the terms and conditions of the contract, including the statement of the services which the Army is buying from KBR. By doing this I will assign responsibilities to KBR and Government entities.

There may be some people who would disagree with my interpretation of these clauses. I am certainly not the final word on how they may be interpreted. For contractual interpretation the Armed Services Board of Contract Appeals is a prime venue for settling contract disputes. Often the rulings of the Board involve an interpretation of the meaning of contract clauses.

Cases may also be brought before the United States Court of Claims. This is a court specifically established by Congress to hear claims against

6   (Light 1999) p. 24

7   (Erwin 2007) p. 1

8   When reviewing the Pentagon budget, the Procurement section is mainly hardware costs. Services are part of the Operations and Maintenance section, which includes both contracted and organically performed work.

the Government, usually arising out of contractual agreements. Again, the Court of Claims may often be required to provide an interpretation of the meaning of contractual language. Rulings of the Court of Claims may be appealed to the Federal Court of Appeals, but this is rare. In theory, the Supreme Court could hear a contractual case, but this is an extreme rarity. Contractual disputes do not involve constitutional issues and are better decided by the Court of Claims.

All this being said, I base my interpretations of contractual language on my intimate familiarity with the LOGCAP program and contract. I understand the intent of the parties in entering into this contract. I can apply thirty-three years of working in Government contracts, 31 with the Government and two years in a private role. I have hundreds of hours of Government training in contracts, contract administration and contract law. I have thought through these problems on many occasions and have published articles on contract interpretation. I am very comfortable with my understanding of these issues.

ACKNOWLEDGEMENTS

While I have decided to tell this story based upon my personal knowledge and information gather from public sources, I have been aided by thoughtful discussions with a number of people.

Jim Risen got me into this and I appreciate his efforts to publicize my story. I thoroughly enjoyed our conversations and learned much from his approach to these issues. I consider his reporting work in national security issues an extremely valuable contribution to the public understanding of many vital and complex problems.

Dina Rasor and Bob Bauman have shared information and provided support. Their book, *Betraying Our Troops*, is a thoroughly researched and accurate account of many issues surrounding LOGCAP through 2005. The book is also well written and very readable. Their continuing attention to issues of defense contracting should be followed by all policy makers in this area. Ms. Razor's other Books; *More Bucks, Less Bang* [9]and *The Pentagon Underground* [10] are also well worth the read.

Leslie Gross-Davis provided invaluable support for my appearances before the Democratic Policy Committee. She is a fine public servant; smart, dedicated and a wonderful person. I have thoroughly enjoyed working with her.

---

9   (D. Rasor, More Bucks Less Bang 1983)
10   (D. Rasor, The Pentagon Underground 1985)

Debbie Crawford, known as Ms. Sparky, is an invaluable source of information concerning troop support and contractors on the battlefield. She worked in the Green Zone for KBR and now manages a web site "Ms Sparky's Mishaps and Misadventures" (www.mssparky.com). Don't let the title fool you. Having established a large web of colleagues and sources, she often beats the major media in reporting on events involving military support contractors. She is a staunch supporter of the troops and also of the contractor workers, who are often harmed as much as the troops by the actions of these firms.

Mr. Donald Trautner was the head of the LOGCAP program office at Ft. Belvoir during my time with the program. Don shared with me with his extensive knowledge of the history of the program. Don was also the best traveling companion you could ever hope for when in Southwest Asia.

My Army LOGCAP team provided me with constant information and analysis when I managed these contracts. Mary Beth Watkins, Dick Terhune, Val Duhart, Grant Curtis, Greg Tetter, Andre Batson, Justin Hirniak, John Wilson and Pat O'Farrell were the epitome of dedicated public service. These are smart and experienced people who created value for soldiers and taxpayers. The public should know that Army has many such workers, both soldiers and civilians, who always are striving to keep our country safe.

Mr. Randy Barthelome worked with me on the LOGCAP IV strategy team. I have known him for over thirty years and learned many things from his experience in contracting policy and the management of source selection.

Finally, Marshall Collins has been a friend and a sounding board for over 30 years. Much of what I know about effectively managing a contracting operation, I learned from Marshall. My last years in Government would have been impossible without his support.

My family has put up with me throughout all of this, from working for the Government through becoming a public figure on LOGCAP to the completion of this book. It has not always been easy. For their constant support I am proud and grateful.

Of course, any flaws in this book are my responsibility alone.

Chapter 1. Overrun by the Taliban, then by KBR

On October 3, 2009, Taliban insurgents overran Combat Outpost Keating in the Kamdesh District of Nuristan in Afghanistan. Eight American soldiers were killed and 22 were wounded. The Army sent a three star general to investigate the incident. He released a report in February 2010. The report identified several factors which led to the tragedy. An excerpt from the report, printed in the New York Times, stated:

> The investigation concluded that critical intelligence, surveillance and reconnaissance assets which had been supporting C.O.P. Keating had been diverted to assist ongoing intense combat operations in other areas, that intelligence assessments had become desensitized to reports of massing enemy formations by previous reports that had proved false, and needed force protection improvements were not made because of the imminent closure of the outpost," the report said. "These factors resulted in an attractive target for enemy fighters.[11]

Not only did the report describe the failures, but specific individuals were held accountable for these failures through administrative review of their actions. Officers were removed and saw the end of their careers. This appears to be the appropriate response to this event. There was a thorough after action review. Lessons learned identified things that went wrong. Things that went right were also noted. (The soldiers were well trained and fought well.) Finally, individuals were held accountable for poor decisions.

---

11 (Nordland 2010) p.1

In 2004, the Army was overrun by KBR. Leaders attempting to enforce the LOGCAP III contract in the interest of the Army were pushed aside. Defense Contract Audit Agency (DCAA) audits were ignored as unsupported costs were accepted for the purpose of setting fees. High award fees were paid to KBR while the Army ignored any reports of poor performance. Unreasonable dining facility costs were shielded from DCAA post contract audit. In the process soldiers were denied the benefit of wasted resources, KBR was made whole from their own mistakes and Halliburton saw its stock rise.

In a sense, I was one of the casualties of this operation. It was August of 2004. For two days I had been attending various meetings with Government and contractor personnel working on the Army's LOGCAP contract. We were meeting in a typical hotel conference room, round tables throughout, a screen in front with the usual power-point presentation, so beloved of the military playing out. Representatives of the Army Field Support Command, my organization, the Defense Contract Management Agency, the Defense Contract Audit Agency and the contractor, KBR, were in attendance. When I walked into the meeting room after a break, I immediately knew something was wrong! The manager of the Ammunition Contracting Division was in attendance at this LOGCAP contract partnering session. Since in that role he did not belong at this meeting, I was fairly sure I had just been replaced. The fact that no one had mentioned this to me was in keeping with my fairly low expectations for management support, at this point.

SETTING THE STAGE

I grew up in Louisville, Kentucky in the 1950s. My father was a decorated Navy officer, serving in World War II and the Korean War. My mother was a public school teacher who taught at a school with very disadvantaged children. Integrity, loyalty and public service were important, as was education. Thus I earned a BA in Philosophy and Economics and did some graduate study before setting out to earn a living for my family.

I had a wife and a son at this point and so was concerned about building a secure life with them. I took the Civil Service PACE test and began a procurement career in the Army, and I stayed with it until February 2008. I found the career varied, interesting and satisfying. When I negotiated major contracts, I was negotiating in the interest of the public and of the Army. I learned to obtain equipment and services at a fair value, with quality and timeliness taken into account, from savvy, experienced and intelligent colleagues. As they also had high ethical standards, this was an exceptional environment to learn the job of military contracting.

One highlight came in 1981, when I led a team which negotiated contracts priced at over $1 billion for the fire control systems that went into the M1 Abrams Tank, along with spare parts and other services. Prior to this, the M60 Tank series — like the Bradley Fighting Vehicle program — had always received their fire control components late, meaning that most tanks spent their first few months in a parking lot. We were able to negotiate a price that included a solid engineering support unit at Hughes Aircraft, along with an exceptional quality assurance unit. Hughes included a warranty at no cost because they could rely on the quality of the product, and the M1 tanks rolled off the production line with a full set of quality fire control equipment in place. We also reduced the costs of maintenance and repair parts by buying the quality up front.

In 1986, I was granted a long-term training assignment at the John F. Kennedy School of Government at Harvard, where I received a Masters Degree in Public Administration. The ironic aspect of this is that I can truly say that this experience had no positive effect on my career. As long as you have a Masters Degree, whether from Harvard or a degree mill, it counts the same for the Government. Some leaders are also wary of academic accomplishment, which can be seen as a threat. They prefer to promote people who might be more compliant in executing programs.

FIELD SUPPORT

In 1999, COL William Pulscher, the Army Industrial Operations Command director of Procurement, called me into his office. He asked me to take on a new assignment and work with a team which was planning Command reorganization. The Army is really experienced in reorganization; we did it about every three years. This reorganization was to create a subordinate command which would be dedicated to providing various logistics support to troops in the field. This subordinate command would need a contracting division, structured to provide effective support for the mission.

COL Pulscher had already assigned two officers, LTC John Wilson and MAJ Terry Moses to this team. He said he wanted me to provide some "adult leadership" to the group. This was not a criticism of the two officers, who were among the very best I worked with. COL Pulscher recognized that I had over twenty years of contracting experience and that the new organization would be mainly a civilian operation. While John Wilson brought field contingency contracting experience and Terry had worked several acquisition assignments, I had broad experience in contracting and with civilian organizations.

This job offered some new and different work, since it would be an organization contracting mainly for services, rather than the supplies which I usually bought. John and Terry proved to be wonderful people with whom to work, as was most of the larger team creating the new command. The overall team was under the leadership of the Deputy Commander, OSC: BG Jerome Johnson (whom we will meet again).

Our contracting team explored the various ways the new command would use contracts for this support. The main way, at the time, was the re-alignment of contracting for pre-positioned stocks, which the command currently managed. Pre-positioned stocks, or war-reserve stocks, are sets of army material located in places the army may need to fight. At this time there were significant stocks in Europe and Korea. To meet unforeseen contingencies, some stocks were kept aboard ships, available to move to possible operations. Finally, we were working to establish some stockpiles in Southwest Asia, specifically at a base in Doha, Qatar.

Each set of stocks was required to undergo routine maintenance on a set schedule. In Europe and Korea, maintenance workers were provided through Host Nation Support. The maintenance of the stocks on board ship was done through a contract at a maintenance base in South Carolina. Reflecting the lack of host nation support capabilities in Southwest Asia, the stocks in Qatar were maintained by a contractor.

A Fateful Suggestion

In one of our meetings, I made a recommendation which was to have extensive consequences for me and for the Command. I was familiar with the LOGCAP program, which provided logistics support to deployed troops. The current LOGCAP II program, which was at the end of its five-year contract period, was managed by the Communications and Electronics Command (CECOM). Since CECOM primarily developed and procured communications and electronic equipment, I voiced the opinion that the new Field Support Command was a much better fit for LOGCAP. My superiors agreed and so did our HQ, Army Material Command.

We immediately established a team to put together a solicitation for the LOGCAP III contract. Mary Beth Watkins, a contracting officer who had worked for me earlier, volunteered to be the PCO on the source selection. A specialist named Richard Terhune was also assigned to the team. Together they led the team which competitively awarded LOGCAP III to KBR, a subsidiary of Halliburton, in December, 2001.

Prior to award of LOGCAP, I had my introduction to life in southwest Asia. I traveled several times to our pre-positioned stocks base in Doha, Qatar and to another Army base in Kuwait. Prior to the war, Qatar and Kuwait were relatively safe places to be. Crime was virtually non-existent and you could walk the streets alone at any time of day or night. Much of the population was comprised of contract workers from other countries. The number of actual Qatari or Kuwaiti citizens was comparatively small. These other country nationals knew that any incident would result in immediate deportation, with loss of a good income (compared to conditions in their own countries). Even worse would be prison time, for the conditions were quite harsh.

Qatar was my first introduction to 120°F temperatures (think Phoenix in August). Water was available everywhere on the military base, since you need some after walking one hundred yards outside. This harsh environment necessitated that all vehicles were stored and maintained in warehouses. Maintenance of equipment at this location proved to be an important contribution to the up-coming war in Iraq.

City Centre was the town's combination of modern buildings and traditional-style souks (market places) where everything was sold—including cooking pans that were big enough to roast a whole camel. The most impressive buildings in the city were the palaces of the emir. They were residences for the large royal family and the home of critical government offices.

September 11 Changes Everything

On September 11, 2001, we all knew that life had changed for us. We commenced immediate planning to use LOGCAP resources to support operations in and around New York City. We offered to set up a small base for relief and recovery workers under the contract. As it turned out, the New York National Guard and FEMA were able to handle the situation.

My team started to plan for operations in Afghanistan, where the Taliban were sheltering Osama bin Laden, who was considered the mastermind behind the 9/11 attacks. It was obvious our response would be there. Under LOGCAP, bases were setup in Uzbekistan and the Republic of

Georgia to serve as platforms for Special Forces operations. Early in 2002, I also became quite aware that planning was underway for operations in Iraq.

On October 30, 2002, White House Spokesman Ari Fleischer declared that, "The only interest of the United States has in the [Persian Gulf] region is furthering the cause of peace and stability, not [Iraq's] ability to generate oil."[12] Almost immediately thereafter, I was asked to attend a meeting of a group that was planning for restoring Iraq's ability to generate oil following the planned invasion.

The group was chaired by Michael Mobbs, deputy to Douglas Feith the DOD Under Secretary for Policy. The group was comprised of former oil company executives, CIA intelligence agents, State Department officials and DOD officials. They seemed to accept as a fact that a war with Iraq would take place. Their mission was not just to put our fires, as it had been in the first Gulf war, but to restore Iraqi oil production.

Based upon their intelligence, this would be a hard job. Even if the fields were not fired and the plants destroyed, the oil infrastructure was in terrible condition. Saddam had not put any of the oil revenue into maintaining the oil system. Instead, he built palaces and distributed enough food to keep the population in check. If the mission involved oil field fires and replacing dynamited facilities, it would be a big undertaking.

While some legal analysis disagreed, I determined that the planning for this eventuality was within the scope of the LOGCAP contract.[13] I had an affirmative legal ruling from DOD counsel, and I was satisfied that the planning portion of LOGCAP supported this effort. I was firm in demanding that the planning scope require a plan which any qualified company could execute. I later approved buying pre-positioned equipment for this mission under LOGCAP.

As the war approached, we were asked to write the order that would assign the mission to KBR. At this point I balked.

We could do that, but not as a task order within the scope of LOGCAP. Some official would have to sign a justification document stating why only KBR could do this mission. We thought this would be hard to justify as we had done market research and identified several companies who could perform this work. I assured the team we could do a quick, secret solicitation and have a contractor ready for the operation. Shortly after stating this position, I was informed that the Army Corps of Engi-

---

12 (Fleischer 2002)
13 I will describe the LOGCAP contract in detail later.

neers would execute the contract. My Commanding General was very appreciative when I told him we were out of the oil field business.

Later Ms. Bunnatine Greenhouse, the highest ranking contracting official at the Corps, lost her position because she also agreed that it was not a valid requirement to merely assign this to KBR. She recommended a one year contract with competition to follow. This was absolutely the right call, but the Corps punished her for making it. Ms. Greenhouse is an exceptional public servant who retains my admiration for her actions.

I also used my pre-positioned stocks contracts to prepare for the war. We had quite a bit of equipment in Qatar which could be moved to Kuwait to meet a deploying Army division and then move into Iraq. This would leave the maintenance personnel in Qatar with nothing to do. I used a clause in their contract to move their maintenance effort to Camp Arifjan in Kuwait. They would be available to work on equipment arriving in Kuwait and moving into Iraq. They would also be available to do repair on battle damaged equipment when the war began.

It was clear that the Administration had planned to go to war in Iraq in the summer of 2002. Whether I agreed or not, this was going to happen and it was going to involve thousands of US soldiers. My job was to provide support for them in any way possible.

Like other US citizens, I have a personal view about whether this war was correct or not. In my position, I was able to put aside personal views to ensure effective and efficient troop support. As a member of the Vietnam generation, I have been very pleased to know that the US public have supported the troops no matter what they think about the war itself. Soldiers heading to the Area of Operations (AOR) know that they go abroad with the support of their family and neighbors. When they return, they are also met with appreciation by their fellow Americans. While we need to do more for these veterans, this is a positive change from the 60s and 70s.

INTO KUWAIT AND IRAQ

My first trip to Iraq was directed by my Commanding General, when he was asked about effective support to the Multi-National Division. About twenty-four countries were offering troops to support operation. They were combined in one combat division, Commanded by a Polish Major General, as Poland sent the most soldiers. Since they were not a constituted unit of any country, unlike US and British units, they needed even more support than our troops. LOGCAP would not only provide base camp support, but would provide all non-tactical vehicles. This included trucks, ambulances, fire trucks and an assortment of miscellaneous vehicles.

Don Trautner, the manager of our Washington, DC, LOGCAP office, and I traveled to Kuwait and on to Iraq.

We traveled on commercial airlines to Kuwait City. At that point one did not need a passport or visa to enter Kuwait as part of the U.S. military. I showed the immigration officer my military ID card and was waived through. We were met by KBR personnel upon our arrival at the Kuwait airport, one of the many tasks they performed under the LOGCAP contract.

We were taken to the grandiose and infamous Khalifa Resort, where KBR had set up their local headquarters, including their purchasing operations. KBR employees generally flew into Kuwait City and were billeted in high style. There they received their equipment and assignment, and after a couple of days they moved on. While at the resort, they lived very well. Rooms were spacious and meals were excellent. My team worked to correct this situation and by my last trip KBR employees were bunking four to a room and the meal quality was under control.

Don and I moved on to Camp Arifjan, the major US base in Kuwait. Here the accommodations, while certainly good by military standards, were not resort quality. We met with officers of the Coalition Forces Land Component Command (CFLCC). Kuwait was the staging area for forces entering and leaving Iraq. It also contained the port of entry for supplies and the staging area for convoys moving into Iraq. Operations of the bases, airfields, port of entry and movement of supplies was all contracted out to KBR under LOGCAP. I was able to observe some of KBR's performance at camp Arifjan, especially the dining facilities. While the facilities operated in an effective manner, employees seemed to have a lot of down time.

KBR was running their regional purchasing from the resort. I visited the operation and found it to be poorly organized and chaotic. This later became a major problem during the DCAA auditing of KBR purchasing, as records were hard to find, if they could be found at all. A KBR purchasing agent, Henry Bunting, testified before Senator Byron Dorgan's Senate Democratic Policy Committee about the abuses he found at this operation. Many purchases were non-competitive, when competition would have reduced the cost. KBR evidently worked hard to avoid DCAA auditors.[14]

---

14 (Chatterjee, Halliburton's Army 2009) pp. 183-186 provides additional detail.

Forward to Baghdad

After a couple of days we flew to Baghdad. We arrived late in the evening. The temperature had hit 137° that day. We where billeted with some 40 Ukrainians on cots in a grand ball room in the Al Faw Place building, a part of the sprawling Camp victory complex. This palace was the building where Steven Colbert later performed for the troops. Unfortunately, power was out, due to very accurate Air Force bombing. The temperature in our room at night did not drop below 110° and there was little air circulation. We slept an hour or so, awoke and drank a quart of water and dozed off. This former ball room was already occupied by about forty of our closest Ukrainian friends, who had staked out cots by the windows. Our cots, in the middle of the room, had no air circulation. We slept an hour or so, awoke and drank a quart of water and dozed off. After the first night I found a space on an outdoor balcony to put my cot and slept a little better after that.

We met with KBR managers to work on the issue of obtaining and moving non-tactical vehicles into Iraq and to the Multi-National Division. At this point any delay was too much for the military. The mission was in progress and the vehicles essential. I believe that a large part of this problem was the lack of planning for the multinational aspects of the operation.

A couple of days later we arranged security to travel to the Multi-National Division headquarters. The Army provided about 18 soldiers, three HUMVEES armed with two fifty cal machine guns and one MK19 Grenade machine gun, and a couple of unarmored SUVs. Since I had been responsible for buying these weapons about 15 years before, I sure hoped that I had done a good job. A soldier informed me that there was a 9mm pistol underneath my seat, just in case.

In the camp at Babil, we met Polish Major General Andrzej Tyszkiewicz who was commanding the Multi-national Division. It occurred to me that this officer had spent most of his military career planning to attack NATO forces in the Fulda Gap in southern Germany. Now he was commanding a division in support of U.S. military action. With twenty-four different nationalities under his command he had a tough assignment. He told me that unlike most division commanders, if something went wrong he did not hear from his military department but from the Polish State Department. A casualty among any of the other nations' soldiers could be an international incident.

MG Tyszkiewicz was an intelligent man with a lot of logistics problems. His first had to do with port-a-potties. US Marines had formerly run the base and had contracted with a local service for placement and maintenance of port-a-potties. They were not emptying these facilities on a regular basis. Even seasoned soldiers had trouble using the facilities due to the smell. LOGCAP and KBR were able to quickly solve his problem (this is one example of the many things KBR employees did well). KBR knew that they had to keep the base commander happy. Unfortunately, that seemed to be one of their few guiding principles.

His next problem was food. He had troops from 24 nations. Some troops expected bacon and eggs for breakfast. European troops expected cold cuts, cheese and bread. There were troops from Thailand and Nicaragua to be fed. The commander had already imported bakers from the Polish army to work on the European bread problem. The logistics of supporting a 24-nation division had never been planned for, let alone executed.

We spent the day working with a great DCMA Administrative Contracting Officer and a good KBR site manager. On other occasions, we came across KBR managers who ignored things which were not on the CG's radar, such as basic camp infrastructure maintenance. This was to create major problems later on.

The return trip to Baghdad, Camp Victory was by a different route, as travel operated on the principle of using several routes, in a random pattern. The opposition knew what was the best route just as surely as we did; should we always use the best route, they would always target it. Using random routes provided better security. This approach was an outgrowth of the economic discipline of game theory.

The highway we took was built like a US Interstate highway; the only difference was that Iraqi drivers did not feel that they had to drive in a specific direction on a specific side of the road. Luckily, there was not much traffic.

THE GREEN ZONE

Back at Camp Victory, we headed out on Route Irish and into the Green Zone to meet with our counterparts in the Coalition Provisional Authority. They had just taken over from the Office of Reconstruction and Humanitarian Assistance (OHRA). Providing base camp support to diplomats is another situation all together. The Republican Palace complex in Baghdad had suffered significant destruction during the air campaign. State department officials were not happy sleeping in sand filled rooms with no air conditioning. It did no good to remind them that the troops, at that time, were in tents with no air conditioning.

When one State Department official called home and a friend asked what it was like living in a palace, all hell broke loose. State wanted their quarters brought up to their desired standard and bought up fast. My leadership directed that we support the State folk, so KBR was directed to do it and do it quickly. As you might expect, cost was no object. I was rather concerned about the soldiers in tents, but to no avail. At least this was paid from State Department funds and did not cost the soldiers any support.

One of the problems which we experienced in the Green Zone was the state of plumbing and electricity. Not only were they knocked out by the attacks, but they were totally inadequate for the buildings. While the buildings could hold hundreds of people, under Saddam they rarely held 50 or more. Saddam did not spend much time at the Presidential Palace, so neither did many government workers. The support systems had been built for these low levels of staffing.

Of course Iraqi electrical and plumbing work was generally substandard by US standards. Pipes were too small to take on the waste disposal of hundreds of people in the Presidential Place, which can lead to inconvenient and odorous issues. Electricity was of course a much more serious problem. Poor wiring can lead to death and injury and had to be immediately corrected. This was part of the scope of work for all LOGCAP camp support task orders, and will be discussed in some detail in chapter 8.

With a dining facility operated to State Department standards, the Green Zone became a favorite stop-off for soldiers stationed elsewhere. All they needed was a plausible excuse and good timing, to be there for dinner. When I visited to coordinate LOGCAP work, I was also happy to have a good meal on State. Later, security was tightened and you needed a State ID to eat in certain facilities.

Rajiv Chandrasekaran has given a wonderful description of the Green Zone in his book *Imperial Life in the Emerald City*.[15] He notes that KBR was slow in providing some of the essential services needed by ORHA under LTG (Ret) Jay Garner and then CPA under Paul Bremer.[16] Water for showers and laundry were considered essential for State but were slow

---

15 (Chandrasekaran 2006)
16 (Chandrasekaran) p.49

in coming. Back in Rock Island, IL, I received phone calls from State over the laundry issue. I would let KBR know of the problem and then work with the Defense Contract Management Agency (DCMA) to monitor the situation. Some of the problems with supporting State were more a matter of managing expectations than correcting failures.

Many State Department workers eventually moved out into the field, often working from small Army Forward Operating Bases (FOBs) which might house 400 or so soldiers, contractors and other American civilians. Peter Van Buren provides an excellent account of performing this work in his book, *We Meant Well.*[17] These field personnel quickly lowered their expectations and we received few complaints concerning their living in what the Army calls "austere conditions."

CAMPS SLAYER AND CROPPER

We were providing some unusual support at another base in the airport complex, Camp Slayer. This camp was the location of the Iraqi Survey Group, which was looking for Weapons of Mass Destruction (WMDs). LOGCAP provided a state of the art operations center, capable of doing top secret work. KBR electricians wired the complex equipment and did the entire interior work at a large palace complex building.

This palace complex was one of the more interesting in the Baghdad area. Camp Slayer was located at a palace and amusement complex adjacent to the Baghdad airport. A large man-made lake, filled with carp, was a centerpiece of the complex. Since there was no natural food for the fish, this lake at a number of floating feeding stations scattered across the lake. I was told soldiers managed to find food to place in the stations and keep the carp alive. Occasionally they fished for the carp, but did not eat their catch.

However, Saddam used to like to fish for the carp and then have a cookout on the side of the lake. Friends and distinguished Baath Party members attended these picnics. The complex contained other entertainment for the guests, such as a large boat house with a movie theater. Intelligence at the start of the war placed important officials in that theater, so it had received two cruise missile strikes in the opening minutes of the conflict. The theater had been thoroughly destroyed by the strike.

Much of the complex had suffered from bombing and ground fighting. Bullet holes in the guard towers indicated that Iraqi soldiers had

---

17 (Van Buren 2011) passim

mounted some defense of the complex. After the fighting, looters had taken away many of the palace ornamentations and destroyed other aspects of the grounds. Plumbing and air conditioning was out. Electricity was provided, initially by portable generators. Given the importance of the Iraqi Survey Group mission, this camp had a priority on getting electricity, air conditioning water and plumbing up and running.

Another large building on the complex had been designed at a smaller scale than normal. This building was a gigantic play house for the young children of Saddam's family members and favorites. It was larger than most good size mansions in the United States. There was also a play house for adults, adorned with hearts as a design motif. This building was dubbed the Pleasure Palace.

The camp has also hosted other classified operations. The camp population consisted of operational troops, covert Special Forces teams, CIA operatives, FBI agents, civilian intelligence experts who specialized in WMDs.

Adjacent to Camp Slayer was Camp Cropper. This was basically a prison camp which was used to hold high value targets. Survey group agents at Camp Stryker had ready access for questioning scientists and government officials. We did not know this at the time, as this was a classified matter. However, I did notice Tariq Aziz there during a visit, which was kind of a give-away.

CAMP ANACONDA

On later visits I went to other bases in Iraq. Camp Anaconda (later known as Joint Base Balad) became the major US logistics hub for the country. Located at a converted Iraqi Air Force training base, it was refreshing not to see another palace complex. Since it had good runway both Air Force and Army aircraft operated from the base. There was a field hospital which could receive casualties, stabilize them and send them on their way to Germany.

Truckers brought supplies in from the east (Turkey) and the south (Kuwait). From Anaconda supplies were distributed throughout the country. Other contractors had areas for the repair of the combat vehicles they manufactured such as M1 Tanks and Bradley Fighting Vehicles. Fuel, food and ice all moved through Anaconda. There were approximately 18,000 troops there at any time.

The base had a one star general in command and so received some attention from KBR. The base had an Olympic size swimming pool which

KBR had turned in to a resort operation. Next store was a workout area which offered the latest exercise equipment, basket ball courts and running track. The camp movie theater was up and running as was an indoor swimming pool. The dining facilities provided plenty of good food with a wide variety. The ice cream bars were especially popular.

Unfortunately the base water system was not yet up and properly functional. An Army unit was sucking water from the Tigris and filtering it for some uses.[18] Drinking water was, as at all bases, bottled water. The general and I had a long talk about priorities, but he wanted Anaconda to be a local morale and welfare site, so he was pleased with the above mentioned amenities.

We had a number of problems with the supply line through Turkey. These trucks were driven by Turkish nationals and were not treated as well as the American ex-pats who drove up from Kuwait. They, of course, resented this. As they were often well armed, we narrowly avoided some really dangerous incidents.

During this trip, in 2004, I also met with State Department and Army officials managing the Green Zone. One officer assured me that Baghdad was now safe for Americans, and he traveled outside the Green Zone often. Two days after my trip, the armored State Department bus (dubbed the Rhino) hit an IED. No one was killed, but after that all travel from Camp Victory to the Green Zone was by helicopter for awhile.

During this last trip to Iraq, the deteriorating security situation was apparent. My C-130 plane from Kuwait to Baghdad was shot at by some form of rocket. Our pilot fired infrared flares to divert the rocket as he took evasive action. (I'd had a role in sourcing those flares, too, so again I hoped we'd done a good job.) The landing was a sharp descending corkscrew ride known as a combat landing. We did this on every landing in Iraq; however this one was a bit more nerve and body wracking.

While I was at Camp Anaconda, we received several rocket and mortar attacks. Sirens sounded, and we all put on Kevlar jackets and helmets and headed indoors. These random attacks had become fact of life at most major bases during 2004. One of the mortars hit an Apache helicopter sitting on the runway. This was pure luck on the part of the insurgent, who took out a multi-million dollar piece of equipment with a round costing a hundred dollars or so. I wondered if he got the insurgent of the month award. This incident clearly demonstrated the asymmetrical basis of such actions in an insurgency action.

---

18 More of this in chapter 7.

Finally, while at Camp Anaconda I ran into a very troubling aspect of our contract. While driving on the base with a KBR manager, I noticed people who were apparently living in shipping containers. Some men were cooking and cleaning clothes on the ground outside of the containers. The KBR manager informed me that the men were from Bangladesh, working under the LOGCAP contract. They were part of the largest group of KBR workers, those who were dubbed "Third Country Nationals" (TCNs). The KBR workforce was comprised of American workers (known as Ex-Pats), TCNs and a few Host Country Nationals (HCNs), that is, Iraqi citizens. (At the time, the security situation did not allow for many HCNs.)

TCNs are a major source of labor throughout Southwest Asia. When I established the pre-positioned stocks base at Qatar, I learned that most labor in Qatar is done by TCNs. Labor brokers arrange the hiring from a variety of countries, depending on the labor involved. Our contractor had used a broker to provide mechanics for the Qatar mission. The labor broker was himself a TCN living in Qatar, though he had a silent partner from the royal family. It appeared that those TCNs were treated fairly well, and the mechanics on our base were housed and fed the same as American workers.

Iraq was different. Prior to the war, Iraq had a large internal supply of workers and did not use TCNs. There were no Iraqi labor brokers. KBR therefore used off-shore brokers to supply the labor for projects in Iraq. These brokers treated workers from some countries almost as slaves. The workers took out loans to cover their transportation to Iraq, loans which they could never seem to pay off.

When I saw this situation at Camp Anaconda, I found myself in an odd position as a contracting officer. I demanded that KBR incur more costs under the contractor. For both practical and moral reasons, my contract was not going to treat workers in this manner. I directed KBR to give me a report on the situation along with corrective actions to upgrade the treatment of TCNs. I was removed from management of the contract before I received the report, and I am not aware of any additional actions on the part of KBR or the Army to correct this situation.

After visiting with the Green Zone officials I flew to Doha, Qatar, where CENTCOM had its headquarters. The logistics managers there gave a fairly positive assessment of LOGCAP support, as was usual at this time, and noted the quick response of LOGCAP in meeting the needs of soldiers. The major problems in performance and cost were yet to be revealed in the field.

The Army had, however, created its own problem for support. During the first part of the war, commanders could ask for most anything and get it. They had no budget and were not responsible for the funding. Logistics requirements continued to escalate. This had two important impacts. Costs were much higher than they should have been. Also, the logistics system was strained by bringing in unnecessary supplies. Michael Hastings described the impact of this scenario in Afghanistan, later in the war, noting, "What that meant to McChrystal: Flights that could be bringing in supplies to those in the field were getting wasted in shipping burgers and ice cream and Xboxes."[19] This affected operations in both Iraq and Afghanistan throughout the wars.

Following a visit to our pre-positioned stocks installation (which I had last seen in 2002), I started the 25-hour journey back to the States. Given the events of June with MG Johnson, I was fairly sure this was my last visit to the theater, and subsequent events proved me correct.

19 (Hastings 2010) p.

CHAPTER 2. "TOOTH TO TAIL"

LOGISTICS

The classical Greeks had the word "logistike", generally meaning "calculations" — which is a good place to start with logistics. Logisticians make innumerable calculations in planning the support for any military operation. The LOGCAP contract required such calculations on the part of the military planners and the contractor in devising a logistic support plan and managing its implementation. Auditors were constantly plowing through data to determine if we were getting what we paid for and if we were paying a reasonable price, taking operating conditions into account.

Logistics support essentially means providing soldiers with water, food, shelter, ammunition and fuel; this has been a central problem for warfare since ancient times. As Alexander the Great marched his soldiers from Greece through Persia and on to India, he faced these same problems. Water had to be obtained from whatever country his troops were in. Crossing a desert was an enormous problem. Food came either from the occupied country or from supplies off-loaded from ships. This limited the options to marching routes close to the sea. Fuel, in those days, included fodder for the pack animals, and it generally had to be available in the occupied country. The animals carried the essential baggage, including spare weapons and siege equipment.

The ships which supplied Alexander appear to have included vessels under his direct control and merchant ships owned by traders who were making a profit on the campaign — they were contractors and they provided the food and other supplies, along with the transportation. Already, contractors were playing a role in supporting warfare.[20]

Napoleon was able to set up a fairly effective supply chain in Europe for his initial campaigns. Supply depots at the French border were the starting off place for moving equipment and food to his troops. Of course the troops also took supplies from occupied territory, along with fodder for their horses. But Napoleon learned a tragic lesson when he invaded Russia. The Russians for the most part denied him food and fodder and the supply chain from France was too long to be effective. Napoleon barely escaped with 10% of the forces he'd set out with on these invasions.

In modern warfare, it has become possible to maintain longer supply chains. In the Pacific in World War II, the US maintained one of the longest supply systems ever. Production, movement and distribution of supplies were hard but the Army and Navy were able to accomplish the mission. During the Korean War, logistic support by the U.S. military supply system was supported locally by the South Korean government. Planning for war against the Soviet Union in Europe has counted on support from our NATO allies. In Vietnam, a combination of American firms and host country nationals provided many services under contracts with the military. Laundry, food and some camp maintenance services were provided by Vietnamese. These are services that are now under the LOG-CAP contract.

US Logistics after Vietnam

After the Vietnam conflict, the U.S. military had to reassess the manner in which expeditionary troops would be supported in future conflicts. During Vietnam, as mentioned, the military relied on the South Vietnamese to supply US forces with a variety of services, from laundry to food.[21] There was some degree of improvisation as to how this was accomplished, as the campaign progressed, but it was not an essential part of doctrine. Organic Army units continued to also provide these services, as they had done in past conflicts.

Organic support for troops was the accepted theory, if not always the actual practice. When I refer to organic support, it means the soldiers do the job. The operations were similar to those depicted for the Korean War in the television show *MASH*. Soldiers cooked and served food in

---

20 (Engels 1980) p. 26
21 This is called Host Nation Support by the Military.

---

the mess tent and repaired equipment in the motor pool. When the camp was set up or taken down, when a new latrine was dug or when supplies were delivered, soldiers did the job.

During the post-Vietnam era, the military was under heavy pressure to reduce forces and costs. Funds, as is often the case, were available for development of new systems, to be produced by major defense contractors with significant lobbying clout. But there were no such powerful lobbyists to protect funding for Combat Support/Combat Service Support (referred to hereafter as "support") for wartime and other contingency events; "support" was an easy target. This led the military to consider outsourcing some of this support to low-cost providers in the host nations where U.S. military were stationed and expected to fight. According to Laura Dickinson, "Official military reports after the war [Viet Nam] make the case for continued and increased use of contractors to provide logistical support on the battlefield."[22]

An additional problem was the manner in which the military handled logistics. In the sixties, the military had eliminated the Technical Services Chiefs, clouding the issue of who was responsible for the adequacy of support services.[23] Most support units were moved to Reserve units and by the early eighties some had been moved to what the military calls COMPO 4, components which are not resourced and must be constituted when needed.[24] This led the military to look for other means to provide support.

Ways were found to reduce the organic support in favor of low-cost or free support from other countries at little or no cost to the United States. Primary examples of the first initiatives were Mutual Support Legislation, Wartime Host Nation Support (WHNS), Status of Forces Agreements (SOFA), Assistance-in-Kind and other foreign nation burden sharing agreements and arrangements. This eased the strain on the U.S. military budget. Europe and Korea were the principal venues for exchanging organic support for host nation support, especially during peacetime. Such arrangements were depicted as positive U.S. foreign relations. The logic was that, since we were defending these countries, it was fair that they should provide this support.

---

22 (Dickinson 2011) p. 29
23 (Vann 1997) p. 776
24 Contractor provided support is under COMPO 9.

However, in other regions foreign nation support could be difficult to obtain. The military recognized a need for risk mitigation methods to better insure adequate, flexible and timely support when required.

In the late 1980s, while studying at Harvard, I was involved in analysis of the Army's "Tooth to Tail" issue. At the time the numbers indicated that an Army division slice[25] contained approximately 17,000 combat troops and 31,000 support troops, and about a third of the Army's total budget went to providing that support. This ratio indicated a military that might be short on combat power compared to support. If we waged a conventional war in Europe against the Warsaw Pact, massive numbers of troops would have to be moved into theater, and that presented a dilemma. If only combat power was hurried to theater, those troops would find themselves without the vital support necessary to fight and win. Troops that are tired, hungry and thirsty are reduced in their combat effectiveness. However, if some of the available air and sea lift were diverted from troop movement to support organizations, the actual warfighters might not get to theater in time.

Also, at this time Secretary of Defense Casper Weinberger was publishing a yearly analysis of Soviet military power, and his numbers indicated that the NATO forces would probably collapse within about eleven days after a Warsaw Pact attack through the Fulda Gap and across the north German plains, if additional combat power was not immediately deployed. It only became apparent that these DOD figures were grossly overstating the fighting potential of the Warsaw Pact when the Soviet Union collapsed. Secretary Weinberger and President Reagan's desire was to upgrade forces across the board, but especially to develop new, more sophisticated systems. Cuts could be made in support forces, with planned outsourcing as the solution. Rather than spend current dollars on support troop units, support money would only be spent during operations, when a contractor was hired to do the job. This concept freed money for systems, and freed troops for combat, cutting the enlarged "Tail" of our force structure.

The general discussion involved how to set in place a process to obtain the contractor support. Support would be needed immediately in the event of a conflict, so mechanisms would have to be in place before any such emergency. In 1992, Richard Cheney was Secretary of Defense under George H. W. Bush. The Pentagon solicited bids on a contract to

---

25 A "division slice" was a combat division and the support troops necessary for that division to operate effectively.

study how the military could provide support to troops in the most effective manner. This report was to examine the military's likely deploy-
ments and recommend how bases could be built and support provided.[26]
KBR, a subsidiary of Halliburton at the time, beat out 36 other companies to win the contract.

KBR's study remains classified. However, it is clear that the study
was used to justify the LOGCAP Program; one umbrella contract to provide this support in any contingency operation. It may be only coincidence that Mr. Cheney later became president of Halliburton.

This military initiative coincided with initiatives in private industry
to outsource non-core business functions. It became a standard of business books to claim that firms should concentrate on their core competency and outsource other functions. For the military, combat was certainly the core competency. It was thought that an approach that was
seen to be cost effective for private industry would also provide benefits
to government functions, including the military. In chapter 11, we will
re-examine this analysis.

Another important factor came into play. A defense reform in 1983–85
created regional commands that would be the organizations responsible
for fighting in their respective theaters. For the U.S. Central Command
(USCENTCOM) with Southwest Asia (SWA) as its Area of Responsibility (AOR), relying on various forms of host nation support for combat
operations presented a definite risk. Unlike Europe and Korea, in this
region we had no significant numbers of forward deployed ground forces
and few on-shore support installations with prepositioned stocks. It was
difficult to attain signed foreign nation support agreements and ground
force exercise training in the SWA AOR. Infrastructure in this region
would be insufficient to provide the U.S. military with necessary support
during operations. If organic support was eliminated to reduce the tail,
and host-nation support were unavailable, then contractors would have
to fill in.

Most USCENTCOM combat and support forces would have to be
deployed over long distances and support would have to be provided as
operations were being conducted. Headquarters, USCENTCOM and the
U.S. Army, USCENTCOM (ARCENT) (Third U.S. Army) were located
in CONUS (the Continental United States) with no permanent forward
presence. It was becoming evident that a non-traditional means for providing support would be required in this region. No such means had been

---

26 (Briody, 2004) p.184

created when CENTCOM was established and located at McDill Air Force Base, in Tampa, Florida.

An additional complication was the ever increasing closures and re-alignments of U.S. and overseas bases. As these bases were closed, some of the functions which they supported were reduced or eliminated. Therefore, force mobilization and support power projection capabilities were significantly decreasing.

LOGCAP IS BORN

In the Defense Appropriations Law passed in 1983–84, Congress directed the Department of Defense to establish a contingency contract capability that would support U.S. mobilization and overseas force support deployment needs (such as those of USCENTCOM). The U.S. Army was designated as the Department of Defense Executive Agent for this mandate. U.S. Army Regulation 700-137 (December, 1985) established the Logistics Civil Augmentation Program (LOGCAP). LOGCAP was now mandated in law and promulgated by regulation. Funding was provided for this program to develop support capabilities through deliberate planning in support of the U.S. Army.

At this time, LOGCAP was generally conceived as a planning program which would lay the groundwork for providing support in the event of a conflict. Theater operational plans would include LOGCAP analysis in preparation for operations. Plans would include sourcing various kinds of supplies needed for support and moving those support services into theater. When the first major exercise of this concept occurred in Operation Desert Storm, there was no LOGCAP contract to utilize. The use of contractor support was rather *ad hoc* and was not a major success.

During Operations Desert Shield and Desert Storm, the Army used civilians and contractor personnel for troop support. Saudi Arabia provided some Host Nation Support, particularly oil, trucks and food. The Army also hired contractors on the international market. The United States hired 76 U.S. contractors who deployed about 9,200 employees to the AOR for operational support.[27] These contractors provided vital support, as many combat units deployed without their normal support units.

By 1990, HQDA recognized that the initial decentralized approach for this untraditional program did not work. Commands continued overt resistance to the program. The orientations of MSC LOGCAP contracts were too narrow; they were limited to functional area support such as

---

27 (General Accounting Office, 1994)

oil supplies, transportation and individual meals with no provision for an overall dining facility, for example. Most LOGCAP MSC funding was used for general support — like tires for administrative vehicles, or Temporary Duty travel.

Also by 1990, HQDA saw that LOGCAP should be a centralized program that had one umbrella contract as supported by one LOGCAP Prime Contractor. The contract should have the potential to rapidly provide nearly every area of functional support over vast regions. Additionally, HQDA planners were visualizing a "One Stop Shopping and Single Point of Contact" concept. A "turn-key" base camp, for example, with a wide spectrum of functional area support, was a prototype goal. This base camp would have one contractor Project Manager for all support matters and be supplied through seaports and airports within a worldwide commercially resourced LOC.

Operation Desert Storm (ODS) provided a great opportunity to bring this LOGCAP vision and concept closer reality. HQDA LOGCAP planners were deployed with the ARCENT advance party into SWA for Operations Desert Shield/Storm (ODS) (Gulf War I) in 1990–91. Their wartime mission was to augment ARCENT Senior logistics and engineer staff capabilities and refine and field test the LOGCAP Umbrella Support Contract concept on an ad hoc basis.

After ODS, HQDA planned to solicit and let a LOGCAP Umbrella Support Contract, as it is known today. The only challenge was to identify and select a command or agency that could assist with the solicitation of a contract of such magnitude, and then be able to provide LOGCAP contract administration and execution support for HQDA under very demanding event conditions, worldwide.

HQDA chose the U.S. Army Corps of Engineers (USACE). Both agencies are located in the Washington, D.C. area and USACE has extensive experience with contracting international construction and engineering services, with the development and maintenance of the CONUS environmental infrastructure, and with the establishment of numerous USACE field offices globally.

HQDA conducted a LOGCAP Worldwide Requirements Conference in July, 1991, at the USACE Russell Building in Atlanta, Georgia, to gather information and recommendations for drafting a comprehensive Umbrella Support Contract solicitation to cover most U.S. Army Event support needs as presented herein. USCENTCOM, ARCENT and other ODS personnel were key participants in this conference. A unique concept of requirements was developed that became a basis for the Umbrella Contract Statement of Work (SOW) within the solicitation.

Given these dedicated and concerted efforts since 1990, the first LOG-CAP Umbrella Support Contract was awarded competitively by HQDA, through USACE, to Brown & Root Services Corporation (BRS) (Houston, Texas) in August 1992. The contract was intended to support three simultaneous Events, two Major and one Minor. "Major Events" were envisioned, for example, to be wars in Europe and Korea with "Minor Events" being humanitarian relief efforts such as hurricane disaster relief in Bangladesh.

LOGCAP contractors were to be deployed into the Event Area of Operations (AO) within 72 hours of receipt of a written Notice to Proceed (NTP) and ramp up requirements soonest given funds availability and Event conditions. Contractor efforts were managed entirely for the supported force by HQDA/USACE Team LOGCAP Forwards and had a worldwide "Reach Back" capability to bring in support offshore that was not available in the AO.

In the original design intentions, the Contract was meant only to provide basic life, facilities (e.g., Base Camps) and LOC (e.g., local and line haul motor transport, supply points and sea and aerial ports) support until other force support capabilities arrived or could be arranged. Such support examples are Host Nation Support, local contacting and Active and Reserve military units.

LOGCAP was not envisioned to stay in place for years, but it has, given the realities of Event executions since 1992. LOGCAP is externally driven by Event support requirements deemed essential to U.S. national interests. Unilateral application or termination of LOGCAP support is not an internal program support option.

Reality Intervenes: LOGCAP Immediately Diverges from Original Intent

Less than four months after the Contract was awarded, President Bush initiated the action in Somalia designated Operation Restore Hope. Task Orders were awarded under LOGCAP I to provide base camp support. Within a short time, LOGCAP became the largest single employer in Somalia.

KBR supported additional operations in Haiti, Rwanda, Saudi Arabia and Bosnia under LOGCAP I. The most extensive of these operations was in Bosnia. Following the Dayton Peace Accords, the U.S. initiated

Operation Joint Endeavor, providing 25,000 troops to augment 40,000 other NATO troops in the Balkans. This was a peace keeping measure and would be centered on Bosnia. The LOGCAP contract was used to create six staging bases in Hungary near Kapsovar and Taszar. Twelve bases were to be created in Bosnia, but that number tripled because the tactical situation required smaller bases distributed throughout the area.

As with current operations in Iraq, Afghanistan and Kuwait, this operation in Bosnia was planned for a one-year period. As appears to be the standard case, NATO was unable to leave after one year and Operation Joint Endeavor was succeeded by Operation Joint Guard and Operation Joint Forge. In 1998, the administration determined that there would be an indefinite U.S. and NATO presence in the Balkans.

The history of events did not cooperate with the original LOGCAP vision for temporary bare base support operations. LOGCAP was quickly selected, 2 December 1992, to support the U.S. incursion into Somalia. In less than 24 hours, 5,000 U.S. Marines were steaming on two U.S. Navy assault ships toward Somalia for over-the-beach hostile landings. International media were already in Somalia awaiting the U.S. landings. LOGCAP was the only option found that could provide the complex, rapid and diversified area support required for this Event.

Even given this crisis condition, the U.S. Services could not agree who would fund the contractor efforts. OSD intervened and directed payment. Within 11 hours, LOGCAP Contractor rallied the necessary support from business contacts in Africa and nearby countries and were operating at the Mogadishu Seaport and two nearby airfields.

LOGCAP was immediately cast into its first complex Military–Political operation. LOGCAP initially supported the U.S. Navy and Marines, and then it was handed off as support to the U.S. Army, and then to the United Nations (UN) with U.S. financial backing. The episode ended with several LOGCAP contractors being killed and wounded, along with the "Black Hawk Down" incident.

LOGCAP went on to support most major U.S. military Events from 1992–96 under this first LOGCAP Umbrella Contract. Event support was provided in Rwanda, Haiti, Saudi Arabia, Kuwait and the Balkans.

As a result of these Events, another of the original intents of LOGCAP was not to be fulfilled. The U.S. Army was not going to be supported as an independent force by LOGCAP. The U.S. Army would be supported as a member of a U.S. Joint, Foreign Coalition or United Nations Force. The spectrum of LOGCAP support was not to culminate here, by any means. Yet LOGCAP remains today the largest U.S. Army contingency support program in modern times.

LOGCAP II: DOWN A SLIPPERY SLOPE

In 1996 the LOGCAP contract was re-competed, and DynCorp won LOGCAP II. At this point we see one of the major problems with the LOGCAP program. The U.S. commanders in the Balkans were satisfied with the support they received from KBR. They did not wish to switch to a new contractor. Rather than having DynCorp take over LOGCAP support in the Balkans, the United States Army Europe (USAREUR) awarded a new Balkans Support Contract to BRS (the company that was later called KBR) in 1997 on a sole source basis. They competed for this work in 1999 and BRS won the new contract and remained as the Balkans support contractor.

This phenomenon of commanders' unwillingness to change support contractors was a powerful constraint on inducing competition into the LOGCAP program. Change can be disruptive and commanders naturally avoid it. The contractor also becomes adept at integrating his staff into the commander's staff. The contractor becomes the staff expert on service support. As officers rotate through the operation the contractor personnel often become the most experienced members of the staff. In 2010, the Army made a significant decision to retain KBR as the life support LOGCAP contractor in Iraq, even though savings from competition were available. We will examine this phenomenon further later in this book.

The contractor also becomes quite good at doing those things that make the commander happy. However, that the commander and his staff are happy with the contractor does not mean the contractor is doing a good job. It is difficult for the commander to judge whether the contractor is spending money wisely. The contractor's business systems are not visible to the commander. Overstaffing, faulty subcontracting, redundant systems, etc. will not register as problems for the commander. Under LOGCAP III, commanders were consistently pleased with KBR work, even while auditors, administrators and whistleblowers were identifying major problems.

CONTRACTOR VS. ARMY COST ANALYSIS

Following the Bosnia experience, the Army had Logistics Management Institute (LMI) perform an analysis of the cost difference between contractors versus troops performing support functions. (I have not seen the earlier KBR study, but I have seen the LMI study.) Total cost, including salary, training, and lifetime benefits were calculated. It was assumed the contractor would not have lifetime benefit costs. The analysis showed about a 30% savings from using contractors.

The analysis did not include:

- The cost of administering these contracts (Contracting agency, DCMA, unit technical Representatives and DCAA.)
- The risk of Contractor failure or inability to perform in a conflict environment.
- Security for contractor personnel in theater.

The study compared the costs of regular army units to contractor support, but when Army units provide this type of support, generally reserve units are used; they cost less than regular army units. These analyses worked from a standard military concept of a forward line of battle and contractors operating in a secure rear area.

Of course, this did not happen in Iraq or Afghanistan.

In 2005, the Congressional Budget Office conducted the most extensive analysis of using contractor personnel as a substitute for organic support. I will discuss this analysis in chapter 10. Given the report of a 30% savings, organic units were reduced and it was planned to rely on contractors to provide CS/CSS support.

During operation Desert Strom, contracting was mainly through contingency contracting offices in Saudi Arabia. Negotiations were difficult and prices high. After this operation Perini Corp received a contract to provide CS/CSS in a precursor of the LOGCAP contract. As noted above, LOGCAP I was awarded to KBR, who provided support during operations in various locations, including Bosnia. DynCorp received LOGCAP II, but had little use during the five years of this contract. KBR was awarded LOGCAP III in 2001. By this time there was significant reduction in organic capability to provide CS/CSS with the elimination of regular army units along with reserve units (Army National Guard units are generally combat units).

There have been major increases in CLS and CS/CSS contracting in the past 20 years. LOGCAP, at $5 billion per year, represents a major increase, mainly due to the operations in Iraq and Afghanistan. CLS contracting has replaced soldiers as the prime maintenance support vehicle. I am not sure where numbers would be available to compare the size of contracting now to 20 years ago.

The combining or integrating of the non-traditional LOGCAP with the traditional military operations support created a turbulent relationship from the beginning. LOGCAP was immediately identified as a significant force structure threat. Many commanders believed that accepting contractors in the deliberate operations planning would lead to a reduction in uniformed support forces.

Others displayed a great distrust of contractor event performance. Contractors were thought to be too slow; too expensive; and, not controllable or useful as military personnel. Contractors were seen also as a deletion of individual combatant capacities and an increase in life and force protection support requirements for the operational commanders. LOGCAP support also was perceived as too centralized above the Event commander level.

To the Officer Corps and Enlisted members, outsourcing education, training and indoctrination was for the most part a strange idea that was hard to accept. Although dependence on external force support was obviously increasing, the military institutions, command exercises and other training did not embrace outsourcing. Therefore, until more recent years, for most military personnel and commands LOGCAP was basically relegated to an "On the Job" training situation during the execution of an operation.

Headquarters, Department of the Army (HQDA) attempted to reduce these operations support concerns in 1987–1990 by allowing the active numbered Armies (e.g., Third, Seventh, Eighth) to develop, award and administrate their own LOGCAP contracts under the policy and regulatory provisions of the program. HQDA would provide funds and Team LOGCAP specialists to assist the commands with their respective LOGCAP Event support contracts. LOGCAP training would then be made available for Event execution.

Under substantial HQDA pressure, ARCENT let the first such LOGCAP in July 1989 to Perrini, Inc. The contract was called the SWA Petroleum Distribution and Operations Pipeline (SWAPDOP). ARCENT allowed the contract to expire in June, 1990, without exercising option years. The primary reasons for the contract expiration appear to be the lack of bonding and communications between the contractor and the command.

Iraq invaded Kuwait in August, 1990. Shortly thereafter, SWAPDOP was put in place on an emergency acquisition basis *at much higher costs* to support Operations Desert Shield/Storm (ODS) (Gulf War I) in 1990–91.

LOGCAP II AND THE MOVE TO AMC

A very dramatic change took place for LOGCAP in April, 1996. The Vice Chief of Staff, Army, directed the U.S. Army Materiel Command (AMC) in Alexandria, Virginia, to take over contract administration, management and execution responsibilities for the LOGCAP Umbrella Contract from G-4, HQDA and USACE. Along with this direction came the necessary program management responsibilities. However, HQDA (G-4) would remain the overall LOGCAP proponent and maintain all regulatory, fiscal, and force structure matters, including contract execution approval authority. Later in 2000 under an AMC internal reorganization, LOGCAP was aligned under the newly activated U.S. Army Field Support Command (Provisional) at Rock Army Arsenal, Moline, Illinois.

LOGCAP was providing most support for military forces in Southeastern Europe, including the Balkans, when AMC assumed this LOGCAP mandate. Consequently, most people thought was that AMC would be immersed in the expanding Balkans support with the emerging Yugoslavian War on the horizon. This assumption proved false.

By the end of 1996, U.S. Army, Europe (USAREUR), with USACE, sole sourced the Balkans contingency support efforts to BRS with the concurrence of HQDA and the Office of the Secretary of Defense. This decision was said to have been made to protect continuity of USACE contract management and fend off any risk of changing to AMC, given the expanding Balkans crisis and probability of war. AMC LOGCAP efforts in the Balkans then became a USAREUR contract under USACE administration of the same LOGCAP Prime Contractor, BRS.

AMC also re-competed the LOGCAP contract during this time and awarded the contract to DynCorp Services, Inc. in 1997. However, AMC LOGCAP was now relegated to the conduct of extensive readiness exercises, assistance visits, deliberate plans development and support of minor Events. Benign Event support was conducted in East Timor, Panama, Colombia and Haiti. This minor support ($23 million) combined with the short period of Balkans support only came to approximately $42 million.

LOGCAP III: SLIDING AWAY

Like everyone else, life changed forever for AMC LOGCAP on 11 September 2001 (9/11). AMC at this time was concluding another recompete of the LOGCAP contract and again (KBR) was to win the LOGCAP contract with a selection date of December 2001. AMC made very important changes to the previous contract SOWs for Event support enhancement while maintaining the Indefinite Delivery-Indefinite Quantity capability of the contract.

Two of the more major changes would accommodate the support of future Events which were to occur shortly. First, the definition of "contingency" in the solicitation was changed to potentially expand the application of LOGCAP during an Event; the prior definition was more limited toward military force involvement. The current definition basically can be interpreted as supporting most operations deemed in the national interest, with the approval of HQDA. Secondly, the new contract was also expanded from a possible five years to ten years. This decision was based upon DOD Acquisition Reform initiatives which encouraged long term relationships with contractors, like those which private industry was pursuing. This period consisted of one base and nine option years, a timeframe that is more adaptable to long or consecutive Event periods.

Besides the contract, AMC had made another dramatic change to program support capabilities in 1999. A 66-member LOGCAP Support Unit (LSU) (U.S. Army Reserves) was activated in direct operational support of the program. LOGCAP now had a much expanded capability so that it might support several Events over extended periods and vast regions. Also, the LSU provided a much-needed uniformed member presence for integration into supported forces, especially in harsh and hostile areas.

LOGCAP soon became the contract of choice when fighting "America's Global War on Terrorism". LOGCAP proved on a grand basis to be rapid, responsive and flexible. The LSU mobilized and joined AMC LOGCAP employees and contractors as one team forward to provide unprecedented support early on, no matter the location, supported military force or civilian agency. This support remains today and is still expanding.

Since "9/11", LOGCAP has provided support with over 134,000 contractors at an estimated cost of $32 billion (Rough Order of Magnitude) in CONUS and 10 foreign countries, with most support being under harsh and hostile conditions. This LOGCAP support is unprecedented, if not unique. In addition to the extensive U.S. military support, LOGCAP supports the Polish Multinational Division and a diverse range of U.S. Government civilian agencies such as the Iraqi Survey Group, Coalition Provisional Authority, Threat Analysis Agency and the Department of State.

The strength of AMC LOGCAP lies first in the architecture of its program capabilities for globally rapid, vast and flexible Event support. The foremost LOGCAP strength lies, however, in the dedication, innovation and perseverance of LOGCAP personnel — military, government employees and contractors alike. They earned the currently dynamic LOGCAP Legacy and are the ones who insure that LOGCAP remains the program of choice for Event support in securing our nation's security and other interests.

CHAPTER 3. LOGCAP III

GOVERNMENT CONTRACTS

The LOGCAP III contract, DAAA09-02-D-0007, is an ID/IQ contract. What on earth does that mean? You are going to learn some contracting here and there is nothing I can do about it. In the process you will understand what an umbrella contract does, what Task Orders do, and the role of the Procuring Contracting Officer (PCO). You will also learn why there is no television show named PCO and devoted to the exciting world of defense contracting.

The LOGCAP contract is an ID/IQ contract, an Indefinite Delivery/ Indefinite Quantity contract. In practice, this means that the LOGCAP contract was awarded with minimal actual requirements and minimal actual funding. The LOGCAP III contract contains the potential for additional work and funding — without any additional competition. Under LOGCAP III, the winning contractor was required to provide several management plans. One was a very general worldwide plan, while others were more specific plans for operations in several regions. Under the initial contract, the contractor was paid several million dollars for formulating these plans . The major potential for work on the contract was to actually conduct the operations that were contained in the plans. But we did not know when and where these operations would take place, and how much support would be needed; thus the indefinite nature of the contract.

When LOGCAP is needed to support an operation, task orders are awarded against the contract. Many people have written and continue to write that these tasks are not competitive. This is formally inaccurate; yet it is a fairly correct account of the situation. Task Orders are awarded without any additional competition. However, under the Federal Acquisition Regulations, these are considered to be competitive awards since the basic contract was competed. KBR won the LOGCAP III contract through a competitive process, providing a better proposal than the other firms who competed. Since this initial award was competitive, all non-competitive follow-on task orders were counted as competitive awards. The Army was allowed to take credit for over $40 billion in competitive awards under LOGCAP III from 2002–2009. This enhanced the Army's status when reports on competition were provided to Congress.

When operations commenced, the Army awards Task Orders under the contract for the actual support. Under LOGCAP I, Bosnia was the major operation supported. Under LOGCAP II there were only small operations in the Philippines, Sri Lanka and Colombia. LOGCAP III became a huge contract as over 150 Task Orders were awarded to support operations in Afghanistan and Iraq, with support operations in several other countries, mainly Kuwait.

How was LOGCAP designed to operate in Iraq? Suppose that a Combatant Commander had a requirement to station 5,000 troops at a specific location for a long period of time. The G4 (logistics) on the Commander's staff would coordinate with the LOGCAP Support Unit (LSU) Representative to write a statement of work (SOW) for this proposed camp. The SOW would state the number of troops to be stationed at the camp, the date for their arrival and the commencement of support and the services needed. Those services were fairly standard, including housing, dining facilities, sanitation, laundry, water, ice, pest control, distribution of fuel, and morale, welfare and recreation (MWR) facilities.

There might be special requirements based upon the function of the camp. If this was a supply point, LOGCAP might be required to run a supply distribution facility with warehouses, loading equipment and inventory control processes. If aircraft would use the base, LOGCAP might run the air traffic control, fueling and other airfield operations. Several bases had hospitals and LOGCAP provided the maintenance and support operations for these facilities.

The LSU officer would assist the G4 in putting these requirements into a LOGCAP format and transmit the requirement to the contracting officer. In theory they would evaluate possible trade-offs between solutions to the requirements problem. Housing could be provided in the form of tents, containerized housing (trailers) or constructing hard stand buildings. Of course there were cost and comfort differentials to these solutions which required resolution.

Feeding troops also required tradeoffs. Meals Ready to Eat (MREs) are the new version of K-rations. While they have improved in quality and taste, most people would grow tired of these quickly. (I recommend the lasagna.) Construction of dining facilities (DFACs) that provided cooked meals was the preferred option for a major base. While feeding the troops on the base, the DFAC also served as the supply point for hot meals to be taken to outlying small bases. Receiving such a meal was a definite improvement over MREs.

Once the PCO received the scope of work, they would review the document, possibly obtaining legal analysis. After any changes necessary to make it work under the LOGCAP contract, the PCO would then forward it to KBR requesting a Rough Order of Magnitude (ROM) estimate of the price and a Technical Execution Proposal (TEP) explaining how the contractor planned to accomplish the mission. This was expected, generally, within 48 hours, due to the urgency of supporting operations. At that point, if funds were available and the customer approved the TEP, the PCO would issue a Notice to Proceed (NTP) which authorized KBR to start work and expend funds which would be reimbursed by the Government.

Shortly thereafter, a formal Task Order (TO) would be issued against the umbrella contract to memorialize the NTP. At this point the Task Order would be considered unpriced. KBR was required, by contract to submit a price proposal, containing the proposed cost of the operation and auditable data to support that estimated cost. The PCO would have DCAA audit the proposal and, within 180 days of award of the TO have negotiated the estimated cost for the work. KBR's fee would be based upon this negotiated estimated cost, not on the actual cost of the work. However KBR would be reimbursed for all actual costs that were allocable to this task order, allowable under cost accounting rules and reasonably incurred, even if they exceeded the estimated cost.

This is another area where there are misunderstandings regarding the LOGCAP contract. KBR was paid fee on the negotiated estimated cost of the task order. Exceeding the estimated cost would not produce additional fee for KBR. It would, in fact lower their profit margin on the task order. The problem was the period between starting work and negotiating the fee cost base. During this period KBR had some incentive to increase costs, assuming they would be accepted into the cost base.

Once placed, the actual administration of the order in theater would become the responsibility of the Administrative Contracting Office (ACO) provided by the Defense Contract Management Agency (DCMA). DCMA would also obtain the services of technical Representatives from the supported unit. For example, the supported unit would not operate the DFAC, but would provide an expert (usually a non-commissioned officer) in the Army's requirements for a DFAC. This person would be appointed as the Contracting Officer's Technical Representative (COTR). Such an appointment required training and certification in the basics of contract management. Throughout operations from 2002 to 2010 the Army was unable to provide the required number of certified and trained COTRs. Only in the last year has the Army trained and certified significant numbers of specialists who are part of supported units.

CONTRACT TYPES

This part is a bit technical also. The theory of contract types played a major role in the LOGCAP process. You may choose to skim a bit until we get to the good parts, how the LOGCAP Task Orders were actually constructed. You will miss some really great factoids about contracts, though.

There are different types of Federal Government Contracts, distinguished by how the contractor is to be paid for the work. One contract type is "firm fixed price", another type is "cost reimbursable".

Choosing the proper contract type for procurement of a Government requirement accomplishes two different but related functions. The type of contract allocates cost risk between the two parties and it provides incentives for the contractor to perform in a certain manner. Both of these factors must be taken into account in the choice of the contract type. The decision is based upon the requirement (supplies or services), the ability of the Government to explicitly define the requirement, and the relative importance to the Government of various goals (time, quality, cost).

Appropriate risk allocation is the first of these factors. A contractor will assume some degree of risk in the contractual agreement, based upon the contract type. The type must be related to the overall ability of the contractor to control risk while performing the contract. Under a firm-fixed-price contract the contractor assumes all of the risk of performance. Under a cost reimbursable contract, most of that risk is transferred to the Government. The range of contract types forms a continuum from fixed-price to cost reimbursable, with each type allocating risk in different proportions between the contractor and the Government. The Government's stated preference is for the contractor to assume most of the risk, so that fixed price is the preferred contract type. This means, however, the Government will pay a risk premium if the contractor considers the risk of fixed price contracting to be excessive.

The choice of a contract type is also an approach to providing incentives for influencing contractor behavior by correlating profit with performance. Contract type attempts to approximate the determination of price in a free market through the dynamics of supply and demand, which do not exist in the Government contracting process. The Federal Government is often a monopsonistic buyer. No other buyer buys CS/CSS for combat troops or aircraft carriers. The seller may be a monopolist, an oligopolistic firm, or at best engaged in monopolistic competition.

In this analysis we will ignore the incentives which attach to competition. A firm which must compete with several other firms has a different set of incentives for proposing lower prices and for providing excellent service and products. Generally, competitive incentives correlate growth, and the potential for future profit, with performance. The firm will evaluate how other firms will price and how significant a low price is within the evaluation criteria. During performance, the firm will also take into account how future competitions will evaluate past performance. There is significant data that suggests firms discount past performance as an evaluation factor and concentrate on price. This is often counter to the goals of the Government.

Government Contracting Officers are responsible for choosing the appropriate contract type when constructing a solicitation or a contract. They may be supported by price analysts and policy analysts who are part of the contracting office. The requiring activity can provide information on the cost risks associated with the procurement, along with the desired non-monetary goals of the procurement. Market research may determine the willingness of the pool of potential contractors to accept various contract types for this requirement. All of this information should support the final PCO decision.

In the following paragraphs I will discuss some of the major types of contracts.

Firm Fixed-Price Contracts (FFP)

In order to understand cost reimbursement contracts, like LOGCAP III Task Orders, it is helpful to understand fixed-price contracting. Under a fixed-price contract the Government will pay an agreed upon price upon successful completion of the contract. Many government contracts are firm fixed-price; the price quoted in the proposal is final and should include all costs which will be incurred by the contractor during performance including a profit. If the contractor finds ways of doing the job more efficiently and saves money, this becomes more profit. If the contractor overruns their cost estimate, they lose profit and may take a loss on the contract. In either case the Government pays the agreed upon firm fixed price.

A standard case of an appropriate firm fixed-price contract is the production of an item in accordance with a Government technical data package, containing all the specifications and drawings for the product. The contractor can price the labor, materials and overhead necessary for a production run with a high degree of confidence. The price may be established through competition or be negotiated on the basis of a DCAA audit of the contractor's proposal. Most production contracts are done this way.

Many service contracts may be done on a fixed price basis. The key is the transparency and stability of the requirement. Only if the contractor can arrive at a price without the risk of unknowns (let alone those pesky "unknown unknowns" of Secretary Rumsfeld), will they take a fixed price for the work. Similarly, if the risk is high, the contractor may price contingencies into the fixed price, for which the Government does not want to pay.[28] The operations and maintenance of a military base, for example, may be done this way. The conditions for using a fixed price would be:

- The base size and population are stable.
- The Government can specify the services required in detail.
- The period of performance is set, usually at least a year, with options for additional yearly increments.
- There is some history of costs at the base to provide a sound basis of estimate for the prospective contractor.

Since the contractor's basic economic incentive is to save money on a fixed price contract, the Government must be able to oversee performance and determine if the product or service delivered is exactly what the Government paid for. Production contract usually require that the

---

28 (Gansler, Affording Defense 1989) p. 165-166

product pass inspection and acceptance quality assurance testing before the Government will accept the product and pay the contractor. The product must contain the specified material, be manufactured in accordance with the technical specifications and perform as intended.

This kind of control is more difficult for a service contract, as the specifications are much broader. A service contract requires continual monitoring of contractor performance during the life of the contract. For example, the Government should have quality assurance specialists who can determine if contractor maintenance is performed in accordance with required standards. Electrical maintenance must use the appropriate wires and be performed in accordance with National Electric Code (NEC) standards as specified in the contract. Similarly dining facilities must be operated in accordance with the Government meal plan, serve the required number of troops and maintain comply with specifications for cleanliness and food preparation. All of this must be subject to verification inspection by quality assurance inspectors and technical Representatives.

In general, under a firm fixed-price contract the Government does not need financial oversight since they will pay the specified price for completion of the contract. However, performance oversight is critical, given the contractor's incentive to save money, possible by cutting corners, purchasing non-conforming material, using cheaper and unqualified labor or other methods which result in less than full performance.

Every purchase you make at a store is a fixed price contract. If you think the price is good, you will buy the product. You do not know, nor do you care, how much profit the contract makes. In your judgment this is a good price and you will pay it.

Cost Reimbursement Contracts

In some cases, however, it's difficult or impossible to know exactly how much certain items or services are going to cost. The requirements are not as well defined as on most production contracts. There may be some inherently subjective aspects to evaluating performance. In these situations, the government will usually use a cost-reimbursement format for the contract. Cost-reimbursement contracts are less desirable because in most cases the government assumes the risk of cost overruns.

In a cost-reimbursement contract, the final pricing will be decided when the contract is completed, or at some other agreed-upon time in the contracting period. A total cost estimate will be determined at the beginning of the cost-reimbursement contract, to allow the government agency to budget for the project and to establish a maximum amount for reimbursement. Cost-reimbursement contracts come in several different forms, described below.

All cost type contracts require that the contractor have a cost accounting system which will generate accurate data for the Government to audit costs. DCAA reviews these systems and provides a recommendation to the Corporate Administrative Contracting Officer from DCMA who approves the system. At the end of the contract DCAA will audit the actual costs incurred by the contractor. They will be evaluated to see if they are allocable to this contract, allowable under Cost Accounting Standards and were reasonably incurred. DCAA may reject costs under each of these three criteria and advise the Procuring Contracting Officer to initiate action to recover these costs from the contractor. This requirement, along with the roll of DCAA became a significant issue in LOGCAP III contract management.

Cost-Plus-A-Percentage-Of-Cost Contracts

This type of contract is illegal! We became aware of the problems with this type of contract rather early in American history. The commission supporting George Washington's Revolutionary Army entered into contracts with agents to supply the army with various goods. The agent was to be paid the cost of the goods and a percentage of that cost. It did not take long to understand that the agent was incentivized to increase the cost of the goods to the maximum possible, to maximize his fee. General Washington quickly revised this policy to pay agents a salary to purchase goods and to encourage them to negotiate the best deal for the Continental Army.

Unfortunately, the experience was repeated in World War I, with the exactly the same results. This is what happens when you do not really learn from mistakes. Congress then passed legislation prohibiting this type of contract. No contract may be written by the Government which contains this perverse cost control incentive.

Even so, some very competent analysts writing about the contracts in Iraq assume that the contractor is paid all costs and a profit which is a percentage of those costs.[29] This is not the case. Fee is generally a percent of estimated costs, calculated beforehand (though this arrangement can and did lead to some abuses).

---

29 (Dickinson 2011) p. 83

Cost-Plus-Award-Fee Contracts (CPAF)

The LOGCAP program uses this type of contract almost exclusively, leaving the Government holding most of the cost risk. Cost control is always a criterion for award fee payment, so the contractor loses some fee when there are cost overruns and thus has some incentive to control costs. The incentive is based upon the size of the award fee pool and the percentage of award fee based upon cost control.

The contractor receives reimbursement and a fixed-base fee, with the potential to earn all or part of an additional award fee. The government will decide the amount of the award following an assessment of the contractor's performance, based on factors such as cost management, timeliness, and quality of work. CPAF contracts are intended to motivate contractors to complete the contract in an effective and efficient manner. Unfortunately, there is significant evidence that these incentives do not operate in a generally effective manner.

Cost-Plus-Award-Fee Contracts under LOGCAP

When the Acquisition Strategy Decisions were made for the LOGCAP III contract, a range of contract types were included as applicable to individual task orders. The yearly planning order was to be done as a firm fixed price order, for example. However, it was anticipated that most task orders for support to contingency operations would be done on a cost plus award fee basis.

The factors which led to this decision were:

- There would be significant uncertainty regarding the initiation of performance in a contingency environment. Contractors would find the risk associated with an estimate of the costs of performance would be unacceptable for a fixed price contract. This judgment was based upon market research conducted among potential contractors
- Performance would be initiated within 48 hours of receiving a requirement. The contractor would provide a Rough Order of Magnitude estimate of the costs of performance prior to initiating work. This ROM could quickly become the basis for a cost estimate suitable for a cost type contract.
- There would be significant changes to the requirement during the period of performance. Dealing with these under a cost contract is administratively more efficient under a cost contract.

- An award fee provision would provide incentives for the contractor to execute the requirement in a manner which would meet Government performance goals, including cost control. Under a fixed price arrangement the contractor would concentrate attention on reducing costs, which was not the Government's prime contract objective.

Most of the task orders, and all of the significant ones, under LOGCAP III were awarded as CPAF contracts. As noted above, under this type of contract the Government agrees to pay all of the reasonable costs associated with the contract and a two-part fee. Part one is the base fee. This is a percentage of the estimated cost, not the actual cost, of the contract. Part 2 is an award fee. This fee is a percentage of an award fee pool, which, in turn, is a percentage of the estimated cost of the contract. Some additional explanation is in order.

When we solicited for the LOGCAP contract, we asked bidders to propose the fee structure they would accept for CPAF work. Final proposals were accepted after September 11, 2001, by which time it was apparent to bidders that there might be more potential work under LOGCAP than had been anticipated. One bidder in particular, KBR, appeared to believe that the workload would be large and they radically lowered their proposed fee structure. This made their proposal much more competitive, though they would earn less under the contract. They proposed a fee structure of 1% base fee and 2% award fee pool.

For each CPAF task order, KBR would receive 1% of the estimated cost of the order as the base fee. They would earn this fee by performing acceptably in accordance with the requirements of the contract. The estimated cost was to be established early in contract performance, through negotiations between the contractor and the Government. It should be emphasized that this is the fee for doing the work as called for in the contract. That means meeting all quality standards, meeting the timeframes required, providing all data required and meeting any other requirements of the contract.

For each CPAF task order KBR would be eligible for up to 2% of the estimated cost in award fee. This award fee would be determined by an award fee process which was set forth in the contract. This process included the evaluation of KBR performance on a quarterly or semi-annual basis. DCMA, DCAA, the Combatant Command and the contracting office would participate in this process. The process was set forth in a contract clause of the basic LOGCAP contract containing the Award Fee Plan.

THE LOGCAP AWARD FEE PLAN

The award fee plan contains the direction for the award fee program as defined in the contract. The award fee process provides a performance incentive for the contractor and gives the Government a tool to identify and reward superior performance. The amount of award fee the contractor earns is based on a subjective evaluation by the Government of the quality of the contractor's performance as measured against the criteria contained in the plan.

Plans are developed with the objectives of providing for evaluation of the contractor performance levels taking into consideration contributing circumstances and contractor resourcefulness. The intent was to focus the contractor on areas of greatest importance for program success. The award fee plan was to be a vehicle to clearly communicate evaluation procedures and provide for effective communication between the contractor and the Government evaluators who make the award fee performance evaluations

Our intent was to keep the plan as simple as possible commensurate with the complexity and dollar value of the tasks performed. Obviously a $5 billion Task Order would have a fairly complex award fee plan. We also intended that the award fee plan be a living document that should be continuously reviewed and updated as experience was gained in monitoring performance. The plan would also be adjusted to reflect changes in the objectives and priorities of the Combatant Command.

ORGANIZATIONAL STRUCTURE FOR AWARD FEE ADMINISTRATION

The award fee organizational structure would consist of the Fee Determining Official (FDO), the award fee review board, and performance monitors. The FDO approves the award fee plan and any significant changes. The FDO reviews the recommendations of the award fee review board, considers all pertinent data, and determines the earned award fee amount for each evaluation period. The decision of the FDO is final and is not subject to any appeal by the contractor. The decision of the FDO is documented in the Award Fee Determination Report and is final.

The chair of the Award Fee Board is an individual designated by the Fee Determining Official. The Chair of the award fee board is responsible for gathering contractor observation reports from the performance monitors for each evaluation period and preparing the award fee board recommendation. Generally, the performance evaluators and the contractor will provide their evaluation to the board. Often this is done as a briefing package. Upon completion of the board session, the Chairman of the board will draft an award fee recommendation report,

The award fee board's report, the performance evaluation report and contractor's self-assessment will be available to the FDO for consideration in determining the award fee. The FDO will consider the results of the award fee board's evaluation of the contractor's performance against the criteria identified in this plan, as well as information provided by the contractor.

The Award Fee Board reviews the results of the performance monitors' evaluation of the contractor's performance, considers all information for pertinent sources, and prepares an earned award fee recommendation for the consideration of the FDO. The award fee board will also recommend changes to this plan. The FDO may accept this recommendation or make a different determination based upon additional information and analysis.

The contracting officer acts as the liaison between the contractor and Government personnel. The contracting officer ensures that the earned award fee is provided to the contractor as directed by the FDO. The contracting officer will notify the contractor of the FDO's decision including explanation of the assessment of the contractor's performance as measured against the evaluation criteria and the amount and percentage of the award fee earned. The notification will identify significant areas of performance and include the reasons why the fee was or was not earned. Given the importance of communication in the award fee process, the contracting officer, assisted by the performance monitors, will be available to "debrief" the contractor to ensure all parties understand the performance assessments.

Performance monitors document the contractor's performance against evaluation criteria in their assigned evaluation area(s). Performance monitors' primary responsibilities include (1) monitoring, evaluating and assessing contractor performance in assigned areas, (2) preparing evaluation reports (contractor observation reports) that ensure a fair and accurate portrayal of the contractor's performance, and (3) recommending changes to the plan to the award fee board.

Additionally, unearned award fee does not carry over and is not made part of the subsequent award fee pool. The Government may unilaterally change the award fee plan and evaluation criteria at any time prior to the start of an evaluation period. In fact, the Government is encouraged to continuously fine-tune the criteria and areas of emphasis as lessons are learned and better performance metrics are identified. Award fee programs are most successful when they are continuously reviewed and improved.

LOGCAP III AND SUPPORT TO OPERATION ENDURING FREEDOM
AND OPERATION IRAQI FREEDOM

Operation Enduring Freedom (OEF) was the name given the initial military moves into Afghanistan. LOGCAP was immediately given the assignment of providing base support to the deployed troops. Since Afghanistan is a rather isolated place, bases were also established in the Republic of Georgia and Uzbekistan. I was sending contracting personnel to countries that some of us had never heard of prior to the operation.

At this time, OEF was on a much smaller scale than it is today. Mainly Special Forces were utilized to conduct operations, along with troops from several of the indigenous fighting croups, such as the Northern Alliance. Some contracting was done locally, by Contracting Command Afghanistan. This organization tried to buy support services and material from the local economy as a way of supporting the government we were trying to establish.

In our Field Support Division I had the pleasure of working with Ltc Pat O'Farrell. Pat was one of the best military managers of civilians I ever worked with and is still a good friend. Pat was sent to be the Commander of the Afghanistan Contracting Command and was awarded a Bronze Star for his accomplishments. He described the difference between contracting in the U.S. and in Afghanistan. In the U.S., under a solicitation, a losing contractor who feels he should have won files a protest with the General Accountability Office (GAO). In Afghanistan, after Pat announced the winner of a competition, one of the losing bidders fired a rocket-propelled grenade at the contracting office. This was a much stronger protest!

In 2002, planning for the war to come in Iraq was underway. In the fall we became involved in one of the more controversial aspects of LOGCAP support to the war. I was asked to attend a meeting in the Pentagon concerning a proposed mission. The meeting was held in the Secretary of Defense's secure conference room. The meeting was chaired by Mr. Michael Mobbs, a deputy to Undersecretary of Defense Douglas Feith. We met with the Energy Infrastructure Group, comprised of former oil industry executives along with members from the Department of State and the CIA. Their mission was to plan for two actions. One was putting out oil well fires that were anticipated as the Iraqis abandoned the southern oil fields. This was a tactic they used in the first Gulf War and it was expected again. The second action was to get the Iraqi oil industry up and running to obtain revenue to finance Iraq's internal operations and the cost of the war.

The Group had already done a study of the Iraqi oil industry and determined that the infrastructure had deteriorated during the embargo on Iraq. Technology was old and spare parts hard to come by. Re-starting the industry would be a major project. We were asked to issue a LOG-CAP task order to have KBR plan for these two actions.

But wait — was this even within the scope of work of the LOGCAP contract? Planning work was a major part of LOGCAP, but it generally was for combat services and combat support services, such as base camps and transportation. Our legal team in Rock Island thought it was not within the scope of work. Finally, a lawyer at DOD issued an opinion that it was within the LOGCAP scope of work. We issued the task order, requiring that the plans should be such that any qualified contractor could implement them.

During this meeting my lead contracting officer stated that she did not consider execution of the actions — putting out oil well fires and repairing the infrastructure — to be in the LOGCAP scope of work. After the meeting was over, Mr. Mobbs told me he did not want her to attend any more meetings on this project.

We later issued a second task order to purchase some items to be used in putting out oil well fires. We would pre-position them in Kuwait for immediate deployment to Iraq. These two task orders cost a few million dollars and were, at the time, classified.

In February of 2003, I was asked to attend another meeting in the Pentagon. I went, without my lead contracting officer, as Mr. Mobbs directed. This meeting was obviously intended to plan the use of LOGCAP to execute the two missions. This time I stated that executing the missions was not within the scope of the LOGCAP contract. I also noted that my staff had done market research on putting out fires and managing oil fields and found a number of firms qualified to do the job. In fact, the major contractor for putting out oil well fires in the first Gulf War was Bechtel, not KBR. They, in turn, had used numerous subcontractors to complete the job, and many of them were qualified to be a part of this effort. I offered to do a secret and quick competition to select one or more firms for this project. My proposal was not well received.

The next day I was told I could go home as the Corps of Engineers had taken over the project. The Commander of the Corps, LTG Robert

Flowers, had spoken with the Secretary of the Army at a party and the decision was made. When I returned and briefed my commanding general that I had gotten us out of the oil business, he was quite relieved. The Corps negotiated a secret deal with KBR (no other contractors invited to compete) worth approximately $7 billion.[30]

I always felt bad about this, as it led to the Restore Iraqi Oil (RIO) contracting by the Corps which cost Ms. Bunnatine Greenhouse her job. She was an excellent contracting manager who also realized that there was no real justification for giving this to KBR on a sole-source basis. When she made her valid objections known, she was demoted from a senior executive position, which cost her a bit of money. More importantly, it cost her the opportunity to provide excellent value to the Army and the taxpayers through superior contracting management.

RIO continued to be a problematic program for Corps of Engineer's contracting. The Corps of Engineers tried to mitigate the impact of a possible $7 billion sole source award to KBR by focusing on a future competition. LTG Flowers stated, "The government will limit orders under this contract to those services necessary to support the mission in the near term. The procurement strategy is to compete subsequent efforts at the earliest reasonable opportunity consistent with the needs of the mission."[31] The Corps of Engineers published a solicitation for two contracts in Iraq (north and south) in the fall of 2003. It quickly became apparent that the Corps planned to award significant work under KBR's sole source contract and that KBR, involved in the planning for the competition, would receive the largest award.[32]

At this time I was also using my pre-positioned stocks contracts to ensure adequate support to the troops. BG Vincent Boles was the Commander of Army Field Support Command, a subordinate command to our command. He was in charge of the pre-positioned stocks program. In September of 2002 he asked me if I could set up a maintenance activity in Kuwait to support equipment arriving for the war and battle damaged equipment once the war started. I determined that my contract for the maintenance of stocks in Qatar had a provision for work in other loca-

---

30   (T. C. Miller 2006) p. 43

31   (Waxman, Letter to Acting Secretary of the Army Les Brownlee 2003) p. 2

32   See Cheryl Tappan's book about this program *Shock and Awe in Fort Worth*, (Tappan 2004), for a discussion of this procurement. Ms. Tappan was a team member on the Bechtel proposal and eventually decided Bechtel should withdraw as the bidding was rigged.

tions. Since these stocks would deploy to Kuwait and Iraq in the next few months, my contractor in Qatar would not have much to do.

We had money in September which was only useful through the end of the month.[33] Over a weekend, I negotiated a change to the contract which called for this contractor to set up a maintenance facility in Kuwait. As usual, this was a bit controversial. My immediate supervisor thought this action was outside the scope of the contract, despite the clause allowing work at other locations. I believed it was extremely important to have this support ready for the troops. I signed the contracts myself so none of the contracting officers who worked for me would take any heat.

With the opening of conflict in March 2003, the LOGCAP contract experienced a gigantic increase in work. We were tasked with providing support to approximately 150,000 troops involved in the invasion and eventual occupation of Iraq. My team, which was very understaffed, worked long days and nights to ensure that this support was there on time. As the conflict progressed, plans for the location of bases and the number of troops constantly changed, so our contract had to constantly respond. KBR assigned a lot of good people to this effort and made every effort to supply the needed support. Without their efforts, soldiers would have suffered from a lack of housing, food, shelter and sanitation facilities. My quarrels with KBR were not about this initial support effort. They were about costs, business systems and eventually the quality of some of the support at established base camps.

Throughout 2003, our team continued to award and to manage task orders in Kuwait, Iraq and Afghanistan. The Defense Contract Management Agency deployed administrative contracting officers to these locations. The Defense Contract Audit Agency sent contract auditors to Baghdad and Kuwait. All of us were understaffed and managing contracts that were unprecedented in scope and mission. I cobbled together a larger group using military officers and procurement interns, along with our seasoned professionals. They did a tremendous job in trying circumstances.

My lead contracting officer, Ms. Mary Beth Watkins, was in Kuwait prior to the invasion. This was the time that Iraq fired SCUD missiles into Kuwait, which were anticipated to contain biological and chemical weapons. On numerous occasions, she had to put on protective gear as

---

33 The Government fiscal year ends on September 30. Operations and Maintenance appropriations are only good for one year and would expire at the end of the fiscal year.

the alarms sounded. Later she travelled to the plains of Turkey to plan for a possible invasion from the north. Like Ms. Greenhouse, Ms. Watkins was removed from her position in late 2004 because she was supporting troops, not KBR's bottom line.

The whole team was dedicated to making sure the troops received the support they needed. Many good employees at KBR worked with us to achieve this collective goal. Neither the Army nor KBR had anticipated the scale of operations for the LOGCAP contract. Unfortunately, this initial spirit of cooperation deteriorated by the summer of 2004.

Chapter 4. Army Contracts and Reversed Incentives

This chapter will take us back to 2004, a year of major change in the management of the LOGCAP III contract and the program. My Commanding General, MG Wade Hampton McManus Jr., retired. He was replaced by BG(P) Jerome Johnson, who had previously been the Deputy Commanding General of ASC and had led the team which created the Field Support Command. The Commanding General of Army Material Command, GEN Paul Kern, also retired. KBR brought in a new senior leader for the LOGCAP program, LTG (RET) Paul Cerjan, along with several other new managers. And it was at a conference in 2004 that I abruptly learned that I had been replaced as the manager of the LOGCAP program.

Locally, the changes in LOGCAP management began under BG(P) Johnson. My replacement in August of 2004, as described in the Introduction, initiated the change in the way LOGCAP would be managed in the following years. Several months later, the lead contracting officer on the LOGCAP contract was also replaced.

My general assessment of the results of these changes was distinctly negative. This is not to imply that I was personally necessary for good management of LOGCAP. Many others could have provided that. But as I will explain below, these changes resulted in KBR accruing unearned payments in the form of reimbursement for unreasonable casts and award fees which could not be justified by the contract criteria. KBR was provided with exactly the wrong incentives under the contract. Poor performance was rewarded, and poor performance was provided.

Of course, the taxpayer was shortchanged by these decisions. The prime responsibility of a contracting officer is to act as the agent of the government and the taxpayer. The Government should pay a fair and reasonable price for services acquired without wasting the citizens' finite resources.

Worse, in my opinion, was the effect on the troops. When President Bush declared the end of combat, his declaration had a significant impact on the conduct of the war in Iraq. The military often describes operations in four phases. They are:

1. Preparation for Combat

2. Combat

3. Occupation

4. Withdrawal

During the first two phases, the Combatant Commander is not constrained by a budget. The Commander prepares and executes the operation in the most effective manner and the Army or Defense staff obtains the funds. However, after phase 2, the Commander receives a budget for occupation and withdrawal activities.

In 2004, I attended a meeting at HQ, AMC where the Army Deputy for Financial Management, LTG Jerry Sinn, informed us of the budget constraints which would now affect the LOGCAP program. The Commander of the Multi-National Force would receive a budget based on what was, at that time, a separate appropriation for conduct of the war. LOGCAP support would receive a portion of that budget, though the amount was not fixed in advance. The significant impact was that any additional dollar spent on LOGCAP was a dollar the Commander would not have to spend on other support for troops, such as body armor, up-armor for HUMVEEs and so forth.

I later attended another meeting with GEN George Casey, prior to his assuming command of the Multi-National Force. The meeting was focused on logistics support and was concerned with how to control spending. The general was acutely aware of the need for controls and was asking such questions as: Could we limit the number of items available at the dining facilities? My experience of GEN Casey is that he was an experienced soldier working hard to balance all of the needs of his troops while maintaining the most capable force.

These meetings further emphasized my determination to enforce the LOGCAP contract provisions necessary to provide the troops with both effective and efficient support. I was adamant that the contract should have provided for KBR to be paid appropriately for their services, while ensuring that money would not be wasted in the process. The Defense Contract Audit Agency was a strong partner in this task and I relied upon their analysis as I formulated contract management positions. My staff was in agreement with this position, as was MG MacManus and GEN Kern. This position, unfortunately, did not survive the change in leadership.

Part of this change concerned an obscure clause of the LOGCAP contract associated with the need to award task orders on an urgent basis. If it had to make an award within 48 hours, the Government did not have time to negotiate the estimated cost of the order. We worked off of a rough order of magnitude (ROM) to initiate work on the task order. Such task orders were labeled "unpriced" until the cost base could be negotiated.

So that services under the LOGCAP contract could begin immediately upon receipt of a requirement from the Combatant Commander, the task orders were awarded on this "un-priced" basis. KBR was required to submit a proposal to definitize those costs into a negotiated estimated cost for fee setting purposes. While KBR would be paid all costs incurred under each task order that were allocable to that order under their approved accounting system, allowable under cost accounting standards, and reasonably incurred, their fee would be based upon the negotiated estimated costs.

FAR 52.216-26, *Payments of Allowable Costs before Negotiation,* requires the Government to withhold 15% of the amount of the contractor's vouchers for payment of costs incurred prior to negotiation of the contract. This is meant to provide an incentive for the contractor to prepare a qualifying proposal, which will be the basis of negotiation, following audit and negotiations.

Initially, due to the constant and massive number of changes to our scopes of work, KBR was not able to provide adequate proposals and the FAR clause was not enforced as a matter of equity. The main task order in Iraq, Task Order 59, was issued in May 2003. By March 2004, we had issued seven major change orders, which had increased the size of the support and adjusted the locations at which support was to be provided. We had issued 1,400 minor change orders (letters of technical direction) which had an effect on the contractor's proposals.

After March 2004, we did not issue any more major change orders. Letters of technical direction continued. But KBR was in a position to provide sound proposals. By the summer of 2004, we established cut off dates for proposals. At this point, DCAA strongly recommended that we implement withholding under this clause to provide incentive to KBR to improve their various business systems, all of which were currently unsatisfactory. The PCO agreed that it was time to implement the FAR clause and circulated various means of doing so within the LOGCAP, contracting and legal community. By August there was a general agreement on the way forward.

As usual, I informed my chain of command, MG Johnson and HQ,AMC, that we had reviewed all of KBR documentation and were prepared to initiate the withhold under the appropriate clause. I told them that, unless I heard otherwise, the letter would be issued on the morning of the 17th. Since this matter had received a thorough airing throughout the chain, including legal review, I did not anticipate hearing anything and I did not.

On August 16, 2004, the Lead Contracting Officer prepared the letter to KBR which would initiate 15% withhold pursuant to the clause. She informed KBR of this decision during an In-Process Review meeting held in the Quad Cities. During this meeting a KBR Representative informed her that her decision would be reversed. On the morning of August 17 she provided their contracts manager, Ms. Mary Wade, with the written determination. In this determination she referenced the difficulties in obtaining a qualifying proposal from KBR. A press release was prepared for this decision, but it was never issued. It did, however, become a matter of public record and was reported in several newspapers.

Reuters reported that the 15% withhold would become effective on August 17, and Halliburton issued a statement which was reported at HalliburtonWatch.org as follows:

> "At the end of the day, we do not expect this will have a significant or sustained impact on liquidity," said Cris Gaut, chief financial officer, in a news release. "There are very few companies in the world that could or would adapt this quickly while, at the same time, financing an operation of this magnitude."[34]

Note that Halliburton was quite happy to tell the public that this would not have a liquidity effect on the company. They had sufficient resources to support the program, and the Army could trust KBR to live up to contractual requirements and Halliburton to live up to the financial guarantee.

---

34 (Halliburton Watch 2004) p.1

Later that day, the decision was abruptly reversed based upon the direction of the Commanding General of AFSC, Jerome Johnson. He was in Washington at the time and arranged a conference call with me, the Lead Contracting Officer for LOGCAP[35], and COL Tim Considine.

AFSC has later claimed that the Procuring Contracting Officer (PCO) had not issued the letter initiating the 15% withhold. In fact the PCO had issued the letter and was directed by the Commanding General of AFSC to rescind it. The Washington Post reported the confusing matter in this way:

> Only hours after deciding to withhold some payments to Halliburton Co. because of questions about billing for its work in Iraq, the Army reversed itself yesterday and said it would give the giant contractor more time to justify its claims.
>
> The decision capped two days of confusion over whether the Pentagon would withhold 15 percent of payments to Halliburton subsidiary Kellogg, Brown & Root Inc. under federal procurement rules that require contractors to provide clear justification for their bills. On Monday, Halliburton announced that the Army would give KBR a third extension to provide the needed documentation, meaning it would continue to be paid in full. Early yesterday, the company said in a statement that the Army called and apparently reversed itself, saying that withholding on new invoices would begin today. Halliburton estimated that $60 million a month could be withheld, pending negotiations about the bills.
>
> Then in the afternoon, officials at the Army Materiel Command — which oversees the logistical services contract with KBR — did another turn-about and decided not to withhold any payments.[36]

In addition, MG Johnson has indicated on several occasions that there was no influence from higher-ups in Washington to stop the imposition of the 15% withhold. But he told us during the phone conference that he had met with senior leaders in the Department of the Army on this issue and was now directing the Contracting Officer to rescind the letter imposing the 15% withhold.

The Lead Contracting Officer for LOGCAP, Ms. Watkins, sent a revised letter to KBR, merely asking what would be the impact of implementing the 15% withhold. This issue had already been discussed with KBR and was taken into account in the PCO's original decision to imple-

---

35 The program was so big at this time that, unlike most contracts with one contracting officer, we had a lead contracting officer for the main contract and subordinate contracting officers for task orders.

36 (O'Harrow Jr.) p.1

ment the withhold requirement. Shortly thereafter, Ms. Watkins was also removed and the waiver continued for all KBR task orders.

The removal of Ms. Watkins was another of those interesting Army leadership actions on LOGCAP. Ms. Watkins was told in October, 2004, that she would be deployed to Iraq in eleven days for a six-month tour. While she was initially resistant to doing this tour at all, due to family considerations and a belief that the contracting officer did not belong in Iraq, she later merely requested a more reasonable amount of time to prepare. She was told that if she could not leave in eleven days, she would be removed from her position. At this point she said no and was removed. Her replacement never left the country on any extended tour or even on a short trip.

Ms Watkins had previously traveled to numerous locations to support the LOGCAP contract. She performed training exercises in Korea and the United States. She was in Afghanistan early in the support mission to ensure that commanders had a direct voice in managing the contract. Ms. Watkins was in Kuwait prior to the invasion, when Iraq was firing SCUD missiles occasionally, causing everyone at Camp Arifjan to put on chemical protective suits. Ms. Watkins traveled to Turkey when the Army was planning an invasion from the north. She was coordinating the supply routes across the plains where material and soldiers would move and temporary base camps would be built. In most of these missions, Ms. Watkins lived in very austere conditions, often tents. She did this to provide the best support possible to troops.

It is obvious that she was not removed for turning down a deployment which never existed. What she did was to insist that KBR should perform within the "four corners of the contract." This phrase meant they would perform the full scope of work and comply with all of the clauses they signed up for. I firmly believe she was removed because KBR wanted her removed.

The Army stated their reasons for not implementing the 15% withhold in a request for a formal deviation from the Department of Defense. The Army claimed that implementing the 15% withhold would threaten KBR's ability to fully perform on the contract. The request states that KBR had told the Army that imposing the 15% withhold would threaten performance, and the AFSC told DOD that they had no means of making up the shortfall in performance. This claim is directly contradicted by the Halliburton press release quoted above.

Halliburton had issued formal financial guarantees of KBR performance under both the LOGCAP contract and the RIO contract. The question of KBR's ability to finance the contract was a question concerning Halliburton. The Army had already recognized this and had asked DCAA to perform an analysis that included Halliburton. The results of this analysis were summarized in an Army Memorandum:

> Halliburton has guaranteed the performance of KBRSI. The Defense Contract Audit Agency (DCAA) and the Defense Contract Management Agency (DCMA) reviewed Halliburton's financial capability to support KBRSI's performance on government contracts. DCAA conducted a post award financial analysis. DCMA reviewed the DCAA analysis and Halliburton's financial data through June 2004. Halliburton's July 2004 reforecast of their cash flow shows an estimated yearend cash balance increase of $33 million over their May 2004 estimate. The projected cash on hand at the end of the year is $533 million. This cash balance coupled with the lines of credit total $1.2 billion giving Halliburton approximately $1.733 billion in available cash.

> Based on these findings, it is DCAA and DCMA's opinion that Halliburton would have been capable of supporting KBRSI from a cash flow perspective in the current and near term. The 15 percent withhold would not have a financial impact particularly if the withhold flows down to the subcontractors. KBRSI has also stated that the withhold will not have a significant or sustained impact on their liquidity; however they have no reason to believe that this could be true of some of their subcontractors.[37]

The basic explanation of this situation, often accepted explicitly by the Army, appears to be that KBR blackmailed the Army by threatening to allow the 15% withhold to impact performance on the contract. KBR informed the Army that their subcontracts allowed them to flow down to subcontractors provisions of the prime contract. They stated that they intended to do so with the 15% withhold. Now, in no way was KBR relieved from performance requirements under the contract. It was their decision to use subcontractors for portions of the work and it would be their decision to withhold payment from those subcontractors. There was no requirement to pass along this withhold but there was a requirement to continue performance. Should KBR have accepted their subcontractors' ceasing performance, KBR would have been in default on the contract and subject to termination of the contract.

Would KBR really have done this? My review of the situation indicated that KBR and Halliburton could not afford to do so. Halliburton had sufficient financial resources to finance the contract without passing along the 15% withhold to their subcontractors. Halliburton was also engaged in settling a major asbestos suit liability which Vice President

---

37 (HQ, AFSC) p.1

Cheney had incurred when he was president of Halliburton. KBR officials informed me that the settlement was a fixed dollar amount, made up of cash and stock. The higher Halliburton's stock price was, the less cash would be needed for the settlement. If KBR had defaulted on the LOGCAP contract, Halliburton stock would take a major hit. Having a government contract with $5 billion in cash flow per year was a major benefit to Halliburton stock price. If, due to the default, KBR were prohibited from future Government contracts, this would also negatively affect the markets assessment o Halliburton's future earnings potential. Halliburton could not afford to generate such bad news.

KBR also had some flexibility in performing the contract. Under LOGCAP I and under the Bosnia Support Contract, KBR had self-performed most of the work. They had expertise in dining facility operation and other parts of the scope of work that were done by subcontractors. If they shed subcontractors over financial matters, they could have undertaken to self perform the work. If they chose not to do so and sought new subcontractors, we would have worked with them to avoid dislocations in support to troops, if their plans were reasonable.

Many KBR and Halliburton executives were people of character and many had served in the military. It is hard to believe that they would have abandoned the troops in Southwest Asia even for their own financial benefit. Given all of these factors, I considered it highly unlikely that KBR would have allowed performance to cease on the contract.

It is also unclear that the Army had no recourse in such a situation. Should we have terminated the KBR contract, two other companies had bid on LOGCAP III and demonstrated their ability to perform the scope of work. They had also demonstrated the ability to respond in a short period of time. In such an emergency, the Government has the ability to conduct a very quick award process. In essence, we would have pulled out their earlier proposals, asked them to confirm them, and awarded on the basis of the best value. With $5 billion per year on the line we would have received excellent cooperation.

However, this new contract would have been hard on the Army. There would be shortfalls in performance during the transition period. This was not a preferred course of action. While organic Army units could make up some of the shortfall, I would agree that we did not want to go there.

There was also a middle road. My contracting officer had asked KBR for statements of financial impact and on numerous occasions had told KBR that we could structure the implementation of the 15% withhold to account for some of those impacts. Our goal was not to impact performance, but to provide KBR with additional financial incentive to correct their business systems and provide the Army with auditable proposals to definitize the task order cost bases.

Why would the Army then waive the 15% withhold for the rest of the contract? There are two possibilities. First, leadership may actually have believed KBR would cease performance with a harsh impact on performance of mission in Southwest Asia. I find this unlikely. The second possibility is that Army leadership had made a decision to make KBR whole on the LOGCAP contract, and that this was the first step in that direction. Events which followed the issue of the 15% withhold, described in the next chapter, support this second conclusion.

In response to a Senate resolution,[38] the DoD IG conducted an investigation of the decision to change the Army position on the 15% withholds. I met with investigators in April of 2009. The report was issued on February 16, 2010, entitled "Report on Review of Army Decision Not to Withhold Funds on the Logistics Civil Augmentation Program III Contract, Report No. D-2010-6-001," this report is a fairly typical IG report. It finds that some things were done incorrectly. It does not find any real wrongdoing, mainly by not looking. No individual is found accountable and some additional training should solve any problem.

---

38   SENATE RESOLUTION 11—TO AUTHORIZE PRODUCTION OF DOCUMENTS TO THE DEPARTMENT OF DEFENSE INSPECTOR GENERAL, Mr. REID (for himself and Mr. MCCONNELL) submitted the following resolution; which was considered and agreed to: S. RES. 11

Whereas, last Congress the Committee on Armed Services conducted a staff inquiry into allegations regarding irregularities in the administration of a contract for logistical support in Iraq by the Department of the Army; Whereas, upon the completion of the Committee's staff inquiry, the Chairman and Ranking Member referred to the Acting Inspector General of the Department of Defense for review allegations regarding the Administration of this LOGCAP contract; Whereas, by the privileges of the Senate of the United States and Rule XI of the Standing Rules of the Senate, no evidence under the control or in the possession of the Senate may, by the judicial or administrative process, be taken from such control or possession but by permission of the Senate; Whereas, when it appears that evidence under the control or in the possession of the Senate may promote the administration of justice, the Senate will take such action as will promote the ends of justice consistent with the privileges of the Senate: Now, therefore, be it *Resolved,* That the Chairman and Ranking Member of the Armed Services Committee, acting jointly, are authorized to produce to the Department of Defense Inspector General records of the Committee's staff inquiry into allegations relating to the administration of the Army's LOGCAP contract.

An interesting part of this report is the IG's recognition that the Army's request for a waiver of the withhold requirement. "The Army Sustainment Command request for a deviation from the Federal Acquisition Regulation did not include all relevant facts necessary for the approving official to make an informed decision. In the deviation request, the Army also could not support its claim that it had considered alternatives in obtaining the LOGCAP III services."[39] Unfortunately, no individual is held responsible for misleading the DOD executive who signed the waiver. It is obvious that some Army acquisition leaders desired this waiver, even though they knew it was not justified. Their motive appears to be solely to benefit KBR. An Army memorandum indicated that the leadership at AFSC was clearly aware of the situation.[40]

The report also concludes that my removal and the removal of the lead contracting officer were not handled very well, but this is made to appear to be a coincidence. It is also a coincidence that this happened at the time of the 15 percent withhold decision. In chapter 9, I will discuss in detail my perception of the inherent weakness in relying on IGs for independent and accurate reviews of this kind of issue. My understanding is that the 15 percent withhold issue played a major role in my removal along with that of the lead contracting officer.

In the June meeting I had informed KBR that, in addition to the 15 percent withhold, I would commence to unilaterally settle task order estimated costs based on DCAA audits. This would result in about $1 billion being qualified as unrecognized costs. I would, of course, have later recognized them if KBR could provide the supporting documentation. Because of these actions, KBR demanded my removal along with Ms. Watkins. That the Army would allow the contractor to pick the Army contract managers is an amazing cave-in to contractor interests.

---

39   (DoD Inspector General) p. i
40   (HQ, AFSC 2004) pp.1-4

Chapter 5. Negotiation, Settlement and Fee

Setting an estimated cost base for a LOGCAP task order is part of a complicated series of negotiations between the Army and KBR, and it requires some background knowledge. All task orders for major base camp services were awarded as Cost plus Award Fee Contracts. The fee arrangement in these task orders was 1% of estimated costs as the base fee and up to an additional 2% of estimated costs as an award fee. When contracts are awarded on an un-priced basis, as noted above, the estimated costs for fee setting purposes must be definitized. The amount of the award fee would be determined by a Fee Determining Official, after an Award Fee Board met, reviewed performance and recommended the award fee percentage.

As noted, due to constant changes in the scope of work, and KBR's inefficient business systems, and the combat conditions, KBR was late in submitting adequate proposals to definitize the estimated costs of these task orders. When KBR did submit them, the first step in the negotiation process was for DCAA to audit the proposals to determine if they were in accord with KBR's estimating system and were based upon accurate data.

In a normal Cost plus Award Fee contract, DCAA would also audit actual costs at the end of contract performance, to determine if these costs were allocable, allowable, and reasonably incurred. In this case, when DCAA performed their proposal audits, many of the costs had already been incurred, so they reviewed these costs to see if they were allowable, allocable and reasonable. Thus DCAA's questions concerning over $1 billion in DFAC costs had a double significance. DCAA was rejecting a portion of these costs for use in negotiating an estimated cost for purposes of setting a fee and was also disallowing them for payment under the cost contract arrangement.

The main issue concerned KBR subcontracts for DFAC services and the payment, by KBR, for meals which were not served.

In addition, DCAA found that the KBR estimating system and sub-contracting system were deficient, so they declined to issue the required approvals. This meant that the Contracting Officer could not place sufficient reliance on KBR proposals to conduct meaningful negotiations.

As Chief of the Field Support Contracting Division at AFSC, I was not willing to negotiate definitized cost bases until these compelling DCAA findings were addressed. If KBR could not support negotiations through accurate data which addressed the DCAA exceptions, I considered it appropriate to issue unilateral negotiations. If KBR didn't find that acceptable, they could take recourse by filing a claim against the U.S. Government, which they would have to prove in front of the ASBCA or Court of Claims. In this I had the support of MG McManus, the Commanding General of AFSC. He had us establish a negotiation schedule which required KBR to provide proposals meeting our requirements.

However, MG McManus retired in June 2004. BG (P) Jerome Johnson became the new Commanding General. I was requested to meet with him at KBR's Washington, D.C., offices for a conference on the program. The conference was the first meeting which LTG (RET) Paul Cerjan attended as the new LOGCAP program manager for KBR.[41] During this conference, I re-iterated the position to KBR that negotiations required adequate, auditable proposals, especially for the DFAC portion.

Later during the conference, BG (P) Johnson attacked me personally over an internal Government Issue regarding placing the PCO forward in Kuwait. I was astounded that he would do this in front of the contractor. After this conference I traveled to Kuwait, Iraq and Qatar for most of July. When I returned, in August 2004, BG (P) Johnson removed me from my position of management of the LOGCAP contract.

In my place he appointed Mr. James Loehrl, who immediately took actions to negotiate definitized costs. Appropriately, though somewhat late in the game, significant additional resources were provided for these negotiations. Special Cost Analysis Teams (SCATs) were set up to negotiate the two largest task orders (59 and 43). These were led by Ms.

---

41 (Chatterjee, Haliburton's Army 2009) p.9

Lynn DeRoche, and COL S. Grub, respectively. The major issue on both task orders was the questioned DFAC costs, though there were other questioned costs.

A consulting firm, RCI (now SERCO), was hired (at the direction of BG (P) Johnson) to, in effect, duplicate the DCAA audits, but with a different outcome. RCI appears to have taken suspect KBR financial data and projected estimates to complete work. They found that most of the KBR costs were justified! Mr. Loehrl then directed the negotiations which, if I am interpreting briefing charts correctly, allowed most of the questioned costs.

A briefing provided on 25 March 2005 to Ms. Tina Ballard, the Deputy for Procurement to the Assistant Secretary of the Army for Acquisition, Logistics & Technology, notes on page 10 that the Government position is only a decrement of $25 million out of $6 billion in proposed costs. Page 12 notes that cost positions on the DFAC issue are based upon regression analysis, estimates at completion, and KBR proposals, not the DCAA audit position. Chart 13 notes the pursuit of a fixed price settlement. Ms. Ballard was continually briefed on the progress of these actions, approved decisions and provided some guidance. It was clear at this point that the LOGCAP program was overseen and managed by Ms. Ballard, MG Johnson and Mr. Loehrl.

Another briefing to Ms. Ballard, on 30 March 2005, provides a summary of DCAA questioned costs on Chart 11. DCAA found $264 million in questioned costs for DFACs and an additional $189 million in questioned costs on Task Order 59, alone. Task Order 59 was the major Base Camp in Iraq Task Order. Chart 12 shows that of the $264 million in DCAA-questioned DFAC costs on Task Order 59, the government position based upon the RCI analysis was to question only $57 million. The Post-Negotiation Memorandum for Task Order 59 makes it clear that reliance was placed upon the RCI analysis, and the DCAA audit exceptions were ignored. General Accounting and General Audit Standards (GAGAS) state that auditors should be free from influences that restrict access to records or improperly modify audit scope.

When the Army reported these award fees, they apparently issued some misleading information. The initial settlements did not include fee for dining facility costs in the first year of the contract. DCAA had taken exception to about $250 million in costs due to poor subcontracting by KBR. DCAA considered these costs to be unreasonable and decided that the Army should not pay them. When award fees were reported, "... [The Army] said dining facility costs questioned by auditors from the Defense

Contract Audit Agency had not yet been considered by the military's Award Fee Board. The Army said it could not immediately provide more details on when the dining fee bonuses would be resolved."[42]

There would never be such dining fee bonuses! Instead, under the direction of Mr. Loehrl, the Government took the unusual step of converting about $1.8 billion in first year dining facility costs to firm fixed price rather than cost plus award fee.

The effect of this was two-fold. (1) KBR was given 3% profit (not award fee) for these contracts, which equates to the full award fee, without any evaluation of their performance. While 3% is generally a low profit rate for a fixed priced contract, it is not low for a contract in which all work has been performed, there is no contractor risk, and 3% was the highest fee the contractor anticipated from the beginning. (2) More importantly, as firm fixed price contracts the Government lost the right to disallow costs in accordance with the DCAA's post-contract audit findings. On a cost contract, DCAA would perform a post-contract audit and could disallow any costs deemed unreasonably incurred. Given that DCAA had already taken exception to over $250 million in costs, one would expect that DCAA would have disallowed at least that amount. Yet when T. Christian Miller reported on this issue in his 2006 book, *Blood Money*, he stated, "The dispute [over costs of meals] was eventually resolved, with KBR keeping all but $55 million of the disputed amount."[43]

The Post-Negotiation Memorandum gives the explicit reason for this strange settlement. The price negotiation memorandum explicitly states, "It was recommended that the best way to settle the subcontracts at issue was on a Firm Fixed Price basis so they could be finalized through a negotiated agreement and *not subject to further incurred cost reviews*, as would be the case if they remained in the CPAF mode"[44] (emphasis mine).

David Ivanovich, reporting for the Houston Chronicle, puts this in perspective with two quotations. "This is clearly good news for the company," said Bruce Stanski, KBR's senior vice president for government and infrastructure division. "This action is incomprehensible," Rep. Henry Waxman (D-CA) said in a prepared statement. "Once again, the

---

42 (Reuters) p.1

43 (T. C. Miller 2006) p. 82

44 AMSFS-CC Memorandum For Record, Subject: Price Negotiation Memorandum WB-06, Food Service Costs That Remain CPAF, dated July 15, 2008

Bush administration is putting Halliburton's interests above those of the taxpayers," he said.[45]

DINING FACILITY OVERCHARGES

Yet this was not all. The Army did leave another $1 billion in dining facility costs as Cost plus Award fee. But contrary to proper contracting procedure, KBR then received the average fee on these costs without any evaluation of their performance. The record of negotiations, based upon the RCI (SERCO) review, will seriously inhibit the government ever finding any of these costs unreasonable and subject to disallowance.

AWARD FEE BOARDS

Mr. Loehrl then personally set up and managed the award fee boards for KBR's cost plus award fee contracts. At this time the dining facility negotiations were not complete, so these boards did not include those parts of the contracts. Given all the information that is public knowledge about KBR performance, along with Government analysis, it is hard to understand that the overall ranking for KBR was 92% of award fee! A briefing to Ms. Ballard on June 3, 2005, purports to show the award fee earned by KBR on DFAC work on page 10. The total is listed as approximately $50 million in profit and fee. When this briefing was given, I pointed out to Mr. Loehrl that the chart did not include the 1% base fee on cost contracts. Total profit and fee is understated by about $9.5 million. Mr. Loehrl instructed me not to mention this during the briefing.

My understanding is that Mr. Loehrl, at the direction of MG Johnson, continued to personally manage the Award Fee Board process, which is unusual for the Command Director of Contracting and Principal Assistant Responsible for Contracting (PARC). Good ratings on these Boards were important to KBR, as they would be used to demonstrate successful past performance when it came time to bid for LOGCAP IV. And, indeed, based upon this formal record of successful past performance, along with the rest of their proposal, KBR was awarded a LOGCAP IV contract despite problems with transportation, dining facilities, ice production, water treatment and business systems such as cost estimating systems, cost accounting systems and subcontracting systems.

The Army also agreed to give KBR the same fee percentage they had earned on other parts of the contract as the award fee for dining facilities. (This is noted on chart 10 of the referenced briefing.) For their dining fa-

---

45 (Ivanovich) p.1

cility performance, KBR thus earned approximately 92% of the possible award fee without any real evaluation of that performance. As is again public knowledge, based upon the DCAA audits, whistleblower reports and other news articles, their performance was less than stellar.

Every action taken by Mr. Loehrl and overseen by MG Johnson appears to have resulted in KBR receiving more money than the independent reviews by DCAA indicated they were entitled to. Whereas Ms. Bunnatine Greenhouse lost her SES position at the Corps of Engineers for trying to control the Corps' payment of excessive amounts to KBR, Mr. Loehrl was rewarded for his conduct and was promoted to an SES position. In the process, MG Johnson received his second star.

I must make clear that I am not personally aware of any *quid pro quo* arrangements, pressure from higher Army and DOD personnel or other arrangements between Government officials and KBR. These claims would be substantiated by DCAA audits, RCI (SERCO) analysis, AFSC negotiation memoranda, Award Fee Board minutes and memoranda, briefings to Ms. Tina Ballard at ASAALT and other documents concerning these actions. Some GAO and Congressional reports may also shed some light on this. I believe that these actions may have cost the Government over $1 billion. A report by Senator Byron Dorgan and Henry Waxman found a larger number, $1.4 billion.[46]

This is especially troubling in that Army funding to support the war effort is severely constrained. As discussed above, I had met with GEN Casey when he was Vice-Chief of the Army, preparing to deploy to Iraq. He was cognizant that he would only have a fixed allocation of funds for all facets of the war. Economists refer to the "opportunity cost" of spending money on one thing rather than another, under a fixed budget. Any excess payments to KBR resulted in a corresponding loss of funds for other important soldier support, such as body armor or up-armor HUMVEEs.

It is also obvious that the continual waiver of the 15% withhold, the generous settlement of estimated costs for fee purposes, the high award fees generated at the award fee boards, and the fixed price settlement of $1 billion in DFAC costs have been worth a lot of money to stockholders and managers at Halliburton. Prior to these settlements, Halliburton was attempting to spin off or sell KBR as a separate entity, with all of the unit's liabilities, because it was a drag on Halliburton cash flow and profit. After MG Johnson and Mr. Loehrl took over and made all of these

---

46   (B. a. Dorgan 2005) p. i

settlements, I understand that Halliburton spun off KBR as an IPO, re-taining much of the stock. This should be verifiable from public records. The KBR IPO achieved a high stock price, giving Halliburton sharehold-ers a valuable asset, produced significant profit on the IPO stock increase and raised significant cash for the company.

The chart below shows the impact of these events on Halliburton stock. According to Chatterjee [(Chatterjee, Haliburton's Army 2009) pp. 49-50] Vice President Cheney exercised stock options with Halli-burton in 2005, realizing a $6.9 million profit, which he donated to chari-ty. This would, of course, give him a nice deduction against other income.

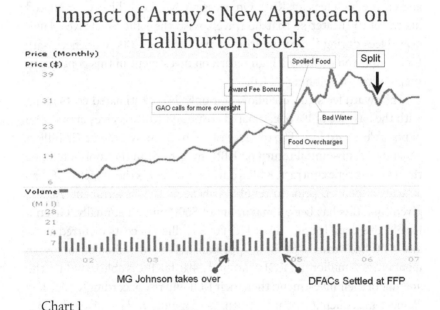

Chart 1

ARMY AWARD FEE BOARD TESTIMONY

Senator McCaskill, at an April 2007 Senate Armed Services Commit-tee hearing, asked MG Johnson to account for the apparently high award fees which KBR has earned under the contract. While MG Johnson stat-ed, "I rely upon the people, the experts, the men and women we put there, who have the experience, just as you have, to make that judgment." In reality, prior to his leaving the Army Sustainment Command in July 2007, the process was under MG Johnson's complete control. As he admitted later, he made the final decision when he reviewed every award fee let-ter. The Award Fee Determining Official was COL Carl Cartwright, the

Deputy to the Executive for Field Support at MG Johnson's Command during this period. COL Cartwright was rated by MG Johnson and responsive to his control.

Of even greater significance, MG Johnson noted the Mr. James Loehrl "has made 11 trips to theater to chair award fee boards." Mr. Loehrl is a Senior Executive who reported to MG Johnson and was dependant on MG Johnson for his annual bonus. MG Johnson insured that he was appointed as a SES after he negotiated contract settlements favorable to KBR. It is highly unusual for the Commander's Principal Assistant Responsible for Contracting (PARC) to chair an award fee board. The reason, in this case, appears to have been to keep complete control over those boards and ensure high fees for KBR. On occasion, Mr. Loehrl has coordinated his travel to theater so that he travels with the KBR executives. High award fees during the period from early 2005 thru 2006 were necessary for Halliburton to show a high return on investment in this contract in preparation for spinning off KBR.

The award fee structure allows for only 2% of estimated costs along with the base fee of 1% of estimated costs, and KBR receives about 90% of possible award fees. The total fee of approximately 2.8% of $17 billion generates a substantial return on KBR investment in the contract. Since this is a cost type contract, KBR's only investment is the money KBR has actually expended prior to reimbursement by the Government. At any given time this has been a maximum of $600 million annually. Given a fee of 2.8% (base fee plus award fee) of $5 billion in costs incurred annually, KBR has earned a profit of approximately $140 million on an investment of $600 million; an ROI of around 24%. If KBR is able to reduce the amount of their investment, then their ROI will rise accordingly. One key element in reducing that investment is to maintain the waiver of a 15% withhold on expenditures made prior to contract negotiation, which will be discussed below.

DCAA audits have substantiated that KBR did not have effective business systems in operation through 2005. They also found numerous instances of poor subcontracting, poor cost control and lack of management control systems. Whistleblowers have documented numerous cases of poor performance, and there have been news reports highlighting lack of performance. Notwithstanding the general satisfaction with KBR-provided food services, living conditions and other bases services, the high award fees are not justified.

Later in the same hearing, MG Johnson launches into a sustained de-fense of KBR in answer to a question by Senator Martinez on weaknesses with the contractor. He states:

> ...the fact is, their business systems were acceptable, and their technical and managerial performance in executing the mission in the field frankly was as close to flawless as you could have for a contractor. We couldn't argue that.

> So, given the procurement rules, they earned their award fee. It was not given to them. In fact, on each one of the award fee boards, Mr. Loehrl went to theater more than 11 times. He sat down with commanders. Before the award fee approving official signed the letter, I reviewed it. I made personal phone calls and visits myself to the field.

There are several problems with this testimony.

MG Johnson's assertion that their business systems were acceptable is false. MG Johnson knew that as of December 2005, the KBR estimat-ing system still required corrective actions to be acceptable. He knew then that for the contract period of performance from 2002 through at least December 2005 the estimating system had been inadequate. The billing system was described by DCAA in March 2005, quoted in a brief-ing to Ms. Ballard, as follows:

- Based upon a draft executive summary, DCAA continues to recommend Inadequate in Part with the following findings:
- KBR does not consistently notify the Procuring Contracting Officer (PCO) or Administrative Contracting Officer (ACO) of contract over-payments.
- KBR does not reconcile and timely submit accurate final vouchers on physically completed contracts.
- KBR does not properly or timely brief its contracts and associ-ated task orders.

KBR's business systems were in total disarray during this period. Yet for this period MG Johnson defends a high award fee as "earned" with acceptable business systems. MG Johnson makes it perfectly clear that he was in control of the process, through Mr. Loehrl. Those "more than 11 trips" were an unprecedented assignment of his PARC to manage the award fee process.

Good ratings on these Boards helped insure that KBR received one of the awards under LOGCAP IV.

MG Johnson's continual praise of Mr. Bruce Stanski, Mr. Paul Cerjan and Mr. Remo Butler indicate a relationship that appears much too close. Proper acquisition management requires both a partnering arrangement with contractors and a healthy separation which recognizes that all each party has its own interests, some of which are at odds. Support for both the troops and the taxpayers requires holding the contractor responsible for controlling costs.

IMPACT OF ARMY AWARD FEE MANAGEMENT

What did this award fee process accomplish? Economists have a term of art called "moral hazard." Once you are insured against the bad outcome of an event, you are apt to take greater risks. Consider health insurance. This insurance is intended to protect you against events which are generally not under your control. But even if we are insured against the financial pain of a heart attack, we have strong incentives to try to avoid one.

Automobile insurance is a little different. Here we are insured against the financial results of our own actions. While we still wish to avoid accidents, knowing that insurance will repair our car and any damage we do to another vehicle makes us a feel a little more comfortable talking on the cell phone while driving.

A final example is the bailout of large banks. In effect, the Government has insured them against the losses from their own reckless investments. If you know you have this kind of insurance, the profitable course of action may be to continually make high risk choices, in this case on risky but potentially very profitable investments. If they turn out well, the bank gets the profit. If they fail, the taxpayer takes the loss. Heads I win, tails somebody else loses.

KBR was sent a strong message that they would not suffer the consequences of poor performance. They would receive high award fees regardless. In effect, the Government would insure KBR against poor performance. The moral hazard is clear, as KBR lost the incentive to manage to high performance standards.

My approach to award fee boards was simple. They were not going to happen until KBR provided sufficient data to negotiate the estimated costs for task orders. Prior to negotiation of an acceptable estimated cost base to set the award fee pool, KBR would be limited to the 1% base fee. Following negotiations, we would hold the award fee boards to allocate fee. This would be one mechanism to provide incentive for KBR to improve their business systems and provide DCAA with acceptable proposals.

When I was removed from my position in August of 2004, KBR was still unable to provide that data and no boards had been held. It was my opinion that if boards were held, KBR would earn little or no fee, based upon their performance. Remember, they had to perform in an exceptional manner to earn award fee. I considered their performance to have been sub-standard in many areas. In late 2003, I was receiving calls from the general in charge of logistics for the Combined Forces Land Component Command (CFLCC) located at Camp Arifjan in Kuwait. He told me, "Charlie, I may not be a motor pool expert, but KBR's maintenance of vehicles for the transportation requirement is very substandard." As it turned out, KBR was not doing much maintenance but instead were buying more trucks than needed, which would run up the cost base.

After I was removed, for work other than dining facilities, the March award fee boards gave KBR $72 million in profit.[47] They then received a 3% fee for dining facility work, for an additional $30 million for work through 2004. By any standard an annual profit of $102 million is good business, especially if you have failed dismally on significant portions of the work.

Use of Cost Type Contracts

Let me say a few additional words about the use of cost type contracts on LOGCAP. When it is difficult to price an effort, because the full extent of the effort is unknown at the beginning, a cost type contract is appropriate. Otherwise, the contractor would have to include all contingencies in a fixed price, to avoid taking a loss. In the end, the Government would pay for contingencies which did not actually happen.

These execution issues with KBR and the Army would have had the same impact on fixed price task orders. Possible problems would have been:

- The lack of functioning business systems would have had a severe impact on attaining fixed prices.
- Pressure to negotiate these prices would probably have led to pricing in costs for all possible contingencies, including some which would not occur.

Since a fixed price contract provides incentives to lower costs, performance oversight becomes even more important. The impact of poor oversight, due to the lack of adequate DCMA resources, would have probably been exacerbated under a fixed price contract. For example,

47   (Reuters 2005)

KBR may have hired even fewer qualified electricians, plumbers, water purification managers and carpenters than they did, relying to a greater extent on cheap labor. Material prices would have been lowered through substandard, cheap supplies available in the region, to a greater extent than did happen.

The major problem with the use of cost type contracts under LOGCAP III appears to have been in the latter years of performance. By the end of 2004, operations had changed from Phase II to Phase III. GEN Casey now had a fixed budget for conducting Phase III operations, including providing for CS/CSS under LOGCAP III. Base locations and populations had stabilized. Required services were well defined and changes had been significantly reduced, though not eliminated. There was no historical cost data on performing in the theater environment. Additional oversight resources should have been available to the Government.

The continued reliance on cost contracts from 2005 to the present does not appear justified. Unfortunately, it probably would not have been possible to change to fixed price contracts, because of three factors:

- DCMA resources were still insufficient to adequately monitor such a large fixed price (or set of fixed price) contracts(s). Without this oversight, cost reduction would have been KBR's main incentive, resulting in poor quality of performance.
- KBR's business systems were not approved by DCMA, following DCAA continued audits, until 2007. Adequate data to negotiate fixed prices would not have been available, probably resulting in higher than necessary prices.
- The Army's position that KBR should be "taken care of" financially would have significantly skewed any attempt at fixed price contracting.

While the use of cost type contracts under LOGCAP is an issue of some importance, it should not be emphasized above the other issues with the Army's management of LOGCAP. As long as the Army was committed to providing KBR with favorable treatment, the contract type hardly mattered.

Chapter 6. Dining Facilities, Fraud and Bribes

One day in 2004, I received a letter from KBR. Enclosed in the letter was a check, payable to the U.S. Government, for $2,000,000.00. This was quite the largest check I have ever held in my hands. KBR was is-suing this check to the Government to account for an instance of one of their employees accepting bribes and steering contracts to favored vendors rather than to the low cost vendor. They had self disclosed the problem and were cooperating with investigations of the employee.

Bribes by KBR procurement personnel writing subcontracts in the-ater were to become a serious problem for the contract. The Army had expected KBR to self-perform most of the work on LOGCAP. Their successful proposal in 2001 had emphasized their abilities to do so, as demonstrated in Bosnia. Instead KBR had used subcontracts to provide major parts of the work in the AOR. With billions of dollars in subcon-tracts to be issued, bribery was a great concern. This was especially true of dining facilities.

KBR's management of dining facilities in Afghanistan and Iraq was one of the most contentious problems with the LOGCAP III contract. Famously, Napoleon is reported to have observed that an army travels on its stomach. Providing troops with food is one of the most important tasks under the LOGCAP program. It may be second only to providing troops with water.

If you ever watched the *MASH* program on television, you may re-member the unit soldiers going to the mess tent for meals. A very dispir-ited soldier put rather unappetizing globs of potatoes, mystery meat and what passed for vegetables on metal trays. Behind the scenes are soldiers doing "KP"; peeling potatoes and opening cans of vegetables. An Army cook is preparing the food. While *MASH* was set in Korea, it reflected, to some extent, the experience of soldiers in Vietnam as well.

Flash forward to 2004, Camp Victory, Iraq. When I visited this camp in 2004, I noticed quite a bit of improvement in the dining facilities (DFACs) from previous visits. At lunch, for example, soldiers had a choice of hamburgers, hot dogs, spaghetti, along with French fries and vegetables on the serving line. As an alternative, they could prepare cold cut sandwiches in the dining hall proper or go to the salad bar. Greens were fresh, along with fruits and tomatoes. Drink choices included milk, juice, and various soft drinks. Ice cream and cake were available for desert.

Breakfast offered eggs to order, pancakes, bacon, and sausage, along with cereal, fresh fruit, juice and milk. Dinner serving lines had several entrees, vegetables, potatoes and cake or ice cream for dessert. There was a fourth meal available at midnight due to the long hours for soldiers and the timing of certain missions.

In Iraq, as opposed to earlier conflicts, soldiers ran the risk of gaining weight during their tour of duty rather than returning home skinny and ready for mother's cooking. The food was not gourmet, nor probably up to mother's standards. The food was, however, plentiful, well prepared and presented a variety of choices.

As a means of improving the morale of troops, who, following their meal, may have gone on patrol in areas of Baghdad where they could expect an ambush or IED, these DFACs served a very useful purpose. One can question the relative value of devoting funds to meals when armor was still an issue, but these were choices for combatant commanders and the Army staff to make.

In spring 2004, when I met with GEN George Casey, he was then Vice-Chief of Staff of the Army and knew he would be sent to Command in Baghdad. GEN Casey was quite concerned with the trade-off between comfort items and military items. I have gained an immense respect for GEN Casey, a soldiers' general who was determined to perform his mission while taking care of the soldiers under his command.

The main issue I had with DFACs was not the level of support for troops; it was whether the Army was paying too much for that support. As usual, my chief ally in dealing with this issue was the Defense Contract Audit Agency (DCAA).

The first indication I received that things were not quite right was when I heard that KBR was issuing subcontracts for the DFACs. As I just mentioned, one of the reasons KBR won the LOGCAP III contract was their experience in providing support in Bosnia under LOGCAP I and the Balkans Support Contract. The selection team considered that KBR's ability to self-perform such requirements as dining halls reduced the Government's risk. Now we learned that KBR would not self-perform in Afghanistan and Iraq.

This decision to subcontract was allowed under the contract and the Government had the opportunity to review the costs of subcontracting to ensure they were reasonable. This review would be conducted by DCAA. DCAA would review the subcontract prices, determine if they were justified by competition or were negotiated based upon cost data supplied by the subcontractors. DCAA would then provide a recommendation to the PCO concerning the reasonableness of the costs incurred.

DCAA's initial finding was not good. KBR's subcontracting system was determined to be unacceptable. In addition DCAA had examined over $1 billion in subcontracts for dining facilities which KBR issued for Task Order 59, support to Joint Forces in Iraq. KBR solicitations and proposed subcontracts contained guaranteed payments for certain amounts of meals, notwithstanding the number of meals served. As DCAA examined the money paid to subcontractors and billed to the U.S. Government, they realized that KBR had agreed to pay for an enormous number of meals which were not served. Their initial finding was that the Government had overpaid by about 20%.

We had over 130,000 troops in Iraq. Supplementing them were civil servants and contractor personnel who were authorized to eat at the dining facilities. (Most subcontractor personnel, especially third country nationals, did not eat at the dining facilities.) Altogether, around 150,000 people ate three (sometimes four) meals per day at the dining facilities. A little math suggests 147,095,000 meals in a year. Twenty percent is a lot of meals.

Additionally, KBR and their subcontractors knew in advance how many people were located on the base. Base populations changed over time, but on any given day it would not be hard to estimate how many meals should be prepared. These subcontractors were (supposedly) experienced in this kind of work and should not have needed a 20% overage guarantee.

KBR, of course, took issue with this analysis. They argued for the heat of war, the uncertainty of base populations, etc. However, KBR re-wrote their solicitations and subcontracts for the second year of dining facility contracts in accordance with DCAA guidance and assistance, and it all seemed to work well. DCAA was satisfied and, while they took some exceptions to dining facility costs on later year task orders, did not have the same problem as with the first year.

KBR then shifted to arguing the amount of the problem. They challenged the figures concerning how many meals were actually served and how many were billed. Once again, DCAA had the best numbers. KBR business systems were so bad that their data could be interpreted several ways and their figures were constantly changing.

Performing some additional math, we find that KBR billed over $1 billion for serving about 147 million meals. The Army was paying about $10 per meal. Comparatively, the British were paying about $4 per meal in their support package for the south of Iraq. Although their meals were less generous than ours, we were paying at least double the amount. A 20% decrement, as recommended by DCAA, still appears to have been generous to KBR.

As always, there were two issues here. This was a cost type contract and we had not negotiated the cost base for fee-setting purposes. The second issue was that DCAA would perform a post contract audit of costs incurred. After this, the DCAA auditors had already indicated that they considered about $250 million to have been unreasonably spent.

How much of these meal costs should be put into the cost base? I proposed settling at the KBR billed amount minus the 20% DCAA recommended decrement, about $800 million. After I learned of the British costs, even this appeared too generous. But KBR would not accept it. We really were never in a position to negotiate, based upon the unreliability of their data. As an example, in July 2003, one subcontractor, Tamimi, had billed the government for 42,042 meals a day while serving only 14,053 meals a day. Eventually, the Army accepted the bulk of the disputed billings, an agreement Rep. Henry Waxman, D-Calif., called "a lousy deal for the taxpayer."[48]

POOR QUALITY MEALS

We also had indications that, at times, the troops were not provided the proper quality of food. At the beginning of the conflict, in addition to running the Dining Facilities, KBR subcontracted for the actual food. A former KBR employee, in a deposition for the Senate Democratic Policy committee, claimed that KBR received outdated and spoiled food from

---

48 (Ivanovich 2005) p. 1

their supplier. KBR employees were instructed to go ahead and use the food.

In perhaps the most extreme instance, citing "Pentagon documents," NBC claimed, "The Pentagon reported finding 'blood all over the floor,' 'dirty pans,' 'dirty grills,' 'dirty salad bars' and 'rotting meats ... and vegetables' in four of the military messes the company operates in Iraq."[49]

Obviously, poor food quality poses a possible health risk, undermining troops' ability to perform mission. In addition, the Government is charged for food which meets standards, while receiving food of lower value. In 2004, provision of food was shifted from KBR to a contractor known as Prime Vendor Food, held by Public Warehousing Corporation (PWC.) Unfortunately, this contract also had numerous problems which will be discussed below.

FRAUD

One of the major fraud issues in Iraq was related to our DFAC operations, but it did not involve KBR. Initially, under LOGCAP, KBR provided a total Dining Facility (DFAC), including the food. In late 2003, LOGCAP was instructed that food was the responsibility of the Defense Logistics Agency (DLA) as the Executive Agent for subsistence and would be provided by PWC under the Prime Vendor contract. The transition took longer than anticipated because PWC, the contractor for Prime Vendor, experienced difficulties in commencing operations in Iraq. By late spring 2004, PWC was providing all subsistence food to Iraq, Afghanistan and Kuwait, with KBR providing DFAC operations.

The Director of DLA has been designated by the Deputy Secretary of Defense as the DoD Executive Agent (EA) for Subsistence. As the DOD EA, the Director of DLA is the focal point for providing continuous, sustainable and global end-to-end supply chain support as required by end users. Department of Defense Directive 5101.1 DoD Executive Agent defines EA as the "head of a DoD component to whom the Secretary of Defense or the Deputy Secretary of Defense has assigned specific responsibilities, functions and authorities to provide defined levels of support for operational missions, or administrative or other designated activities that involve two or more of the DoD components."

Defense Personnel Support Center (DPSC) in Philadelphia, Pennsylvania is responsible for food service. They provide total dining hall support worldwide to military and other authorized federal customers.

---

49 (AFP WAshington 2003) p. 1

Through the Subsistence Prime Vendor (SPV) program and direct vendor delivery, customers can receive their food 48 hours after placing an order. They awarded Kuwait's Public Warehouses Company (PWC Logistics) a billion-dollar contract to supply U.S. forces in the region in 2003. The $1.4 billion contract to supply U.S. troops in Kuwait, Iraq, Jordan and Turkey was initially for 18 months. The contract could be extended for a total of five years and could increase to 14 billion dollars. The actual value of the contract would depend on the number of U.S. troops present in those countries, which could increase or decrease, depending on need. The contract was extended in 2005 and again in 2008 and is currently in effect.

PWC's managing director, Tarek Sultan, is a member of the Sultan al-Essa family. Another member of the family is chairman and managing director of the board of the National Real Estate Company of Kuwait, PWC's largest stockholder.

The Public Warehousing Company (PWC) was established in 1979 as a Kuwaiti governmental entity to provide warehousing solutions and supply chain services to local, regional, and multinational customers. PWC was privatized by the Kuwait Investment Authority in June of 1997 and is currently listed on the Kuwait Stock Exchange with a total market capitalization of approximately 100 million Kuwaiti dinars. PWC has a broad shareholding base that includes prominent private and public sector investor such as the National Real Estate Company (owners of the Free Trade Zone Concession) and the Public Institute for Social Security (PIFSS).

PWC is under investigation for several issues. The first is taking discounts which are not really discounts (bribes/kickbacks) from the food vendors they use. These "rebates" possibly should have been passed along to the U.S. Government.

On July 24, 2007, the U.S. Department of Justice announced that Samir Moahmoud Itani, the owner of American Grocers, Inc., a Houston company that exports food and non-food products to countries in the Middle East, had been indicted for falsifying millions of dollars in costs that were allegedly passed on to and paid by the United States government. This concerns contracts as a vendor to PWC. A Houston Press Article[50] has revealed that this firm may have shipped to Iraq large quantities of food which was spoiled and had passed its expiration date. Since American Grocers was a favored subcontractor of the Sultan family and

---

50 (Knight 2010) p.1

Agility prior to this issue, there is a strong smell of collusion on this fraud issue.

The final issue is the relationship of PWC to The Sultan Center (TSC), a Kuwait supplier of food items. Evidently PWC classifies purchases from TSC as subcontracts and allows TSC profit in those purchases. TSC is also managed by a member of the Sultan al-Essa family. The family owns approximately 40 percent of the company stock. TSC also owns a significant percentage of the National Real Estate Company, mentioned above, which means it holds an interest in PWC. In press releases, PWC downplays the size of the ownership stakes, but a minority ownership may be controlling, especially with family relationships. If this is true, then purchases by PWC from TSC could possibly constitute interdivisional transfers. If so, no profit should be earned on the transfer, and pricing would require justification. In addition discounts from the TSC should be passed on to the Government.

PWC has changed its name to Agility. In July of 2009 they announced two management changes:

> Agility named Dan Mongeon as CEO of its Defense & Government Services (DGS) business group. Agility DGS provides comprehensive logistics solutions to various government entities and non-governmental organizations on a global basis. Mongeon, a retired U.S. Army major general, has been president of Agility DGS since June 2006 and will continue in that role. He also has been named to the management board of Agility, the parent of Agility DGS. Mongeon joined Agility, formerly PWC Logistics, in 2006 after 34 years in the Army. He is former director of operations at the Defense Logistics Agency in Fort Belvoir, Va. He also served as deputy chief of staff for logistics, U.S. Armed Forces Command at Fort McPherson, Ga., and was commander of the Defense Supply Center in Philadelphia.

> Agility announced that retired Army Lt. Gen. Paul Cerjan joined the company as President of its Defense & Government Services business group responsible for Europe, Middle East and Africa. Cerjan will be based in Kuwait and will be responsible for Agility DGS's Prime Vendor contract that covers the supply of most food items to U.S. troops in Iraq and Kuwait. Cerjan also will manage the company's CENTCOM, EUCOM, AFRICOM and NATO contracts and oversee its business with various European ministries of defense. Agility DGS's Gulf Catering Co. and Threat Management Group units will also report to Cerjan, who will sit on the Agility DGS board of directors. Before joining Agility DGS, Cerjan held senior management positions at L-3 Government Services, KBR, Loral and Lockheed Martin.

Agility is a rather large company, but the DLA contract is about $2.5 billion per year. They hired a DLA leader who probably had some influence in that source selection. Paul Cerjan, as you remember, was hired by KBR in early 2004 to turn things around. The plan was that he would be there one year. He was at the Washington DC meeting with MG Johnson, where I reiterated our firm stance to KBR on audits and withholding and Johnson severely criticized me in front of the contractor. Cerjan made a few personnel changes, but nothing much changed in the KBR approach to LOGCAP. The Army, however, radically changed things to the benefit of KBR. Cerjan was quite a success. MG Johnson spoke highly of him in the April 2007 testimony at the Senate Armed Services Committee. This is the testimony where SENATOR. Dorgan believes Johnson lied significantly.

In 1998/1999, LTG (RET) Paul Cerjan was President of Regent University. This is Pat Robertson's Christian University which boasts of over 150 graduates working in the Bush administration; Monica Goodling is one of the outstanding examples. This relationship would give Cerjan credibility as a Bush team player with very high level access.

Unfortunately this cozy relationship with the military appears to be still intact. Recent Department of Justice releases indicate that they are trying to settle this case in a way which will allow the military to continue contracting with Agility. Since there has been no resolution of this indictment, the military has also announced that they may extend current Agility contracts. It appears that fraud, combined with good connections, may really pay in this case.

In a January 2011 Report to Congress on Contracting Fraud, the Department of Defense noted that there was no comprehensive database on fraud in defense contracting. A review of several databases indicated that in the past three years 30 DOD contractors had been convicted of fraud and another 120 contractors had entered into settlement agreements. Frankly, 10 convictions per year does not sound like a lot, given the number of contractors (235,000) and contracts let every year.

The Association of Certified Fraud Examiners was asked to look at the fraud issues in Iraq and Afghanistan. They estimate that 7% of spending was lost to fraud. Applying this number to the Commission on Wartime Contracting calculation of $177 billion spent on contracts in SWA, the amount lost on fraud could be over $12 billion. This number would not include losses attributable to simple waste.[51]

---

51 (Commission on Wartime Contracting 2011)p.1

BRIBES

Bribery was another area where KBR commitments to the Government, during the proposal evaluation for LOGCAP III, turned out to be false. In its bid, KBR had touted its experience in self-performing the broad range of logistics support services and had underscored that a company which did not rely on subcontractors provided the advantages of unity of control and less risk of an unknown subcontractor failing to perform.

With the beginning of the operation in Iraq, we saw a completely different picture. KBR quickly set up a procurement operation in the Kuwait Hilton complex. When I visited this office in 2003, I found a chaotic operation with files scattered everywhere in a large hotel conference room. The Defense Contract Audit Agency later found significant problems with this procurement system, mainly the inability to find documents and files to support the pricing of subcontracts. These were part of the systemic deficiencies in KBR business systems which DCAA auditors continued to find throughout LOGCAP III. It later turned out that some KBR employees had an incentive to hide those files.

Potential subcontractors started visiting this office looking for a piece of the action. Billions of dollars in work was subcontracted by this office. These subcontractors were the source of a continuing stream of bribery problems with KBR work in southwest Asia. David Phinney describes the KBR subcontracting operation this way: "Sometimes, contracts for work were nowhere to be found. Others appeared carelessly written with little or no effort in seeking competitive offers. Many proved to be highly inflated or showed little documentation of work completed or goods delivered."[52]

Those subcontracts for DFACs were a particular source of concern. In addition to the poor contracts described above, acceptance of bribes appears to have been common. Mr. Phinney reports, "Some KBR employees allegedly asked for more than just goods and services in return, according to at least one internal memo from the United States embassy in Kuwait. It was common knowledge 'that anyone visiting their seaside villas who offers to provide services will be asked for a bribe,' the August 6, 2003, memo stated, quoting officials from a local Kuwaiti company named Altanmia."[53]

---

52 (Phinney 2005) p. 1
53 (Phinney 2005) p. 1

Marie De Young spent five months working for KBR in Kuwait in the procurement office. She told Congressional investigators she found significant problems with the contracts with La Nouvelle and other companies.

Miss De Young testified that while reviewing those contracts, she found La Nouvelle had billed monthly for 37,200 cases of soda at a cost of $1.50 per case but delivered only 37,200 cans. She also testified that KBR was paying La Nouvelle up to $1.2 million a month to provide laundry service, equivalent to $100 per 15-pound bag. Under a separate contract with the same company, KBR paid only $28 a bag, she said.

An internal KBR memo dated May 2003 cautioned employees not to "discard, shred, delete or dispose" of any documents relating to La Nouvelle and two other companies, Altanmia and Tamimi. Both companies have also been accused of possible overcharges in their billings. Then, in November 2004, Halliburton filed a declaration with the Securities and Exchange Commission stating that the Pentagon would be investigating two employees who had worked on the Iraq contracts. "The Inspector General's Office may investigate whether these two employees may have solicited and/or accepted payments from these third-party subcontractors while they were employed by us," the company stated. No names were disclosed.

DFACs were not the only source of potential bribes. A bribery case which has received some press attention involved a KBR procurement manager named Jeff Mazon. In February 2003, Mazon was employed by KBR to award subcontracts to supply fuel tanker trucks at a U.S. military airport in Kuwait from March through August of 2003. KBR had estimated cost for this six-month contract at $685,000. Mazon got at least two bids — one for $1.9 million and another from La Nouvelle, for approximately $1.7 million. The Justice Department, in their grand jury presentation, alleged that Mazon fraudulently inflated both bids before the contract was awarded, tripling the first bid to $6.2 million and adjusting the La Nouvelle bid to $5.5 million, ensuring they received the contract. Mazon was accused of receiving a $1 million payment from La Nouvelle. The indictment stated that "Mazon and Hijazi [a La Nouvelle executive] also executed a promissory note as a ruse to make the $1 million payment appear to be a loan from Hijazi to Mazon."

Mazon was arrested in Norcross, Georgia in 2005. His trials have taken place in Rock Island, IL because the LOGCAP contract is managed on Rock Island Arsenal. Mr. Hijazi was also charged, but has not been returned to the United States and was unavailable to testify at Mazon's trials. Mazon successfully fought off the charges twice, winning dead-locked juries in trials in 2009, in April and again in October, arguing that the inflated amount was an error that reflected an increase that precisely matched a reverse monetary conversion between U.S. Dollars and Kuwait Dinars. The error did not come to light until Mazon had left KBR/Halliburton and had explored, many months later, doing business with the contractor, a practice that was not unusual for others at the company.

Eventually Mazon pled guilty to one misdemeanor count of failing to inform his supervisor of a contract that had been inaccurately inflated, but later corrected. It is unclear if prices to the Government were inflated due to this "clerical error."

Similar bribery issues have affected reconstruction efforts in Iraq and even the construction of the U.S. embassy in Baghdad. In Federal court testimony a witnesses confirmed that he was offered a bribe by Wadih al-Absi, a friend of Bush and Cheney Kuwaiti who was given the no-bid contract to build America's new embassy in Baghdad. This surfaced during the Mazon trial in the testimony of another former Halliburton subcontractor, Anthony Martin, who admitted for the first time in public that al-Absi's company gave him a $50,240 bribe.

First Kuwaiti and al-Absi were awarded the contract to build the new U.S. Embassy in Baghdad, Iraq at a cost of under $500 million, still making it one of the largest contracts for any U.S. Embassy anywhere. That has steadily grown since 2003. Additional court testimony confirmed the costs of the embassy billed by al-Absi and First Kuwaiti have skyrocketed, along with all the talk of the bribes, to $736 million.

These cases are prosecuted by the U.S. Attorney's office in Rock Island, Illinois, rather than in Washington D.C. and have only received a smattering of media coverage from two local newspapers there, the Quad City Times, in Iowa, and the Quad Cities Online (The Dispatch, Argus and Leader community newspapers). Occasionally, the headlines are picked up from the Quad Cities Online by the Associated Press.

Bribery as a Prevalent Problem

Bribes was not a new feature of contracting. A recent Air Force scandal has shown the presence of temptation and the willingness to accede to it at the highest levels. Foreign contracting has always been a prime setting for bribery problems. Different customs regarding bribes or kickbacks along with the distance from home seem to contribute to these problems.

When I first became involved in field support, I inadvertently threatened a bribery scheme in Korea. As I had done with LOGCAP, I identified a program called DSAFE, located in Korea, as properly belonging to the Field Support Command. Our head of Contracting, COL William Pulscher, and I began to work the transfer. We ran into immediate and almost violent opposition from the head of Army contracting in Korea. This colonel was adamant that the function would not leave his control.

We were puzzled by this position, as DSAFE was not a core function of Contracting Command, Korea. We also were not happy dealing with this colonel, as we both took a rather instant dislike to the man. It was not that he opposed what we were trying to do; we were used to that situation. We both felt there was something not quite right about him and suspected that he was covering up things.

Our suspicions were confirmed when he left Korea in handcuffs. He had been involved in several bribery schemes, one of which involved using DSAFE to steer work to favored Korean contractors. His main scheme was rather ingenious. When his contracting officers were prepared to make an award, following a proper evaluation and selection of the low cost contractor, he would review the award. He would then call the winning firm prior to announcement of the award. He would guarantee them the award for a price. They would pay, and the proper award would go through. The company would be grateful, even though he had done nothing to get them the award.

The scheme was illegal but hard to detect. There was no trail of improper influence going back to the Colonel. If he could have kept it going until his tour was up, he would have retired with quite a bit of money. However, an honest Korean firm alerted the authorities and it was over. When authorities raided his house, they reportedly found his wife trying to stuff $50,000 into a mattress.

This same pattern affected Contracting Command, Kuwait, during the conduct of operations. A rather sleepy forward contracting Command prior to the war (they only had a part-time commander), with the commencement of work in Kuwait in 2002 this Command became an overworked operation processing millions of dollars. A number of Army officers with scant training in contracting were deployed to work in this office. Numerous cases of bribery have been discovered and processed concerning this office.

Fate gave me a role in this fiasco. The Deputy Assistant Secretary for Acquisition, Logistics and Technology (Procurement), Ms. Tina Ballard, directed us to move some work off of the LOGCAP contract and into what is called sustainment contracting. She was feeling pressure for using a contingency contract for work that was stretching over the course of several years. After I was removed from the day-to-day management of the LOGCAP III contract and given the mission of developing the LOGCAP IV strategy, I was also asked to take on moving work to sustainment. I set up a conference in Atlanta at the Ft. McPherson home of ARCENT and Contracting Command, Kuwait. Representatives from all over theater, along with HQ, AMC and HQ, DA were there. Contracting Command, Iraq and Contracting Command, Afghanistan both made the same presentation. They were understaffed and overworked and could not take on new mission without significant new resources. At that time HQ, DA could not provide those resources.

Contracting Command, Kuwait was a different story. They offered to take on some of the LOGCAP missions in Kuwait, such as work supporting Camp Arifjan and other bases. Following the conference, we arranged for these transfers and felt we had fulfilled the mission. HQ, DA was happy as these transfers relieved some of the pressure on LOGCAP.

It was not until later, when the main bribery scandals broke, that we realized this transfer had been a mistake. The work should indeed have been moved to sustainment contracts, but Contracting Command Kuwait was not the place for it. The Army has since located a Rock Island office devoted to "reach-back" contracting. Major requirements from theater are solicited and awarded in Rock Island, where there is no influence from the culture of bribery in Southwest Asia. The contracting officers in Rock Island are among the most ethical folk you could find. I worked with them for thirty years and was always pleased to find a strong, may I say Midwest, ethical orientation.

As I write about the reach-back contracting, I always think about my initial run-in with MG Johnson. My reluctance to accede to his demand to move contracting officers into theater was based upon issues other than a fear of bribery. However, he was adamant that any contracting must be done in theater, close to the customer. If you are going to work in this business, I recommend developing an appreciation for irony.

A final issue regarding bribes has not been adequately resolved. The Justice Department has prosecuted a number of bribery cases related to LOGCAP, mostly in Rock Island, IL, since the contract is managed at Rock Island Arsenal. Cases have resulted in convictions or settlements; usually with a fine and some prison time. However, the next step would be to recover costs paid under the contract related to the bribe. The existence of a bribe leads to the conclusion that costs were inflated, usually by an amount which significantly exceeds the amount of the bribe. KBR and subcontractors should not be reimbursed this amount. If, as is usually the case, the costs have already been paid, the Government should recoup the inflated costs. Senator Claire McCaskill raised this issue with the Army in Senate hearings but did not receive a satisfactory answer. Based upon that exchange, it appears the Army has not recouped most of these costs.

With respect to both dining facilities and bribes, there remains a large amount of inflated costs which have been paid to KBR. The amount exceeds several hundred million dollars. Pursuing these overcharges will take the will of Army leadership along with the experience of DCAA auditors. Given the Army's current relationship with DCAA, the will does not appear to be there.

FALSE CLAIMS

When a company, such as KBR submits documents for payment, these documents must be true and accurate in support of the requested payment. Seems kind of obvious doesn't it. The False Claims Act codifies this principle and proscribes penalties and a means of recovery for the Government. Given all of the publicity about over payments to KBR, you might expect significant False Claims activity by the Department of Justice. You would be wrong.

There have been relatively few such prosecutions. One such case involved the dining facility contracts which KBR awarded to Tamimi Global Company at the beginning of performance. The U.S. alleges the kickbacks were made by Mohammad Shabbir Khan, vice president of Tamimi, which is based in Dhahran, Saudi Arabia. During the time the payments were made, KBR awarded Tamimi contracts worth more than $400 million, the U.S. says, according to the Justice Department. In a document filed on March 11, 2011 the Government states:

> The two KBR employees most directly implicated in this case are Mr. Terry Hall, who was KBR's head of food services for Kuwait and Iraq from late 2002 through early 2004, and Mr. Luther Holmes, his deputy. Mr. Hall and Mr. Holmes were both receiving kickbacks from a high-level Tamimi employee at the same time that they were making decisions and recommendations that ensured that Tamimi would obtain lucrative dining facility ("DFAC") subcontracts from KBR pursuant to the LOGCAP III contract for which KBR would be reimbursed by United States taxpayer dollars along with a fee determined by the subcontract costs. These actions resulted in, among other things, the submission of falsely inflated

and fraudulent claims to the contracting officer for payment from the United States Treasury.[54]

Ironically, this case was brought as a counter claim to a KBR lawsuit against the Government, in which KBR was attempting to collect $41 million which they alleged the Government had failed to pay. DCAA had questioned this amount on the Tamimi contract, in addition to the overall $250 million on DFAC costs, because Tamimi appeared to have a higher price than other subcontractors. KBR sued to recover this amount and the Government counterclaim appears to support DCAA. Tamimi appears to have received this favorable treatment due to the bribes to KBR employees. The Government's counterclaim may put the entire cost of the Tamimi contracts, $400 million, at risk for KBR.

The other major False Claims Act case which Justice has filed against KBR involves payments for security operations by Blackwater. This relates to the tragic ambush and killing of Blackwater employees in Fallujah. Reports at the time stated that Blackwater was engaged in guarding the transport of dining hall equipment when the attack occurred. Henry Waxman's committee put together the facts. The delivery was for a subcontractor to KBR under LOGCAP. The LOGCAP contract states the Government will provide security and any exception must be approved. KBR had no such approval and had ultimately billed the Government for these private security costs. At the time the cost in question was $19 million.

The Justice Department filed suit in April 2010. While the suit does not mention a specific amount, there is widespread belief that there were other instances of the unauthorized use of private security, so the money at stake could be much larger than the $19 million.

The *Qui Tam* provision of the False Claims Act was an attempt by the Government to enhance recovery from contractors by encouraging private citizens, often company employees, to file lawsuits against the company for submitting such a claim. The Government would review the suit and decide whether to join the suit. Usually, if the Government joins the suit there is a strong chance of winning. The citizen who filed the suit will receive a part of the funds recovered from the contractor.

Unfortunately this device has not been used to a great extent with regard to the LOGCAP program. Apogee Consulting describes a case involving the accounting and control of government property under the LOGCAP contract. They write:

---

54 (Defendant's Amended Answer and Counterclaims 2011) p.1

The latest chapter in this tawdry tale is kind of puzzling, though. The U.S. DOJ announced that it had intervened in a False Claims Act *qui tam* suit filed by a former KBR employee, alleging that KBR had violated the False Claims Act on its LOGCAP III contract "because it was unable to account for materials paid for" under a subcontract with a Turkish company named Yuksel-Reysas. According to the announcement, Yuksel-Reyas performed operations and maintenance (O&M) services at various U.S. Army camps located near Mosul, Iraq.

Which is kind of puzzling, isn't it? Because while failing to account for contractor-acquired material may be a lot of things—such as violations of the property control system, or breakdowns of the material management and accounting system, or even violations of accounting system internal controls—it's hard to picture how that would lead to presentation of a knowingly false claim to the U.S. Government.

But the Project on Government Oversight (POGO) was able to dig up some more details. This organization often supplements the official record with interesting and useful facts. POGO found the *qui tam* relator's original complaint and reported that the relator "alleges that at least $31 million worth of property and materials purchased under the subcontract was lost — air conditioners, refrigerators, generators and motor vehicles, among other valuable items, just vanished into the desert air."

Looking at the complaint, we saw that the relator was a Government Property Administrator employed by KBR, and allegedly tasked to investigate an $80 million "overexpenditure" on the Yuksel subcontract. During that investigation, the relator alleged that the subcontractor had spent at least $31 million in "unauthorized purchases of property and materials"—which had never been entered into the property control system. (The relator's complaint appeared to acknowledge that roughly $5 million of that amount was subsequently located, leaving $26 million of unaccounted-for property.)

Because of KBR's alleged property control system failures and inaccurate property reports, the relator alleged a "reverse False Claim" situation—which is (in layperson's terms) where a knowingly false statement is made with the intention of wrongfully lowering an amount of money normally due to the U.S. Government. The thing is, we're not sure that KBR would normally owe the U.S. Government any money even if $31 million worth of stuff had gone missing.

Obviously, we don't have access to KBR's LOGCAP III contract and we don't know the exact language of its property clauses. But normally, the standard Government Property clause (52.245-1) states:

(h) Contractor Liability for Government Property.

(1) Unless otherwise provided for in the contract, the Contractor shall not be liable for loss, theft, damage or destruction to the Government property furnished or acquired under this contract, except when any one of the following applies—

(i) The risk is covered by insurance or the Contractor is otherwise reimbursed (to the extent of such insurance or reimbursement). The allowability of insurance costs shall be determined in accordance with 31.205-19.

(ii) The loss, theft, damage or destruction is the result of willful misconduct or lack of good faith on the part of the Contractor's managerial personnel.

(iii) The Contracting Officer has, in writing, revoked the Government's assumption of risk for loss, theft, damage or destruction, due to a determination under paragraph (g) of this clause that the Contractor's property management practices are inadequate, and/or present an undue risk to the Government, and the Contractor failed to take timely corrective action. If the Contractor can establish by clear and convincing evidence that the loss, theft, damage or destruction of Government property occurred while the Contractor had adequate property management practices or the loss, theft, damage or destruction of Government property did not result from the Contractor's failure to maintain adequate property management practices, the Contractor shall not be held liable.

Astute readers will notice that there are several scenarios where a contractor (such as KBR) might be held liable for the loss, theft, damage, or destruction of government property. As we said, though, normally the U.S. Government prefers to "self-insure". So it seems to us that the relator and the U.S. Department of Justice will have a tough time proving to a judge and jury *why* KBR would go to such lengths to lie about missing and/or unaccounted-for materials.[55]

Well, we've seen sketchier allegations before. Time will tell whether the prosecution can prove its case. Interestingly, a memoir by a KBR employee seems to confirm the problem. Russell Blair, a KBR billeting manager in Mosul, tells the story of personal refrigerators which were available to KBR personnel but not to soldiers. He was in the habit of giving a few to soldiers, but could not put those on the property books. When the Government threatened an audit, he thought he was in a lot of trouble. Luckily for him, the audit was cancelled.[56]

Property accountability is probably the next big scandal for LOGCAP. As we withdraw from Iraq and Afghanistan, we will have to account for

---

55 (Apogee Consulting Inc. 2011) p. 1
56 (Blair 2007) pp. 85 - 96

billions of dollars in property either furnished to KBR or purchased by KBR for the Government. Under a cost type contract, every bit of material purchased by KBR becomes the property of the Government; after all, we pay the full cost of the item. My sense is that KBR management of property was lax and that Government oversight was almost completely absent.

CHAPTER 7. WATER PROBLEMS

Finding little animals swimming around in your toilet bowl is not a good sign. We certainly expect that the water company will treat our water in such a manner as to eliminate the risk of this type of event. Yet this is exactly what happened at Camp Ar Ramadi, Iraq, on March 23, 2005. A KBR employee reported finding a live organism in his toilet bowl. Mr. Ben Carter, a water purification specialist working for KBR, confirmed that what appeared to be a larva was, in fact, swimming in the toilet bowl.[57]

Aside from the aesthetics of the situation, the key information was that the water was not chlorinated to the degree necessary to kill larvae or other live contaminants such as bacteria. The water in the toilet bowl was the same water used for showers and laundry; though not for drinking (bottled water was the mandate for drinking water in Iraq). When Carter arrived in Ar Ramadi in January, 2005, he found that KBR did not even have a chlorine test kit available, even though the contract required such testing. Two spectrophotometers designed for chlorine analysis were received in February 2005, in response to a requirement at the camp dining facility.[58] When Mr. Carter tested for chlorine, he found zero levels at the site of the incident and at other sites. Carter tested water in the

---

57 *Betraying our Troops* by Dina Rasor and Robert Bauman provides an account of this and other incidents, and I have relied upon some of their research on these events. This very useful book provides a well researched and well written account of KBR operations through the book's publication in 2007.

58 (Rasor) p.148

large non-potable water tanks after discovering the tanks were left open to air contamination. He again found no chlorine.

Mr. Carter took immediate action, on his own, to start to correct the problem. He added chlorine to the tanks and rigged a pump to circulate this throughout the distribution system. In doing this, Carter demonstrated a concern for the troops and civilians at the base which he shared with many other KBR employees. However, KBR managers appear to have been more concerned with damage control than correction of the problem and notification of the Army. At Camp Ar Ramadi, as at all KBR locations, the LOGCAP contract required daily Situation Reports (SITREPS). This type of incident should have been reported to the Army the next day.

Upon further investigation, the situation proved to be worse than expected. An Army unit was operating a Reverse Osmosis Water Purification Unit (ROWPU) to draw water from the Euphrates River, filter the water and supply it to KBR for use in the base water systems. Mr. Carter thought the Army was also chlorinating the water, but the sergeant in charge of the ROWPU unit told him they were not now and had never chlorinated water. They understood, correctly, that it was KBR's responsibility to test for chlorine and to chlorinate to the extent necessary. Mr. Carter also learned that the Army ROWPU unit was located about a mile downstream from a sewage treatment plant, and it was not using the proper filters. Instead of a submicron filter, the Army was using a multi-medium filter which did not achieve the required filtration of very small contaminates. Since the Army unit was located outside the base, military trucks were moving the water to the base, though this was also a KBR responsibility.

Mr. Carter left KBR shortly after this incident, as did several other KBR employees who were frustrated by the company response,[59] and testified to the above before the Senate Democratic Policy Committee in January 2006. Mr. Carter's story is confirmed by internal KBR documentation obtained by the Committee in the form of a report of the findings of an internal review by Mr. Will Granger, the KBR Water Quality Manager for Iraq and Kuwait. His report concluded that: *"This event should be considered a 'NEAR MISS' as the consequences of these actions could have been 'VERY SEVERE' resulting in mass sickness or death"* (emphasis in the original).[60]

---

59   (Chatterjee, Haliburton's Army 2009) p.170
60   (Granger 2005) p.4

The LOGCAP Task Order requirements are clear and simple regarding water. The contractor is responsible for providing all potable and non-potable water required by the supported units. Potable water is water which is fit for consumption. Non-potable water does not have to be fit for consumption and is used in many ways from washing to settling the inevitable dust found on military bases. Obviously, water used for showering and laundry must be free from contaminates which could cause illness from contact or minor ingestion, as opposed to water used out of doors to settle dust. The Army describes this kind of non-potable water as "disinfected fresh (nonpotable)." Unlike water used to settle dust, this water must be treated prior to use by deployed troops and civilians. Showering will inevitably result in some ingestion of the water. Laundry use, showering and hand washing will result in skin contact with the water. Each of these uses poses a health risk if the water is contaminated.

Potable water was generally provided in two ways in Iraq and Afghanistan. For drinking, bottled water was the rule. MNC-I Theater-Specific Requirements for Sanitary Control and Surveillance of Field Water Supplies (MNC-I Operations Order 06-02, September 4, 2006) states that only bottled water is authorized for drinking in Iraq. Some was imported into theater and some was supplied by contractor bottling plants established to support U.S. operations. In general, it appears that the bottling plants operated in accordance with applicable standards. In the heat of southwest Asia, drinking water is a critical resource. I never saw a shortage of bottled water during my trips to the theater.

The other source of potable water was to take water from rivers and purify the water. The ROWPU unit was the vehicle for initiating this process. Water is sucked from the water source, usually the Tigris or Euphrates Rivers, and sent through a micro-filtration process. The water is divided into two streams. One stream washes the residue back into the river, while the other stream goes into a water tanker truck. On major bases the water was taken by truck to the base water system, along with other water distribution points. Soldiers living in tents or containerized housing usually had large tanks which provided the water for showers, sinks and toilets. These were also filled from these trucks.

For major bases, located at former presidential palaces or former Iraqi military bases, the water is pumped into an underground cistern and from there pumped into the base water system. If necessary, chlorination was performed to remove additional bacteria and other organisms. Soldiers and civilians were advised not to drink this water, but to use it for showers, toilets, hand washing, and clothes washing. Base inhabitants would necessarily come into close contact with ROWPU generated water, so it was necessary that the system produced water suitable for this usage.

As I traveled throughout Iraq, I would stop a major military bases such as Camp Anaconda. Anaconda was the main logistics hub for operations in Iraq. Material moved into Anaconda and was distributed to other bases. Maintenance and repair of trucks, tanks, and Humvees was performed at this base. The camp had a population of around 20,000 troops with a similar number of civilians providing support services. The camp was a former Iraqi Air Force base and was used by the military of both Army and Air Force operations. At one point this base had more arrivals and departures than any other U.S. military base in the world.

When I was there, in July 2004, the water system was not fully operational. However, the Olympic size swimming pool was up and running. In addition the base theater was operational, providing air conditioned movie viewing for the troops. The base had the best exercise facilities I saw in Iraq. KBR was very good at responding to issues that interested the highest ranking individual at all bases. In this case a one-star general saw Camp Anaconda as an in-country R&R base and so was pleased to see swimming pools, theaters and other such venues ready to support troops. I personally might have concentrated on the water system first, but the customer determines the priority of requirements.

At Anaconda, in August 2004, I requested a brief on the water supply to the base. KBR showed me the process from beginning to end. Water was initially taken from the Euphrates River by an Army operated ROWPU. Filtered water went to tanker trucks for transportation to the base holding cistern. At the cistern, the filtered water was deposited for distribution throughout the base. KBR was cleaning up the water tower to establish pressure in the total system. At the cistern, necessary chlorination of the water to remove any bacteria which had survived the filtration process was performed. This water was considered potable, but was not used as drinking water. As at all installations I visited, drinking water was delivered as bottled water. The ROWPU-generated water was considered safe for showers, laundry and similar uses.

One of the problems with KBR performance at Camp Anaconda concerned the ROWPU operation. I saw a military unit manning the ROWPU. My interpretation of the contract was that KBR was to obtain the equipment and perform this function. KBR managers did not disagree with this interpretation, but stated they had problems obtaining the equipment and were not ready to perform this function. The military brought in Reserve units which were trained in water purification and had the necessary equipment. I also informed the KBR managers that while the military was making up for their failure, this did not relieve them of the responsibility for water. The contract did not call for the Army to provide filtered water to KBR as a Government Furnished Service. In fact, the Army was acting as a no-cost subcontractor to KBR, with KBR retaining total responsibility for the water.

The DoD IG Report on water issues states that "Through the LOG-CAP contract, KBR is the main provider of bulk water used in dining, medical and personal hygiene facilities."[61] This was a requirement under the LOGCAP task orders for supported sites. As the report notes, at several sites Army Quartermaster Corps units produced the water and KBR took it from them for distribution. The Army was doing this because KBR had failed to establish their contractually required water production facilities.

At Ar Ramadi, actions taken by KBR recognized their responsibility. Mr. Carter was a ROWPU manager for KBR. The internal report, cited above, took full responsibility for the water quality provided to troops and KBR employees on Camp Ar. Ramadi. Evidently this system, where the Army performed the ROWPU operation, lasted for a long time at most bases in Iraq. It is also evident that the system failed to generate appropriate water at several locations.

Rasor and Bauman report that, "Ben Carter, the new KBR water specialist at Ramadi, had been working to get the new KBR-operated Reverse Osmosis Water Purification Unit, universally known by the acronym ROWPU, up and running to replace the smaller, inadequate military ROWPU that had been purifying the camp's water."[62] The military unit was too small for the base population and was only there as a makeshift until KBR was functional. Military units were sized to support battalion sized units during operations. The LOGCAP contract was to provide such support for the large base camps. The operation was similar to the one I described above, suck the water out of the Euphrates River, run it through the ROWPU, deliver it to the base water system, add chlorine as required and distribute the water. Unfortunately there was a fly in the ointment, really a bug in the toilet bowl.

---

61 (DoD Inspector General) p.5
62 (Rasor) p.145

How could a bug survive in properly filtered and chlorinated water? The answer is it cannot and, as we saw, tests conducted by KBR found no chlorination of the water. This was a gross failure on the part of KBR to fulfill the terms and conditions of the contract. It endangered the health of soldiers and, since sick soldiers cannot perform their mission, it endangered mission also. This was a serious problem for military operations in Iraq. Rasor and Bauman report, "By the end of 2005, about 25,800 soldiers had been evacuated to Army hospitals outside Iraq. Of that number, nearly 60 percent had been evacuated due to illness."[63] My own experience included calls from the general officers concerning outbreaks of intestinal illness at the camps and requests that KBR review and improve dining facility and water treatment processes.

Obviously, KBR was not monitoring the water up to this incident. Mr. Carter has stated that the proper test kits were not available. The LOGCAP contract requires KBR to comply with Department of the Army, Technical Bulletin (Medical) 577, "Sanitary Control and Surveillance of Field Water Supplies," March 1986, with revision December 15, 2005 (TB MED 577). A key word is "surveillance." A major part of any process for providing save water is testing and KBR was not doing this at Ar Ramadi. Contractually, they were required to test water at distribution points three times per day.

Ar Ramadi was not the only location which had water problems. In March of 2006, CPT A. Michelle Callahan MD, the 101st Sustainment Brigade Surgeon reported to the DPC the situation she had observed at a Camp named Q-West. She had noticed cloudy water with a foul odor at showering facilities. This was accompanied by an increase in bacterial infections. Water tests showed no chlorine residual and the presence of bacteria. Further investigation determined that KBR was filling tanks with the ROWPU stream that was supposed to return to the Euphrates with the residue from filtration. This water had almost double the concentration of bacteria and other organisms as the heavily polluted river. Troops would have been better off using water straight from the river!

The DoD Inspector General also investigated water problems at Camp Victory. This Camp, located at the Al-Faw Presidential Palace near the Baghdad International Airport, was the main headquarters for the Multinational Corps (MNC) in Iraq. This also was the base camp for troops who performed military operations in the Baghdad area. The DoD IG found that, "KBR did not perform water quality tests on the water it

---

63 (Rasor) p.149

stored in point-of-use containers at Camp Victory from November 2004 to February 2006."[64]

Army Response

One of the problems I have continually encountered with the management of the LOGCAP Program is the Army's willingness to deny the existence of any problems. The response to water problems in theater was no exception. In April 2007 Senior Army leadership was called to the Senate Armed Services Committee to testify about several issues regarding LOGCAP. Senator John Warner raised the issue of water problems at Ar Ramadi. He received a response from MG Jerome Johnson, the Commanding General at HQ, ASC.

From the transcript:

MG JOHNSON:

Sir, we've looked into the water-power problem at Al [sic] Ramadi, and a couple of issues. One, during the time of the allegation, KBR was not operating the water site. I was operated by an Army unit doing road fuel operations.

WARNER:

So KBR was not involved in the water?

MG JOHNSON:

Not during the time that the allegation was made. KBR assumed control of the operation about two months later. Additionally DOD...

(Crosstalk)

WARNER:

Wait a minute, whoa, whoa, whoa. We've got to get this straight. So at the time of the allegations KBR did not have a responsibility. That responsibility rested entirely with, what, the Corps of Engineers?

MG JOHNSON:

It was an Army water unit that had the capability to produce water using an Army RO pure -reverse osmosis.

***

WARNER:

---

64   (DoD Inspector General) p.3

> But so, in any event, the responsibility for the potability and safety of that water rested with the Army as opposed to any LOGCAP contractor?

MG JOHNSON:

At that time.[65]

MG Johnson's assertion that the Army was responsible for the bad water at Ar Ramadi was an incorrect and unfounded interpretation of the contractual relationship between KBR and the Government.

The Scope of Work for Task Order 89 to the LOGCAP contract lists Camp B4, Ar Ramadi as a supported camp in appendix A. The Scope of Work states in paragraph B.11 that, "IAW applicable Army Regulations, the contractor shall provide, install, operate and maintain potable and non-potable water systems, to include plumbing, sewage, gray/black water separation, and gray/black water disposal, to facilitate the operation of facilities provided or operated by the contractor, previously designated by the government or as directed by the ACO for new requirements."

Both the Government and the contractor understood that this clause places full responsibility for potable and non-potable water at the camp on KBR.

The provision of non-potable water at Ar Ramadi involved removing water from the Euphrates River, running it through a ROWPU, putting the water into tank trucks and moving it to the main base water system tanks and distributing it through that system. Base residents were instructed to use this water for washing clothes, showers, toilets; but not for drinking. Bottled water was to be used as drinking water. Residents would come into contact with this water through their clothing and through showers. I am told residents also used tap water to brush teeth and occasionally to make coffee.

When the incident happened in March 2005, a KBR ROWPU unit was not yet operational and an Army unit was providing this service. The Army had to provide this service because KBR had failed to implement its' own ROWPU unit in a timely manner. The Army was acting as a supplier to KBR and KBR was responsible for insuring that the water run through the unit was purified. As a matter of fact the water was not being properly filtered. MG Johnson's own briefing book for the hearing stated that KBR was receiving water from the Army unit, not that the Army was responsible.

---

65 (Senate Armed Services Committee) p.39

KBR was responsible for testing the water at every necessary stage of the operation. They were also responsible for chlorinating the water if necessary. KBR internal documents, in the possession of the House Committee on Oversight and Government Reform recognize these responsibilities, which were based upon applicable Army regulations.

Later on in the testimony SENATOR Warner asks, "Now, was this an isolated incident at one installation, or was this type of problem being experienced prevalent throughout other areas of the AOR?" MG Johnson answers, "Al [*sic*] Ramadi is the only reported incident that we have that I know of."[66]

Still later MG Johnson denies that there really was an issue at Ar Ramadi, "We found no issues with water there. After an inspection, we did not confirm the allegations that were made." At this point the Assistant Secretary of the Army, Acquisition, Logistics and Technology, who is on the panel testifying, speaks up:

> Yes sir. If I may add to what General Johnson has already said, my first visit to AOR was at the time of the allegation. And so I took personal interest in this, and followed it, and as General Johnson has already pointed out, KBR was not in charge of the water at this time. A military unit was. In addition to the checks that were made, we also checked all medical records to see if anyone had gotten ill from tainted water. We found zero of those, and we checked those twice.[67]

Now we know that KBR was, in fact, responsible for water at Ar Ramadi. The military ROWPU was only making up for KBR's failure to bring their unit on line in a timely fashion. Even with the military ROWPU, KBR took control of storage and distribution of the water at the camp. In this role they were certainly responsible for chlorination of the water to meet contractual safety standards.

Unfortunately for the Army, Senator Dorgan had held a Democratic Policy Committee hearing in January 2006 on this issue. This is the hearing that took testimony from Mr. Carter, the former KBR employee who had direct experience of the Ar Ramadi water problem. After the hearing both KBR and the Army issued statements denying a problem. Now Senior Army leadership had testified to Congress, under oath, that there was no problem. Senator Dorgan was not satisfied with the Army testimony at this hearing. With his usual tenacity, Senator Dorgan had already requested that the DoD Inspector General investigate this issue. The DoD IG issued a report on March 7, 2008, SUBJECT: Audit of Po-

---

66   (Senate Armed Services Committee) p.39
67   (Senate Armed Services Committee) p.40

table and Nonpotable Water in Iraq. This was in response to Senator Dorgan's request. The report states:

> From November 2004 to February 2006, KBR did not perform water quality testing at point-of-use storage containers on Camp Victory. From October 13, 2004, to May 23, 2005, KBR did not monitor water quality at point-of-use storage containers on Camp Ar Ramadi. From March 14, 2004, to February 3, 2006, KBR inappropriately distributed chlorinated wastewater from its purification facility at Camp Q-West into personal hygiene facilities without informing preventive medicine personnel. As a result, water quality within those point-of-use storage containers may have degraded to the point of causing waterborne illnesses among U.S. forces.[68]

Did such illness actually occur? The Army had denied this under oath to the Senate. KBR continued to assert that there was no harm. The DoD IG investigated this matter. They report that at Camp Q-West:

> From October 2005 through June 2006, the local brigade medical sick-call records showed 38 cases that an attending medical official said could be attributed to water, such as skin abscesses, cellulitis, skin infections and diarrhea. Of the 38 cases, 24 (or 63 percent) were diagnosed in January and February 2006. The following figure illustrates an increase in medical problems during that period.

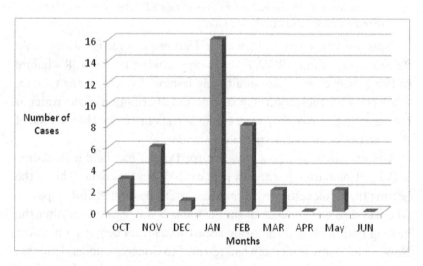

Figure 2. Q-West Medical Cases, October 2005–June 2006

The spike in cases in January and February of 2006 is rather obvious, if you actually look for it.

---

68 (DoD Inspector General) p.6

Army statements that KBR was not responsible, the only incident was at Ar Ramadi and that no illnesses resulted turned out to be highly questionable, at best. Why would Senior Army leaders testify before Congress in such a misleading manner? In Chapter 9 we will look closely at the Army's continual defense of KBR, even when they know otherwise.

The DoD IG states in their report that, "On March 31, 2007, we issued six memoranda to MNF-I, MNC-I, DCMA, and the Army's Logistics Civil Augmentation Program (LOGCAP) officials for their action on the conditions discussed in this report." One week prior to the Senate Armed Services Committee testimony LOGCAP officials, such as MG Johnson and Secretary Bolton had access to the results of the report. The report makes clear why Secretary Bolton's testimony that there were zero troop illnesses as a result of the Ar Ramadi incident is rather disingenuous. Reports of gastrointestinal illness were just not classified this way. The high incidence of such illness, coupled with the identified water problems will lead to a reasoned conclusion that there were a significant number of such illnesses. If you do not count them, then you can report no illness, although this is highly unlikely. When the DoD IG interviewed 251 service members out of a population of 7,225 who were deployed to Ar Ramadi from October 1, 2004 to May 31, 2005, 4 percent said they experienced a water related medical problem.[69] A review of data at Camp Q-West revealed a spike in January and February 2006 of medical problems which could be attributed to water contamination, "such as skin abscesses, cellulitis, skin infections and diarrhea."[70]

If you look at the KBR response it appears to be classic. KBR continued to assert that they did nothing wrong, there was no problem and that that they corrected the non-existent problem. KBR did start testing and chlorinating water at Camp Ar Ramadi by May 2005. Problems at Camp Q-West and Camp Victory, identified by the DoD IG were also corrected.

The water problems also raise questions which we continual find in the Army's management of the LOGCAP contract. The first question is "where was the oversight of KBR performance?" The Army's agent for this oversight is the Defense Contract Management Agency's Administrative Contracting Officer (ACO). The ACO generally has a quality assurance specialist to monitor such issues. In addition the Army provides technical support to the ACO on specific performance matters.[71] It appears that

---

69 (DoD Inspector General 2008) p.9
70 (DoD Inspector General 2008) p.11
71 These personnel are called either Contracting Officer's Representative (COR) or Contracting Officer's Technical Representative (COTR). They

no one in the contract administration caught the water problems until KBR noticed them.

The next issue concerns the consequences for KBR's failure to provide appropriate water in accordance with the contract. KBR had submitted payment vouchers for work at the Ar Ramadi site which would include water provision. Since they had not met the terms of the contract, the Government had the authority to question the reasonableness of these costs and possibly withhold funds from future payments pending further auditing.

Another appropriate venue for consequences would be the award fee boards. It is hard to see how KBR could earn award fee for outstanding performance when they were failing to meet the basic contract require-ments on such a serious issue as water quality. A review of award fee payments for this timeframe indicates that KBR continued to receive over 90% of available award fee, which would indicate outstanding per-formance. This pattern of award fees negated any incentive for KBR to achieve outstanding performance, let alone meet the basic requirements. Their costs were paid and they received their fee no matter what they did.

---

should receive special training in their duties and an appointment letter from the ACO or PCO. At bases like Ar Ramadi there should have been a soldier appointed as COTR for water quality issues.

CHAPTER 8. ELECTRICAL WORK

Another event in Iraq, which affected me greatly, was the death in February 2007 of Staff Sergeant Ryan Maseth. I was not working on LOGCAP any longer and was preparing to retire the next year. Yet it shook me that a soldier would be electrocuted at a facility managed under the LOGCAP program. SSG Maseth was by all accounts a very good special operations soldier, a great American and part of a family which sent two other sons to serve their country. The death of any soldier is a tragedy, and too many have been lost in Iraq and Afghanistan. However, SSG Maseth's death was also a catastrophic failure of the LOGCAP Program and the LOGCAP III contract. Even though I was long gone from the program when this happened, I still felt responsibility that my contracting efforts did not protect SSG Maseth.

In this chapter I will examine this incident in some detail. I wish to place all of the facts from Congressional hearings, Inspector General Reports and other documents, along with my analysis in one place. In addition I am really upset that this incident happened and with the poor investigations which followed.

The facts of SSG Maseth's death are generally well known. On January 2, 2008 he was found by his comrades in the shower of his quarters, dead from electrocution. He was living in a building, Legion Security Forces Building no 1 (LSF-1) located at the Radwaniyah Palace Complex (RPC). There was still strong voltage present on the wet floor. The power was cut to the entire building by a soldier from the unit who was an electronics technician. Unfortunately, attempts to revive SSG Maseth failed

Then the details get a bit murky. The family has stated that they were originally told SSG Maseth took a small appliance (radio) into the shower.[72] The family did not buy that one at all. Ryan Maseth was too smart to do something like that. The family, aided by SENATOR Casey of Pennsylvania and Congressman continued to pursue the questions surrounding SSG Maseth's death. His mother, Ms. Cheryl Harris, was determined to find answers, not only for her peace of mind, but because "I want to make sure that our troops are taken care of that are left on the ground ... [so] they don't have to wake up and worry about taking a shower and electrocution."[73] Having met Ms. Harris, I fully appreciate her dogged fight for other soldiers and other families.

RPC palace complex was one of several in the Baghdad area. It was situated on a manmade hill and was reported to be a complex in which Saddam Hussein actually lived at some times. He ordered the hill constructed in the flat Baghdad area so he would have a high view, something no one else had. The complex had about one hundred buildings and was occupied by Special Forces units in 2003.

SSG Maseth's and another member of his unit occupied quarters in LSF-1 beginning in 2007. Prior SSG Maseth, soldiers occupying these quarters had requested electrical repairs in the building due to receiving shocks while in the shower. The DoD IG report quotes two previous work orders as stating, "Pipes (Shower and sink) have voltage — get shocked in shower and sink."[74] KBR records state that a pressure switch and water pump were replaced. The pump was probably not the one on the roof which caused the electrocution

I watched the Waxman Committee hearings on the electrocutions in Iraq. Both the testimony and the documents which Waxman has on the web-site provided some interesting information.

The document entitled *Memo to DCMA Head Regarding KBR Responsibility to Make Repairs* provides some details. The document states, "The Radwaniyah Palace Complex (RPC) was originally under USACE GRD [U.S. Army Corps of Engineers Gulf Region Division] contract W912ER-04-D-0005; 0010 to perform ground and facilities Operations and Main-

---

72 The DoD IG report on this matter was unable to corroborate the assertion that the Army told this story to SSG Maseth's family. However, this was based on an Army review and the family has much greater credibility on this matter than the Army.

73 (Senate Armed Services Committee 2007) Green Beret electrocuted in shower on Iraq base, May 28, 2008

74 (DoD Inspector General 2009, p.56)

tenance (O&M) (Reference A). The contractor was KBR/MERO and the basic period of performance was from 26 February 2006 to 22 February 2007."[75]

Salient points are:

- All during the hearing the panelists indicated that they had no knowledge of the contract which preceded the LOGCAP task order in question. Yet this document states it was KBR, under a USACE contract. (I checked and the basic ID/IQ contract, W912ER-04-D-0005, is a USACE contract with KBR. The databases, to which I have access, do not have task order 0010.) It is hard to credit that the Government panelists from DCMA, DA IG, and Army Contracting Command did not have this information, along with the KBR panelist.

- In December 2006 the Joint Acquisition Review Board (JARB), a review committee for proposed new contracts, considered whether to extend the USACE contract until August 2007. The decided on an extension of the KBR services, but appear to have decided to shift to LOGCAP. A cost estimate was not requested until 8 February. Since the original contract expired on Feb 22, this created a false Sense of urgency. There appears to be no reason that the USACE order could not have been extended for the full option period or a portion thereof.

- On 23 February the LOGCAP Forward Contracting Officer and Deputy Program Manager signed a change letter adding this site to LOGCAP III Task Order 139. The document labeled *Memo for KBR Regarding Operation and Maintenance for Radwaniyah Palace* is, in fact the initial contractual document to add this location to LOGCAP Task Order 139.

This Memorandum appears to me to be a very poor piece of contracting work. The issues with this document are:

- The KBR prepared planning estimate is made the main description of the services required. The Government should have prepared a document setting out the requirements, rather than rely on KBR.

- Because of the above, the Assumptions listed in the planning estimate become a part of the contract. Assumption 14 notes that the sort time to prepare the estimate did not allow for a complete Technical Inspection (TI) of all the facilities. The

---

75 (DCMA 2007) p. 1

DCMA memorandum cited above indicates that the Scope of Work for Task Order 139 requires complete TIs. Why did the Army proceed with the LOGCAP contract without these TIs? As I noted, above, the USACE task order could have been extended until the TIs were complete. This does not make sense.

- Assumption 14 also states, "KBR assumes the buildings are up to the quality standards of LOGCAP and has based the estimate on assuming O&M on buildings and peripheral equipment that are in acceptable condition." This is absolutely incredible. KBR has been at this site for at least a year. They knew that this set of Saddam era buildings were not in acceptable condition. The Army surely knew this. Anyone who spent any time in a palace complex saw the shoddy construction. When I stayed in the main palace at Camp Victory, portable shower tents were set up outside, because the plumbing and electricity could not be trusted. Why would the contracting officer agree to an assumption in the contract which both parties knew to be false?

- Assumption 15 refers to the "MERO" property books. The DCMA memorandum, cited above, refers to KBR/MERO. Yet the USACE basic ID/IQ contract is with KBR! Where does this MERO come into the picture? This could get really strange. There is some indication that KBR was using planes from a firm called Air MERO to move employees into and around Iraq. Air MERO is thought by some to have links to Victor Bout, former KGB Major now international arms dealer.

- Assumption 16 states, "KBR assumes the building systems to be in good condition and upon discovery of defective systems (Electrical, Mechanical, or Structural) repairs will be made only at the direction of an ACL. KBR has included the cost of known repairs required at the time of the estimate." Both parties to this contract knew or should have known this assumption was wrong. The buildings were not in good repair. KBR had been there at least a year. This assumption is also ambiguous. We are paying them to make know repairs, but these are not specified here. Since KBR had significant knowledge of these buildings, known repairs should cover a lot of repairs. My guess is that KBR means this to include only those repairs discovered in the limited TIs. The Committee documents include *KBR Technical Inspection of Staff Sergeant Maseth's Build-*

ing, which appears to be part of the limited TI and should have resulted in repair of electrical faults in this building.

- The final assumption establishes Level B Maintenance. KBR will not do inspections and repair without a work order. Given the situation at this Camp, the supposed lack of time to do a complete set of TIs, why would you accept Level B.? Documents indicate that the estimate for Level A was about $6 million more than Level B. Given the overall cost of LOGCAP this is an insignificant amount. A risk analysis would have determined that if even one death were projected due to problems at the camp, it was worth $6 million to go to Level A.

If you remember, my initial conflict with MG Johnson, at the KBR offices was over sending contracting officers forward. My main concern is that they would be placed in difficult situations. There would be prior relationships between KBR personnel and the military at these bases. Often the military would share a common interest in the work for KBR to do. A contracting officer would be under pressure to "make it happen" at the sacrifice of good contracts. If this proposed contract had been sent back to my shop for action it would have undergone a thorough review, and questions would have been raised about the assumptions and urgency. One aspect of this issue is that the O&M contract at this camp was poor and this contributed to SGT Maseth's death.

The documents also support the claim that a work order to repair SGT Maseth's quarters was issued by the prior occupant, work was done, and yet the problem was not fixed. The KBR panelist made an incredible claim that the generator described as replaced in the work order was really a different generator, based on some other document. The panelist was quite arrogant in his replies, accusing SGT Hummer of "filing a lot of work orders" as if you could not take him seriously. (That the KBR panelist did not bother to wear a coat and tie to the hearing appeared to send a message that the hearing was unimportant.) The IG seemed to be caught unawares by these documents, as he was about ready to exonerate KBR.

This DoD IG report examines the facts surrounding the death of SSG Ryan Maseth in January 2008 at the RPC, in Iraq. My review of this report suggests that additional facts and analysis needed to provide a full understanding of this situation, what systems and organizations failed, and recommended corrective actions. Since operations and maintenance support at RPC was provided by a DOD contractor, the facts and issues involving contracting actions and practices should be fully understood

in order to avoid future tragedies. In this analysis I will address each of
these issues.

This paper is not intended to be a criticism of the DoD IG's work
in this report. I found this report to be quite thorough and to identify
contracting issues which are very important. The investigation was performed in a timely manner and would, of necessity, have neglected other
factors. My intent is to identify areas in which this report could be aug-
mented to provide a more complete account of the actions and events
which led to the electrocution of SSG Maseth.

The electrocution of SSG Maseth happened on a base under which
operations and maintenance support was provided through the LOG-
CAP III contract, Task Order 139. This base was put under this task order by an Administrative Contracting Officer's Letter issued in February
2008. Prior to this letter the operations and maintenance from February
2006 6o February 2007 were provided by KBR under a Corps of Engineers contract, W912ER-04-D-005, Delivery Order 10. The Army had occupied RPC since 2003 and the DoD IG reports that Washington Group
International/Black and Veatch was the operations and maintenance
contractor during this period. The DoD IG report provides the following
chart:

Date	May 03	Nov 03	May 04	Nov 04	Jul 05	Jan 06	Jul 06	Apr 07	Oct 07	Apr 08
U.S. Special Forces Unit Present at RPC	5th Group	10th Group	5th Group	10th Group	5th Group	10th Group	5th Group	10th Group	5th Group	10th Group
Contract Administrator		U.S. Army Corps of Engineers						Defense Contract Management Agency		
Operations and Maintenance Contractor		Washington International/ Black and Veatch				KBR - MERO		KBR - LOGCAP		

Chart 3

There is a major discrepancy in the documents surrounding this contractual responsibility for RPC. Task Order 59, under the LOGCAP III
contract was written in November 2003. This task order provided operations and maintenance support for the Combined Joint Task Force
7 (CJTF-7) which was conducting the Iraqi operations. SOW Change
6 v10.2 dated 3 November 03, Appendix A identifies the CJTF-7 Base
Camps under the order. On page 14 of this SOW "Radwaniyah Palace
Complex (RPC)" is identified as site D9. Absent some other agreement
between KBR and the Government, KBR was contractually responsible
for full performance of services at RPC beginning on November 30, 2003.
Task Order 59 ran for six months and was extended in 2004 for another
year. In 2005 it was replaced by Task Order 89 for support of the sites

which are now Multinational Force/Multinational Core-Iraq (MNF/MNC-I) sites. Again Appendix A identifies the supported sites and on page 30 "Radwaniyah Palace Complex (RPC)" is identified as site D9.[76] Task Order 89 was replaced by Task Order 139 in 2006.

The DoD IG report does not address this discrepancy which raises questions about who was actually in charge of operations and maintenance at RPC from initial occupancy until SSG Maseth's death. This as a period of about five years and is ample time to find and correct electrical deficiencies in occupied buildings.

WASHINGTON INTERNATIONAL/BLACK AND VEATCH

The DoD IG report does not address the Washington International/Black and Veatch contract for support which appears to have run from Nov 2003 to February 2006. Since, as noted above, LOGCAP III Task Order 59, November 2003, lists RPC as a LOGCAP supported installation, the Washington International/Black and Veatch contract is something of an anomaly. This is apparently a U.S. Army Corps of Engineers contract (chart above) which would not have been an especially prudent action on the part of the Army. As noted on page 38 of the report, the Corps charges supported organizations a 9.2% supervision and administration charge. Under LOGCAP there is no supervision charge and DCMA does not charge for administration,

I do not know the fee structure of the Washington International/Black and Veatch contract, but would assume it is higher than LOGCAP III. Unity of operations and control would suggest that having all installations under LOGCAP would provide some advantages.

Lacking a review of the Washington International/Black and Veatch contract we are left with several unanswered questions. Some of these are:

- Were operations and maintenance at RPC really under Washington International/Black and Veatch in November 2003 or under LOGCAP Task Order 59?
- If it was not under LOGCAP III Task Order 59, who made the decision?
- Why did they make the decision?

---

76 The Scope of Work for Task Order 89 lists an Appendix F which is a "Listing of Facilities that receive Operations and Maintenance." My copy of the SOW stops at Appendix E, page73. It is possible that there is an Appendix F which does not list RPC as a site receiving operations and maintenance support.

- What were the requirements of the Washington International/Black and Veatch contract?
- Were they required to TI all buildings?
- Did they have the equivalent of Level A maintenance?
- What electrical standards were in their contract?
- Are there work orders for LSF-1?
- Basically, what happened at LSF-1 under this contract?

Only with answers to these questions will we have a complete understanding of the circumstances surrounding SSG Maseth's death. Previous contractors responsible for the buildings at RPC had responsibilities for safety and quality in electrical work.

KBR-MERO

There are similar questions regarding the period in which this base was supported by the Corps of Engineers contract with KBR. I would have expected this report to contain a discussion of the contract requirements and KBR's actions under this contract. Some questions are:

- Why was the contract switched to W912ER-04-D-005, Delivery Order 10 under the Corps of Engineers? This would have been a good time to switch to LOGCAP with savings in Corps fees and contract fee structure.
- What were the requirements of the Corps' contract? Were TIs, Preventive maintenance, and LEVEL A equivalent maintenance required? Basically, should LSF-1 have been made safe under this contract?
- What is the significance of a contract with KBR-MERO rather than KBR?
- What happened at LSF-1 under this contract?

If the DoD IG report is designed to provide a complete picture of what happened in the case of SSG Maseth's death, there is more work which should be done.

LEVEL A-B-C-MAINTENANCE

The DoD IG report states on page 9, "For the ten months prior to SSG Maseth's electrocution, LSF-1 received maintenance at "Level B." However, the level of maintenance was not a factor in events leading to the death of SGT Maseth, because none of the above levels of maintaining contemplated the type of "new work" needed to correct the lack of grounding and bonding in LSF-1 electrical systems." This appears to me a rather hasty conclusion, assuming that only a complete rewiring of the building could have prevented the electrocution.

Level A maintenance would have required KBR to do two things which might have prevented this accident:

- KBR would have been required to provide preventive maintenance. Such items as generators, water pumps, etc. may have been checked to insure their continued operability. During such checks, the problem with the roof top water pump may have been discovered. At this point either KBR would have performed a fix which did not require re-wiring the entire building, such as grounding the pump to a metal rod extended to the ground. KBR could also have advised the base mayor that occupancy of the building was unsafe, as KBR had the general requirement for the safety of their employees and all base residents.

- Level A also required "a yearly inspection and punch list for all facilities prioritized Level A." Such an inspection should have resulted in the same remedial actions identified in 1, above.

The DoD IG notes that Level A buildings also had incidents of electrical shock. While this indicates the poor quality of KBR's work and Army oversight, Level A would have provided some additional risk reduction which might have saved the day. The report notes that Level B was somewhat unusual for this type of facility, most major base camps receiving level A. The Army may have saved approximately $6 million (assuming all of the reduction in KBR's initial proposal was due to moving to Level B, though analysis on page 38 of the report suggest the savings could have been as low as $1.8 million), which is a minor saving compared to the $6 billion a year cost of LOGCAP support. To save this money by putting soldiers at risk is an unacceptable contracting action.

The DoD IG report does not identify who made the Level B decision. Since they minimize the importance of this decision, they may not have felt this to be necessary. However, I believe that this decision was critical and should be explored to determine who made it and for what reasons.

Standards in the LOGCAP contract

The controlling contractual documents are the LOGCAP III contract, DAA09-02-D-0007, Task Order 139 including the Task Order Scope of Work and the ACO Letter issued by the PCO Forward which placed RPC on Task Order 139.

To understand the requirements for electrical work we start with the basic contract. Unless otherwise agreed to by the parties, the requirements of the basic LOGCAP III contract are binding on KBR. LOGCAP II incorporates a number of Federal Acquisition Regulation clauses by reference. Some of these clauses are applicable to this issue:

- FAR 52.246-5 Inspection of Services — Cost Reimbursement — This clause gives the Government the right to inspect and reject services not performed according to required standards.
- FAR 52.236-5 Material and Workmanship — KBR is required to provide proper materials, such as generators and pumps and the workmanship to properly install and maintain this equipment. Failure to do so is a breach of the contract.
- FAR 52.236-19 Organization and Direction of the Work — This clause reiterates that KBR is responsible for the management of their workforce during performance, notwithstanding any direction by the Government.
- FAR 52.247-21 Contractor Responsibility for Personal Injury and/or Property Damage

The next document which pertains is Attachment 001 to the LOGCAP III contract, Statement of Work. Relevant clauses are:

- Paragraph 1.4 reads "Unless indicated otherwise, performance standards will be in accordance with Army regulatory guidance." This simple statement indicates that for electrical work, for example, Army regulations, such as Army Regulation 420-1. Facilities Engineering, will apply to work under LOGCAP. By accepting this SOW, KBR assumes a responsibility to be familiar with applicable regulations and perform in accordance with their requirements. As with the law, ignorance is not an excuse.
- Paragraph 1.11 states, "The relationship of the Contractor and the U.S. Army shall at all times be that of independent Contractor. The Contractor shall have exclusive supervisory authority and responsibility over employees." KBR is responsible for the proper actions and workmanship of their employees. If employees perform in an unsafe manner or with poor workmanship, this is KBR's responsibility to control and correct.
- Paragraph 1.14 Quality Control states, "The Contractor shall be responsible for the quality, technical, logistical and financial accuracy and coordination of all aspects of performance." When KBR worked on an electrical pump, as in this case, they were responsible for the work being performed with acceptable quality. This clause should have led to proper grounding

and bonding of any electrical work performed by KBR at RPC. This clause also requires KBR to have processes and procedures for identifying deficiencies in their work and taking corrective action. The paragraph requires, "Corrective action procedures for deficiencies and measures to prevent recurrence. The corrective actions will address the deficiency and an action to prevent future deficiencies." Each time an electrical shock was reported on KBR maintained equipment, this clause should have led KBR to proper grounding and bonding.

- Paragraph 6.2 Facilities Standards states, "...the Contractor may propose the use of commercial or industry standards for facilities comparable ("approved equal") to and compatible with the Government's Army Facilities Component Systems (AFCS) and Theater Oriented Guide Specifications (TOGS) standards."

These requirements, as one might expect of the umbrella contract are general in nature. They do, however, lay the groundwork for requiring standards of performance from KBR when executing a mission. As a contracting officer, my expectations from these clauses would have included proper electrical work, in accordance with Army standards for any operations and maintenance work.

The next document is Task Order 139 — LOGCAP STATEMENT OF WORK (SOW) MNF/MNC-I SITES. Applicable paragraphs are:

SCOPE OF WORK. This paragraph states the requirement for Basic Life Support at these sites.

1.12 WORKSITE SAFETY. The contractor shall be responsible for safety of employees and base camp residents during all contractor operations conducted in accordance with this Statement of Work and Army Occupational Safety and Health Administration (OSHA) safety regulations and guidance as it applies to the Iraq Theater of Operations.

ACTIONS OF THE CONTRACTING OFFICER FORWARD

Under MG Johnson the Army established forward LOGCAP Program Offices in Kuwait, Iraq and Afghanistan. These offices are headed by a Deputy Program Manager and have the potential to provide significant benefits to the Army's use of LOGCAP. These benefits would include:

- Preparation of better LOGCAP task order scopes of work,
- Improved definition of requirements, with large potential cost savings,

- Improved oversight of LOGCAP implementation.

This was a genuine improvement in the LOGCAP program and I fully supported implementation of this initiative, with one exception. MG Johnson directed that the Deputy Program Managers would be warranted contracting officers. I was strongly opposed to doing so and this was the issue which MG Johnson raised in front of KBR in June 2004.

However, placing the contracting officer in theater had several bad consequences without improving contracting in any manner. These were:

- The contracting officer became subject to undue pressure from combatant commanders. They often had colonels and brigadier generals demanding that they issue task orders or modifications which were not ultimately in the best interest of the Army. It is institutional difficult for a contracting officer to resist these pressures.
- This is especially problematic since the combatant commanders are often greatly influenced by KBR. As soldiers and civilians on the Government side deployed and then left after tours ranging from 3 months to a year, KBR was a continual presence. Their personnel become the experts upon which soldiers relied. Their recommendations were in the best interest of KBR and not necessarily the Army.
- The quality of the contracting officer was degraded. My staff in Rock Island was composed of seasoned professionals, who remained throughout the life of the program. They knew the contract, the program, and KBR. They had the support of a similarly experienced legal staff and good management oversight. The forward contracting officers deployed for a year and then left the program, to be replaced by new personnel.

There was no problem with expeditious execution of requirements. My staff could turn around a requirement in 48 hours and give it a contracting and legal review in the process. Staff was in the office at all hours of the day and night and was in constant contact with the LOGCAP Support Unit, DCMA and the combatant commanders in theater.

The result of this decision was poor contracting when done in theater. I firmly believe that poor contracting in theater played a role in the death, by electrocution, of SSG Ryan Maseth. I have relooked at some of the documents which I have seen concerning the death of SSG Maseth and I am still puzzled at the contracting events which are involved here.

According to The DoD Inspector General, "On February 4, 2007, the Commander, Combined Joint Special Operations Task Force — Arabian

Peninsula, requested the LOGCAP Support Unit submit a KBR cost estimate for operations and maintenance services for RPC under the LOGCAP III contract. The commander stated that the request was "strictly part of an on-going effort to reduce the cost of operations at RPC as good stewards of Multi-National Corps — Iraq base."[77]

However, the extension was not issued. Instead, KBR was asked to provide an estimate to include this support under LOGCAP Task Order 139, which had replaced Task Order 89, which replaced Task Order 59, for support of major base camps in Iraq.

KBR provided the estimate on 19 February and the contract was awarded on 23 February through an ACO (Administrative Contracting Officer) Change Letter.[78] The contract was awarded at a negotiated cost base for award fee purposes, suggesting that between 19 February and 23 February the Government reviewed and negotiated the price of this work. This quick action suggests that, in reality, little effort went into review and negotiation of the task order change. The contract was signed by the LOGCAP Deputy Program Manager for Iraq, who was also a warranted procuring contracting officer.

The ACO Change Letter/contract was also on the House Committee on Oversight and Investigations web site. It is, in my opinion, an incredibly bad piece of contracting. It was done in haste when there was no apparent urgency. The JARB had approved extending the current contract until September. The Commander, who requested the change, specifically referenced the extension and award of the work specifically referenced the extension and award of the work to KBR in August. The DoD IG found, "There was no compelling reason to complete the action by February 23, 2007."[79]

While this may be contracting technicality, this action should not have been done as an ACO Change Letter. Since this action was new work and changed the task order price, the proper contractual vehicle should have been a modification to TO 139 or a new TO. It was also not signed by the ACO, but signed by the PCO.

Most importantly, the contracting office accepted KBR assumptions (attached to the letter) which should not have been acceptable to the Government. The key assumptions were:

---

77 (DoD Inspector General 2009) p.37
78 (Weston 2007) p.1
79 DoD IG Report p. 38.

- The short suspense for the PPE does not allow for a complete TI[80] of each building. KBR assumes the buildings are up to the quality standards of LOGCAP and has based the estimate on assuming O&M on buildings and peripheral equipment that are in acceptable condition. (assumption 14) This was identified as issue B3 in the DoD IG report.

- KBR assumes that all existing equipment that exist on the MERO property books will become the property of LOGCAP and that the equipment is serviceable and not in need of replacement. Should equipment be TIed and found to be LDD a replacement will be procured at the direction of an ACL as an additional cost. This includes the IT equipment and CAP-ROCK system (Assumption 15)

- KBR assumes the building systems to be in good condition and upon discovery of defective systems (Electrical, Mechanical, or Structural) repairs will be made only at the direction of an ACL. KBR has included the cost of known repairs required at the time of the estimate. (assumption 16) The DoD IG report identifies this problem in issue B5.

- KBR assumes FACILITY MAINTENANCE will be level B. Limited maintenance does not include inspections, preventative maintenance and upgrades. Any repairs that need to be done on the facility will be initiated with a service request by the customer. Upon receipt of service request, the contractor shall conduct an assessment to determine feasibility of repair replacement of existing items. The assessment shall be provided by the Mayoral Cell. If the assessment determines repair or replacement is warranted, the contractor shall repair or replace. However, if the assessment exceeds the scope of repair or replacement; the contractor shall return the service request to the Mayoral Cell for disposition. Repairs on emergency items (i.e. No power or no AC in the summer) will be initiated within two hours of the request. Normal repairs initiated within 24 hours of the request (Assumption 27). The DoD IG report identifies this problem in issue B5.

Let's look at these assumptions which the Government accepted. Assumption 14 has several problems:

---

80 TI is Technical Inspection.

- It claims a short suspense precludes Technical Inspections of all of the buildings. Section 8.1.2 of the TO 139 SOW states, "8.1.2 states "Technical Inspection of all facilities not initially designated as "Level A" in appendix F (Facilities) shall be completed before the contractor assumes O&M responsibilities." I do not understand the urgency for giving KBR a short suspense. The current task order against the USACE delivery order was approved for extension. Why were the TIs sacrificed in haste?
- KBR has been on this base since at least 2006. All of the TIs should have been performed long ago. Why accept an assumption that buildings do not have a KBR TI.
- KBR is allowed to assume buildings are in LOGCAP condition, when obviously they were not. KBR should have known this. By accepting this assumption, the stage is set for Level B maintenance rather than level A. The Government appears to take responsibility for the buildings being in acceptable condition and waives KBR's responsibilities. The DoD IG states, "By approving the administrative change letter on February 23, 2007, the Army Procuring Contracting Officer Forward accepted the KBR assumption and waived the contract requirement for technical inspections at RPC."[81]

Assumption 15 incorporates the serviceable status of all equipment on the property books at RPC, which may include equipment, such as a water pump, involved in the electrocution. KBR should have known the status of this equipment.

Assumption 16 reiterates that the buildings are in good condition (specifically including electrical systems), which we know was not true, and places the burden of identifying defects for repair on the Government, to issue an ACL. KBR should have known this was not true and the PCO should not have accepted this.

Assumption 27 formalizes Level B maintenance. This is only appropriate if all of the TIs have been performed and the Government is happy with the current condition of the buildings. Since the TIs were not done, at least according to the contract, this assumption sets up the facility for failure. It is incredible to believe that there was either a time or money issue to force this hasty acceptance of Level B in this contract. The DoD IG

---

81 DoD IG Report pages 30-31.

quotes the Commander, DCMA Iraq/Afghanistan as realizing that Level B was a problem.[82]

The DoD IG report identifies a number of issues which contributed to this tragedy. The actions of the contracting officer in Iraq played a significant role. I firmly believe that my office would not have issued the ACL to Task Order 139, as it was done, which placed RPC on this contract in this manner, with the very unfortunate results. Our competent and experienced contracting team would have recognized the issues which the DoD IG identifies. They would have obtained solid legal review of the consequences of the proposed modification. They would not have been influenced by a false Sense of urgency. I realize that this is easy to say in hindsight. However these are precisely the issues I raised concerning a PCO Forward with MG Johnson in 2004.

This DoD IG Report does not clarify the issues of responsibility and accountability associated with the death of SSG Ryan Maseth. While it is true that several Government organizations could have stepped in and corrected the situation, the ultimate responsibility appears to me to rest with KBR. They had a contract to provide operations and maintenance support at RPC under the LOGCAP contract. KBR received work orders which notified them of an electrical hazard in building LSF-1. KBR Sent teams to correct the problem, and what is very important, billed the Government for this work. The failed to correct the deficiencies and failed to provide a safe environment for soldiers, as required by the contract. There is evidence they used unqualified electrical maintenance personnel and did not provide proper oversight. They did not comply with their own operating procedures, which gave the Army a false Sense that work would be done properly.

Yet the DoD IG report fails to establish KBR's and individual KBR managers as accountable for this incident. Given the ambiguity of this report, it is not surprising that Army CID has, again, recommended not prosecution for negligent homicide. In fact, the DoD IG Report will provide useful documentation for KBR to defend a lawsuit initiated by the family of SSG Ryan Maseth.

On page 13 of the report the DoD IG states, "The final section presents our conclusions with respect to accountability for the underlying causes of SSG Maseth's electrocution." Nowhere in the section do I find any individual or really any organization held accountable.

---

82 DoD IG Report page 39.

The report mentions the "hasty" contracting action which placed RPC under Task Order 139. They note that the PCO effectively waived the contractual requirement to perform a Technical Inspection on any building receiving level B maintenance. However, the DoD IG does not ask the next set of questions regarding how and why this happened. We do not know the circumstances of this poor contracting. I firmly believe that it was mainly the result of establishing contracting authority in theater. Coupled with an inexperienced PCO this was a disaster waiting to happen.

Finally I note that Mr. Frank Bruni, a KBR manager, testified under oath, before the House Committee on Oversight and Reform, that "Though we cannot be certain who installed the water pump, we do know that KBR did not do so, and that it was most likely Iraqi-installed." The DoD IG report states that KBR did, in fact, install the water pump under the previous COE contract.

RESULTS

In January of 2009 CNN reported that an Army CID investigator had recommended that SSG Maseth's death be classified as negligent homicide. The investigator apparently pointed at the failure of KBR employees to properly ground the water heater during repairs as a result of work orders prior to SSG Maseth's death. This finding appears to have been a result of the additional documentation found by the House Committee on Investigations and Reform.

However, in August 2009 CNN reported that the Army CID had determined "there is insufficient evidence to prove or disprove that any one person, persons or entity was criminally culpable" in the death of SSG Maseth. This is in line with the DoD IG report, discussed above, which raised issues of contract standards, and level A and B maintenance as contributing factors. As I stated, above, I disagree with the DoD IG report, finding there was sufficient direction in the contract to require proper bonding and grounding and since work orders under level B maintenance were issued, the level did not play a role here. Since I have not seen the CID documentation I cannot comment on their decision. I do feel the IG report played a role in issuing that decision.

The only venue left to pursue this issue is the family lawsuit against KBR. This will be made harder by both the IG report and the CID decision. I wish them good fortune.

OTHER ELECTROCUTIONS IN IRAQ

SSG Maseth is not the only soldier who was electrocuted in Iraq while engaged in normal activities at a LOGCAP supported base. The DoD IG reviewed a number of these and, as usual for the DoD IG, came up with ambiguous findings.

TABLE 1. ELECTROCUTIONS IN IRAQ (CASES INVOLVING EQUIPMENT)

Rank, Name	Service	Date	Incident	Location
Specialist Marvin A. Campo-Siles	Army	04/17/04	Electrocuted while attempting generator repair	Pad 9, Forward Operating Base Brassfield-Mora, Samarra, Iraq
Specialist Chase R. Whitham	Army	05/08/04	Electrocuted while swimming in outdoor pool,	Forward Operating Base Patriot, Mosul, Iraq
Private First Class/E-2 Brian K. Cutter	Marine Corps	05/13/04	Electrocuted while attempting air conditioner repair	Al-Asad Airbase, Camp Fallujah, Iraq
Specialist Marcus O. Nolasco	Army	05/18/04	Electrocuted while taking a shower,	Operating Base Summerall, Bayji, Iraq
Hospital Corpsman Third Class David A. Cedergren	Navy	09/11/04	Electrocuted while taking a shower, Outdoor Shower	Camp Iskandariyah, Iraq
Sohan Singh	Civilian Contractor	07/19/05	Electrocuted while attempting to enter his room	Fallujah Surgical, Camp Fallujah, Iraq
Sergeant Christopher L. Everett	Army	09/07/05	Electrocuted while using a power washer	Camp Taqaddum, Iraq

Sergeant Michael J. Montpetit	Army	06/22/07	Electrocuted while attempting generator repair	Forward Operating Base Prosperity, Iraq

Chart 5

Let me discuss one of these cases, the electrocution of Sergeant Christopher L. Everett. Below is the complete DoD IG Report on this death:

Sergeant Christopher L. Everett, United States Army

Sergeant Christopher L. Everett was electrocuted while using a power washer at Camp Taqaddum, Iraq, on September 7, 2005. The death scene is shown in the figure below.

Figure 10. Area Where Sergeant Everett Was Electrocuted (from Army photographs)

INVESTIGATIONS

The Naval Criminal Investigative Service conducted the investigation until the U.S. Army Criminal Investigation Command arrived at the scene on September 11, 2005. NCIS continued logistical support until USACIDC completed the investigation and departed the area on September 28, 2005. Investigations were completed in the case as follows:

INVESTIGATIONS COMPLETED IN THE EVERETT CASE

Type Report # Report Date

Command Both an AR 15-6 Investigation and a Line of Duty Investigation were started, but combined into a single investigative report. 9/18/2005

Armed Forces Institute of Pathology ME 05-0841 10/15/2005 USACIDC SSI-0239-2005-CID259-36338-5H8 12/15/2005

(Reopened) Accident 2005-09-07-002 5/10/2007 Review of Electrocution Deaths in Iraq: Part II — Seventeen Incidents Apart from Staff Sergeant Ryan D. Maseth, U.S. Army July 24, 2009 Report No. IPO2009E001

The Incident

In early August 2005, a contractor moved an electrical generator to replace an ineffective diesel generator. The new generator provided power for various nearby activities, including a power washer used to clean vehicles. Almost immediately, a military member without electrical or generator training connected the power washer to the new generator. Over the next 2 weeks, people who used the power washer received electrical shocks, including Sergeant Everett and a member of the base's generator repair team. A military maintenance supervisor told the same generator repair team member (who had no formal training in electricity or generator repair) to ground the generator. The team member inserted a grounding rod and connected it to the generator. The power washer continued to shock Service members, and they reported it. On September 7, 2005, Sergeant Everett was electrocuted using the power washer to clean a vehicle.

Observations

Our review of investigations into this matter disclosed significant unresolved testimonial conflicts between witnesses in the different investigations. Those conflicts included questions about how often and who connected or reconnected the power washer; the qualifications and training of the generator maintenance personnel; the efficacy of grounding techniques used; the protocol used in testing for ground; and the extent to which military leaders knew about the specific electrical hazard. Additionally, the investigations did not affirmatively establish responsibility for installing, maintaining, or connecting items to the generator.

Equipment

Power Washer:

Gerni brand, Model 482A, Serial Number: 030401000326 2003; Green, Black and Yellow in color, plastic and metal construction. Power washer had a black rubber hose and handheld washing wand attached.

Generator:

Model and Serial Number: AX91375 and GAUJC027M, respectively.

(Note: In some instances, the contractor's Power Generation Dept. Fault/ Repair Sheets have the two numbers inverted, so we are unsure which is the model number and which is the serial number.)

KW = 400. KVA = 500.

Engine Model Number: 2806C-E16TA

Engine Serial Number: 2PXL15.8H16 or HGB061025U0 (Note: Some

Power Generation Dept. Fault/Repair Sheets list the engine serial number as 2PXL15.8H16. Others list it as HGB061025U0. Also, some identify the engine as a "Perkins" brand name.)

Site Visit

On October 7–8, 2008, we visited the site. The maintenance area where the electrocution occurred no longer existed. Current personnel identified the area where the vehicle washing area had been located. The area is now a large empty lot used for parking vehicles.

Government Contractor Involvement

Questions remain as to whether a Government contractor was contractually responsible for maintaining the generator involved in the electrocution.

Conclusions

We concluded that further investigation was warranted and on December 5, 2008, referred the case to the Army for further examination and appropriate action. Based on our referral, USACIDC reopened its investigation. Conclusions concerning accountability and responsibility await completion of the investigation.[83]

---

83   (DoD Inspector General 2009) pp 22-24

This report lists several investigations[84], conducted by the military, which failed to arrive at a reasonable conclusion. The investigation was only reopened after Congressional questions as to the number and causes of electrocutions in Iraq. Previous to this, the investigators appear to have been concerned with closing the investigation quickly and assigning no blame.

The IG also notes discrepancies in testimony but does not indicate any action to resolve them. Such discrepancies generally indicate somebody is lying. Lying in a criminal investigation is a crime and should be itself investigated and prosecuted. There appears to have been little or no effort along this line. The report also notes that documentation by the contractor's power generation department was faulty.

The IG finds that "questions remain about contractor responsibility." This was a KBR LOGCAP site from the beginning. In the scope of work for Task Order 59, appendix A this site is identified as B6 Ridgeway Al Taqaddim. In Task Order 89, which succeeded Task Order 59, this site is identified as Camp Al Taqaddim in Appendix A. In both of these Task Orders the initial paragraph of the Statement of Work (SOW) states, "The Contractor shall be responsible for safety of employees and base camp residents during all operations in accordance with the Army and OSHA safety regulations and guidance." Could this responsibility be made any clearer?

Yes it could, and it was. Paragraph 8.2 of the SOW covers work orders and repairs. It states, "The contractor shall establish work order procedures and response capabilities to begin emergency repairs within 2 hours of notification (e.g. failure in water, sewage, electric, or general utility networks) and normal repairs within 24 hours."[85] The IG Report notes that there had been earlier reports by Sergeant Everett and a member of the base generator repair team. Certainly these incidents should have resulted in work orders and repair.

Additionally paragraph 8.3 reads, "POWER GENERATION. The contractor shall provide, operate and maintain power for all camp facilities as directed by the ACO, and monitor equipment for proper load and phase balancing."[86] Unless there are other considerations, not stated in the DoD IG report, KBR was the contractor responsible for this incident. The faulty paper work on repairs would have been KBR's Power Genera-

---

84 I still have Freedom of Information Requests pending for these reports. The initial response was that they do not exist in the files searched.

85 (US Army 2003) p.5

86 (US Army 2003) p. 6

tion Department, in accordance with paragraph 8.3 of the SOW, cited above.

The mother of Sergeant Everett filed a wrongful death suit against KBR and another contractor, Arkel International LLC. (McGee et al v. Arkel International, LLC et al) In July 2009 she dropped her lawsuits against KBR. While KBR claimed vindication, the mother described the result differently:

> Larraine McGee, mother of Staff Sgt. Christopher L. Everett, said Tuesday she felt she had no choice when she agreed to KBR's request to dismiss federal complaints filed against the company in Texas and Louisiana. She said she feared "losing the whole case," which also names as a defendant Arkel International LLC, a defense contractor based in Baton Rouge. "KBR had us tied up in appeals, and Arkel didn't appeal anything," said McGee, of Huntsville, Texas. "I was afraid of losing it all. I felt I had to do this so the case against Arkel could continue."[87]

KBR, for their part, feels vindicated in this action and so states on their website. This is what they have posted:

> For the remaining two incidents, involving Staff Sergeant Christopher Everett and Hospital Corpsman Third Class David Cedergren, the IG Report did not suggest any involvement by KBR, but noted that investigations were ongoing.

STAFF SERGEANT CHRISTOPHER EVERETT

> Staff Sergeant Everett was electrocuted while using a power washer that was connected to an electrical generator. The IG Report found that "a military member without electrical or generator training connected the power washer to the generator," and "[a] military maintenance supervisor told the same generator repair team member (who had no formal training in electricity or generator repair) to ground the generator." (p. 23)

> A prior report by the Army did not implicate KBR in any way and stated that another contractor, unrelated to KBR, performed maintenance on the generator involved.

> Lawsuits that were filed against KBR relating to Staff Sergeant Everett were dismissed with prejudice, voluntarily, by agreement with the plaintiffs. A "with prejudice" dismissal is a final resolution that forever bars plaintiffs from suing KBR on these claims. [88]

The first paragraph does not include a following statement by the IG that, "The power washer continued to shock Service members, and they

---

87 (Pittsburg Tribune-Review 2009) p. 1
88 (KBR 2010) p. 1

reported it." What did the KBR Power Generation Department at the site do about this? KBR does not say. The second paragraph is ambiguous. That a government report did not implicate KBR is just business as usual. As for implicating another contractor, one would like to see the report. So far I cannot find such a report. As for the third paragraph since the site is now a parking lot, the investigations received conflicting testimony and did not resolve discrepancies and nobody appears to have read the contract, it is no wonder that KBR could tie up this in appeals until dropping the suit is the only recourse.

Some vindication!

Now you would think that given the impact of these electrocutions and the attention they received, the Army would be quite sensitive to avoiding such results in the future. Of course the Army should accept the responsibility to keep soldiers safe because it is the right thing to do. Future LOGCAP Task Orders which include electrical work should have sufficient contractor and government oversight to ensure work is done correctly. However, if you are reluctant to admit problems at all, then you will repeat them in the future,

Under the new LOGCAP IV contracts, on January 7, 2011, the Army issued a formal "Letter of Concern" stating that DynCorp is neither properly performing nor inspecting electrical work. In addition, the letter asserts that DynCorp is claiming work complete when this is not the case.[89] The DynCorp response apparently admits that jobs were listed as complete when repair parts were still on order. Such "completed" jobs were not in compliance with National electrical Code Standards. DynCorp promised to end the practice.

A LOGCAP contractor provides substandard electrical work and, in some cases, hides the fact. Finally the Army catches on and issues a "Letter of Concern." Won't we ever learn! The poor work should have been flagged immediately by the inspection process. If the work could not be immediately corrected, due to a lack of parts for example, then the Army could have taken actions to safeguard soldiers from the bad wiring.

The contracting officer has other tools beyond a "Letter of Concern" to get the contractor's attention in resolving the problem. The PCO can issue a "Show Cause Letter" which requires the contractor to immediately advise the PCO why the Task Order should not be immediately terminated for default and assigned to another of the LOGCAP IV contrac-

---

89 (Capaccio 2011) p. 1

tors. This was one of the reasons for having multiple contractors under LOGCAP IV.

The Administrative Contracting Officer from DCMA can issue a Corrective Action Report (CAR) as was finally done with the electrical problems on LOGCAP III. All of this should have a negative impact on DynCorp award fees, as was also finally done on LOGCAP III. Instead, it appears the Army is not taking this seriously and making many of the same mistakes we saw under LOGCAP III.

MORE MORAL HAZARD

In Chapter five I discussed the impact of KBR receiving high award fees without meeting the required performance standards. This situation created, what economists call a "moral hazard." KBR did not have to perform successfully to receive high award fees. The appropriate incentives had been removed by the Army, and KBR reacted exactly as one might have anticipated.

The most egregious example is the electrocution of SSG Maseth after the RPC complex was placed under Task Order 139. Having operated there for at least a year, KBR was aware of the condition of the base. They had the reasonable expectation that award fees would be high whether they met the requirements of the scope of work or not. So electrical problems which existed were left without repair and the death of SSG Maseth was the result.

Even then, KBR did not take actions to correct the situation. They instead referred to the lenient terms and conditions of the Task Order modification issued by the PCO forward and claimed it was not their responsibility. They never changed this position, assuming the Army would support them.

Only after a Congressional hearing, did the DCMA issue a corrective action report. Still, the Army had to initiate its own corrective action initiative, Project SAFE, to improve the electrical condition of bases in Afghanistan, Kuwait and Iraq. Even then, KBR appears to have been paid to be a part of this project and correct their failures. Unfortunately, the contractual language with KBR has not been released by the Army.

It took another Congressional hearing, in which I participated, to actually prod the Government into taking away award fee from KBR. The poor wiring conditions had existed for years in various camps. They existed for at least a year at the RPC camp where SSG Maseth was electrocuted. KBR, in a 2008 financial statement footnote anticipated losing one year's award fee, valued at $100 million. Instead, the Army denied just one quarter of a year's award fee, $25 million. I have been told that KBR blamed me and my testimony for losing even this amount. I would not make that claim, but am pleased they gave me the credit.

Chapter 9. Transportation

One of the worst days of my time in LOGCAP occurred on April 9, 2004, when a KBR convoy, carrying military supplies, was ambushed in Iraq. This was a mile-and-a-half-long convoy of 26 vehicles — 19 KBR trucks and seven military vehicles, moving fuel to Baghdad International Airport along a route nicknamed by KBR truck drivers as IED Boulevard."[90] Reports we received indicated only six KBR trucks eventually reached the airport. Six KBR truck drivers were killed, one was kidnapped and two are missing presumed dead. Three soldiers guarding the convoy were also killed. While the death of any person during these operations is a tragedy, soldiers do sign up to risk their lives to defend the country. By contrast, civilian employees of contractors normally expect to serve in behind-the-lines positions.

I started receiving calls and reports the next morning as we were faced with a number of questions. Following the ambush, KBR had ordered their convoy operations to stand down while a security assessment was performed. This was standard military procedure for such an event. While some Army officers wanted KBR to continue moving, I argued that the stand down was appropriate but required immediate resolution. KBR needed some mix of additional security, better armed army support vehicles, better direction on which routes to use and more support troops. After a couple of days of intense analysis and discussion, the Army provided KBR with enhanced security and the trucks rolled again.

---

90   (Hamill 2004) p. 33

The Army also began to make arrangements for soldiers to drive the trucks that KBR had acquired. Based upon the premise that there would be situations in which a contractor could reasonably decline to move due to security concerns, soldiers could be ordered to drive. This backup plan required training soldiers on the trucks and these convoy procedures. This was not a KBR problem, but one of the many complications of using contractors in a combat zone.

Iraq, of course, had evolved into a conflict where there were no behind-the-lines positions. While the concept of using a contractor to provide transportation services may have originally envisaged work in relatively protected zones far from the forward line of battle, this was not the case in Iraq. Civilian truck drivers crossed the border in Kuwait and moved from there to various camps in Iraq. Any time spent on the road and not in camp was essentially travel through a combat zone. The military did not have enough forces to secure these Major Supply Routes (MSRs) so convoy security was provided to the KBR truckers who moved the essential goods which allowed the military to perform their mission.

The transportation requirements of the LOGCAP contract were much broader than providing truck drivers. KBR purchased the trucks, provided the drivers, set up and operated maintenance facilities for the trucks, with mechanics and spare parts, and set central staging areas for their convoys in Kuwait. The standard distribution functions of scheduling and dispatching were done by KBR, working with military logistics specialists.

When up and running, KBR trucks loaded in Kuwait and moved to a KBR maintained base near the Kuwait-Iraq border called Navistar. This base was possibly the largest truck stop in the world. (I apologize to the I-80 Truck Stop, near my home, which also makes that claim.) At Navistar military security joined the convoy, final routing information and intelligence was received and the convoy moved north into Iraq.

I traveled to Navistar in 2003. This base was close to the Iraq-Kuwait and when we arrived we were forced to spend about an hour crouched in a ditch as a security exercise was taking place. Inside the base, I observed a full military complex with housing for troops and truckers, MWR facilities, dining facilities and operational buildings. Of course, KBR ran all of this in addition to the transportation mission. Already, there appeared to be problems with the level of training and experience of KBR personnel. Cynthia Morgan, a KBR truck driver and convoy manager wrote,

"Part of the new job's excitement was my lack of preparation and training — they just threw me into the job without a whole lot of guidance."[91]

The usual destination of KBR convoys from Kuwait was Camp Anaconda, the main logistics base north of Baghdad. Here other convoys would be staged to move supplies throughout Iraq. The distribution of bases in Iraq required KBR to operate throughout the country. Eventually trucks also came into Camp Anaconda from the west, from Jordan.

However, various commodities moved in different ways. Fuel had to be moved to special supply points on the way to Anaconda. From there it was moved to various locations, including the Baghdad International Airport. At the beginning of the conflict through spring 2004, KBR moved food throughout the area in refrigerated trucks. Ice was also moved in these trucks. Perishable goods required special treatment in scheduling their movement in theater.

From the beginning, even prior to the invasion of Iraq, the Army had problems with KBR's execution of the transportation mission. Rasor and Bauman describe the experience of Roger Lambeth, hired by KBR to be a transportation manager in Kuwait as preparations for the invasion were ongoing.

While on the morning checks of the trucks and tractor-trailers, Lambeth discovered what he believed to be a major impediment to providing transportation support to the Army. He felt that more than 80 percent of the vehicles were overused and defective. The Army wanted the vehicles up to Department of Transportation standards, and they were not. There were trucks that did not have gas caps — they had rags stuck in the hole instead; seats that were not mounted — they were loose or would slide; transmission problems — some trucks would not go into reverse; speedometers and other gauges that did not work; serious engine problems; oil leaks, bald tires; defective brakes, fifth wheels that would not release; exhaust leaks; and the list went on.[92]

This creates a disturbing picture of poor support as the military was weeks away from the invasion. This description also corresponds with reports I was receiving from Camp Arifjan. BG Vincent Boles had been our immediate commander at Field Support Command, and had deployed to manage the Coalition Forces Land Component Command (CFLCC), logistics operations. This was the logistics hub in Kuwait and would be the point of entry for U.S. forces invading Iraq. BG Boles was one of those

---

91 (Morgan 2006) p. 71
92 (D. a. Rasor 2007) p.16

fine soldiers I was privileged to work with during this period. He was a smart soldier who cared about troops and his mission. If any of my kids went to war, I would be happy with BG Boles commanding them.

I would receive occasional calls from BG Boles about support by LOGCAP. One of these concerned the transportation mission. As I recall the conversation began, "Charlie, I may not have much motor pool experience, but this does not look like the way to run this operation." General Boles was concerned by exactly the same situation described by Mr. Lambeth. KBR "motor pool" operations were poorly managed with a large number of out of commission vehicles. He observed that KBR bought some poor quality trucks and the KBR response seemed to be to buy more vehicles rather than maintain those they had. This was both a cost and mission problem. At the height of the mission, KBR had over 700 trucks on the road.

David Wilson's testimony submitted to Representative Henry Waxman's committee confirmed this situation. He stated:

> As every other trucker working on these convoys will tell you, KBR had virtually no facilities in place to do the maintenance on these trucks. There were absolutely no oil filters or fuel filters for months on end. I begged for filters but never got any. I was told that oil changes were out of the question.[93]

I discussed this with KBR leadership and worked with the DCMA to issue Corrective Action Reports, requiring KBR to fix the situation. While the situation improved, the management of this part of the transportation mission appeared to waste quite a bit of money. The DCAA auditors later would take exception to a large amount of costs related to truck purchases, verifying this analysis. Unfortunately, I do not believe the Army ever sustained the DCAA questioned costs and retrieved the money.

EMPTY TRUCKS ON THE ROAD

In 2004, we received reports of some KBR convoys containing empty trucks. I was asked about this by a reporter from NPR and I explained that some trucks might not pull a trailer as a security matter, so they could replace a damaged or disabled truck on the route. The convoy could not wait for repair or recovery vehicles to arrive because that made them a sitting target for too long. Trucks might also carry empty trailers,

---

93 (D. Wilson 2004) p. 1

if there was not a return delivery to be made. In making these remarks, I was overly optimistic and defensive of my contractor.

Later investigation revealed a serious problem which was costing the Army needed funds. A KBR employee who had commanded over one hundred convoys stated that they often took an empty trailer to a location and then picked up an empty one for the return trip. Trailers that could hold twenty-six full pallets ran with only one on board. At times, one in three trailers was empty.[94] This was during the period when the cost base was un-negotiated, so building up costs could have increased KBR profit.

The April 9 Incident

T. Scott Allen, a lawyer representing the KBR truckers in a suit against the company, provided a summary of their allegations against KBR in testimony before the DPC:

> Rather, we have sadly discovered evidence and testimony which proves that Halliburton/KBR knew well before my clients were Sent from Camp Anaconda on April 9th that the roads they would travel were engaged in active combat, that the areas were closed and off limits to civilian personnel, and that other Halliburton/KBR convoys had been attacked at or near the same location which had already resulted in multiple civilian casualties.[95]

Documents disclosed in the case indicate that within KBR there was knowledge that this convoy represented extreme risk. The LA Times reported that KBR memos stated, ""[I] think we will get people injured or killed tomorrow," warned KBR regional Security Chief George Seagle, citing "tons of intel." But in an e-mail sent a day before the convoy was dispatched, he also acknowledged: "Big politics and contract issues involved." Keith Richard, the head of KBR's trucking operation, agreed in an email, writing, "Another day like today and we will lose most of our drivers." He also wrote that KBR's civilians are different from soldiers and that truck drivers who signed up with the company expected dangerous conditions "but they did not expect to be in the middle of a war."[96]

Jeff Wendell, of Group News Blog (groupnewsblog.net) reported, "On the day in question the road had been opened and closed repeatedly. The KBR manager who'd been in control of operations for damn near for-

94 (Chatterjee, Iraq, Inc. 2004) p. 35
95 (Allen 2006) p. 1
96 (L. A. Times 2007)

ever had threatened to resign if his drivers were ordered to push a load through. Yet after a while, there the order came... push through."[97]

Craig Peterson, KBR's top official in Iraq at that time, said KBR couldn't decide on its own to suspend convoys and must respond when the military called for delivery of supplies. "Only the army can stop convoys," he wrote in an email. On April 9, Richard ordered that no convoys were to move out. But 25 minutes later, a separate order from the company's communications system ordered the convoys to proceed as planned, the newspaper reported. Later that morning the convoy of 26 left for Baghdad International Airport to deliver the fuel, driving through an obvious combat zone. Just six KBR trucks eventually reached the airport.

Families of the dead truck drivers sued KBR in 2005. Last September, U.S. District Judge Gray H. Miller dismissed the lawsuit, saying courts have no jurisdiction over cases involving military orders. Deciding the case would require "the court to examine the policies of the executive branch during wartime, a step the court declines to take," Miller wrote. The families' lawyers have appealed, arguing KBR has authority over the civilian truck drivers it employs.

Transportation is one of the LOGCAP missions that were never conceived as operating in this manner. Combat would take place along a forward line of battle. Immediately behind the combat zone would be supply stations from which water, food and other critical support items would move to the front line. Behind these would be the major supply depots and base camps operated by KBR. KBR would transport supplies from ports to these major supply depots and perhaps to the supply stations. All movement would be behind the forward line of battle.

Of course the situations in Iraq and Afghanistan turned out differently. There is no forward line of battle. Most of each country is a combat zone. The contractor must transport supplies throughout this zone. Exposed to mush more risk than was originally contemplated when LOGCAP was developed.

In addition, due to this situation and the lack of sufficient troops, the contractor must transport supplies over unsecured routes. The Army can handle such supply routes in two ways. The best way is to secure the route. Most routes behind a forward line of battle would be secure routes. Even in a combat zone some routes may be secured by removing potential staging grounds for assaults and stationing soldiers along the route.

---

97   (Wendell) p. 1

The other way is to travel unsecured routes in secure convoys. When I traveled from Baghdad to Babylon, nineteen soldiers in three vehicles were assigned to escort me there. There were several possible routes to choose from and we travelled on two randomly assigned of these routes; out and back. KBR supply convoys were given convey security to travel on unsecured routes. As we saw, such convoy security is not always adequate. Over time it did improve. The introduction of the Stryker vehicle into Iraq provided much better convoy security when utilized. Insurgents did not want to take on these vehicles with their firepower and resistance to some IEDs. However, the inability to secure routes presented contractor transportation with a major risk.

REEFERS

No, not that kind of reefer! In my travels in theater I never noticed that old familiar aroma from the 60s. Here we are speaking of refrigerated transportation trailers. These were uniformly known as "reefers" in theater. Reefers were a major transportation headache, for a couple of reasons.

The first was that they were I short supply. KBR was slow in procuring enough for all theater missions. The ones they did procure were difficult to maintain, and on any given day a significant number were not usable. Since they were needed to move food, ice and medicine around theater, they were a critical item for us.

The second issue was that KBR tended to lose them. This was generally not KBR's fault. In a typical situation a KBR truck driver would deliver some ice to a unit in his reefer. Soldiers in the unit would quickly notice that the trailer, powered by a unit generator, would make a fine refrigerated storage facility for the unit. They could keep more ice on hand and perhaps, keep some ice cream around.

The troops would politely ask the driver to unhook the trailer and leave it with them. The truck driver would say no, he or she had to return the trailer. The troops would remind the truck driver that they were the customer and this trailer would fulfill a genuine need. This argument might sway some drivers as KBR was quite interested in making the customer happy. I was told that some units resorted to the final argument, pointing out they had weapons and numbers on their side. As a result, a number of reefers were left with the units.

In late 2004 the Army realized something had to be done. They organized a team to locate all such reefers, remove them from the units and get them back into service for transportation. This was generally successful, though some reefers needed a lot of repair.

KBR suggested a partial solution to the shortage of reefers. At the beginning of the war, ice was moved into Iraq from plants in Kuwait. KBR proposed building several ice plants throughout Iraq. This would reduce the number of ice delivery trips and free up reefers for other duty. This would also reduce the risk for drivers by reducing trips and miles driven to supply ice.

The Army agreed to the upfront cost of this proposal for the reasons noted above and because it would ultimately be a more cost effective way of providing ice to troops. Operations always require provision of ice, but operations in Iraq, especially in the summer required a lot of ice. Once the Army made this decision they wanted their ice plants and they wanted them now!

My first trip to Iraq included the mission of finding out why the ice plants were not up and running. KBR had contracted for several suppliers to build the plants and all were behind schedule. KBR gave me a familiar story about how their suppliers were late and I gave them my standard speech that I paid them to manage their suppliers. I impressed upon them that this had high level attention and might ultimately affect award fees. They gave me a plan for greater oversight of their suppliers and a new schedule for getting the ice plants running. By and large they met this new schedule.

OTHER TRANSPORTATION CONTRACTORS

When I was last in Iraq in August 2004, I realized that the existence of other transportation contractors was causing both KBR and the Army problems. PWC, who had taken over the provision of food under their Food Prime Vendor Contract, issued by the Defense Supply Center in Philadelphia, was moving trucks into and around Iraq. Reconstruction contractors were also moving material by trucks. Even the Corps of Engineers was using KBR for transportation, but not under LOGCAP. Unity of control was missing in action.

I saw this at Camp Anaconda where trucks were now arriving from Jordan along an eastern route. Almost all KBR LOGCAP trucks came up from Kuwait in the south. The trucks from Jordan all appeared to be driven by Turkish truck drivers. These drivers were treated very differently from the KBR truck drivers. KBR drivers slept in camp housing when they stayed overnight. Turkish drivers slept in their trucks. KBR drivers ate at the DFAC while Turkish drivers ate their own food. KBR drivers had access to showers, while Turkish drivers did not. This later difference resulted in some Turkish drivers attempting to use the hand wash stations outside of the DFACs to bath.

Unfortunately, this difference in treatment was quite apparent to the Turkish drivers, who wanted the same treatment as the U.S. drivers for KBR. KBR had no authorization to provide anything to drivers operating under different contracts. They tried their best to reach some accommodations in the name of peace, which I supported as a proper practice. One of my goals upon returning was to resolve this issue, but I did not have time before I was removed.

This difference in treatment was not unique to truck drivers. When driving around Camp Anaconda I saw some workers from Bangladesh living in squalor in a simple shipping container, with no sanitation visible and cooking their meals in front of the container. I asked who they worked for and was told they worked for a subcontractor to KBR. I informed KBR that this was unacceptable under LOGCAP and they needed to change this situation. When unacceptable did not seem to work I appealed to their practical Sense. It would do none of any good if a picture of these workers appeared on the front page of the Washington Post. They agreed and promised to correct the situation. However, I did not have a chance to follow up on this matter. A number of these issues were in my trip report, but I received the distinct impression that the report was ignored.

The Army's transportation issues with KBR are not over. Some of the families of dead truck drivers are suing KBR, though their suit has had initial setbacks. Should the families ultimately win, KBR will probably try to bill the settlements as an allowable cost. These suits and other labor issues involving truck drivers will be in court for a while and the Government may have a financial stake in the outcomes. Overall, litigations issues seem to be a part of contractors on the battlefield and I will discuss them further in chapter 11.

TACTICAL VEHICLE MAINTENANCE

An interesting and troublesome offshoot of KBR's transportation role in Iraq was their involvement with tactical vehicle maintenance. As part of the transportation mission, KBR performed maintenance on non-tactical vehicles such as semi-trailers and the numerous SUVs found on all major bases. This function was well within the LOGCAP scope of work.

However, under task order 159 (period of performance from September 1, 2008, through August 31, 2009), the Army added maintenance of tactical vehicles at Joint Base Balad (also known as Camp Anaconda.) My interpretation of the LOGCAP scope of work is that this mission was outside the scope.

There were already sufficient maintenance resources at Balad. Most of the manufacturers of Ml Abrams Tanks, HUMVEEs, M2/3 Bradley Fighting Vehicles, and Strykers were in place in Balad with maintenance teams. These contractors operated under what are called Contractor Logistics Support (CLS) contracts. In fact, the distinction between the CLS contracts and the service support under LOGCAP is this distinction between tactical and non-tactical responsibility. I know of no need for a KBR tactical vehicle maintenance mission.

This is especially true because my staff had created a backup contractual vehicle for tactical vehicle maintenance. This contract established a set of maintenance contractors who agreed to operate on a worldwide basis providing maintenance support to tactical vehicles. We called the contract Global Maintenance and Support Services (GMASS pronounced G-Mass; it always helps a program to have a nice sounding acronym.) This contract already operated at Balad and there was no reason for an out of scope KBR mission.

Of course things then got worse. LOGCAP is a performance based contract. The Army specifies the task and outcome, the contractor determines the best method of performance. There award fee depends on performance in an effective and cost efficient manner. DCAA will not alloOw payment of costs unreasonably incurred by the contractor. However, for this mission the Army specified the staffing of the maintenance operation, which was highly unusual.

In March of 2010 the DoD IG issued a report entitled, Contracting for Tactical Vehicle Field Maintenance at Joint Base Balad, Iraq (Report No. D-201 0-046.)[98] This report found that the utilization rate for the Army required KBR staff at this site was "was less than the 85 percent required by Army Regulation 750-1. Specifically, from September 1, 2008, through August 31, 2009, the rate ranged from a low of 3.97 percent to a high of 9.65 percent. "For most of the time the KBR staff sat idle and the Army paid for them and paid KBR fee for them sitting idle. The loss to the Government was stated in the report in this manner, "As a result, about

---

98 (DoD Inspector General 2010)

$4.6 million of the $5 million in costs incurred by DOD were for tactical vehicle field maintenance services that were not required."[99]

On a total basis this is not the greatest waste on the LOGCAP contract. On a percentage basis, it is staggering. Yet the Army disagreed with the report, claiming that the contract was effective in support of surge operations. The DoD IG, in turn, found the Army justification to be untrue, stating:

> We disagree with the Assistant Chief of Staff's position that DOD was effectively contracting for tactical vehicle field maintenance at JBB. Effective contracting requires monitoring the level of maintenance services purchased and a reduction of those services when they are not required. As discussed in the report, Army internal controls were ineffective in monitoring the level of contractor-provided tactical vehicle field maintenance services. The surge ended in July 2008, when the last of five U.S. surge brigades left Iraq. As identified in the report, KBR provided the 3rd ESC with man-hour reports on July 10, 2008, for April, May, and June 2008. These three man-hour reports were for months within the "surge" period and grouped tactical vehicle, small arms, communications and electric, and fuel and electric field maintenance together. The combined utilization rates for these four areas ranged from 8.10 percent to 9.45 percent.[100]

Unfortunately, the DoD failed to identify the root cause, the out of scope mission and the specification of a manning level. They instead blamed a reporting failure and general oversight problem. All of their recommendations involved improvements to man-hour reporting by KBR and reading these reports by the Army. The mission will evidently continue, with some specified man hours. A good outcome is unlikely. That the whole effort was designed as a windfall for KBR did not cross their mind.

---

99   (DoD Inspector General 2010) p. 3
100 (DoD Inspector General 2010) pp. 8-9

Chapter 10. The Struggle for Congressional Oversight

The first Congressional oversight hearing on LOGCAP was held in 2003 by the House Committee on Oversight and Government Reform. I was there to support the testimony of two Army general officers. Several other Army leaders were on the panel. I was struck by the number of members in attendance, as I did not anticipate LOGCAP had this much interest, especially on the Republican side. After the hearing was opened by the Republican chairman, Tom Davis, the senior minority member, Henry Waxman introduced several motions to issue subpoenas for relevant documents and testimony. On a strict party line vote the motions were denied. At this point there was a vote on the House floor and the Committee recessed temporarily. When they returned, most of the Republican members were absent. It was clear they were there in the beginning to vote down the subpoena requests, not to participate in the hearing.

That this hearing was held at all was a somewhat remarkable circumstance. With a Republican majority in the House and control of committee agendas, oversight hearings were infrequent. The Republicans saw little benefit in oversight of Bush Administration programs, even when they were non-political. The effective and efficient management by the Army of a contract which would grow to over $32 billion and provided essential support to soldiers was, in my opinion, about as non-partisan as you could get.

The Republican minimal oversight position was also consistent with the Bush Administration assertion of the "Unitary Executive" doctrine.

This doctrine considers all of the agencies of government part of the executive branch as described in Article II of the Constitution. The President is the Chief of the Executive Branch and may operate the branch according to his interpretation of the laws. Congress must appropriate the money and authorize programs, but at that point they are essentially done. Through signing statements and his management of the agencies, the President asserted that he should not be subject to additional Congressional review. This doctrine, along with partisan politics, effectively ended most oversight during the time when Republicans controlled the Presidency and both houses of Congress. In his book, *The Waxman Report*, REP Waxman put it in this manner:

> As bad as things were on oversight during the Clinton years, they got much worse when George W. Bush became president. Suddenly, the Republicans lost all interest in holding the executive branch to account. Their approach to oversight changed entirely. When it concerned Bill Clinton, nothing was too small to investigate; but if it involved George W. Bush, it seemed as if nothing was so big that it couldn't be ignored — even if doing so had global consequences.[101]

Congressional oversight of the executive is not a new concept. The first instance occurred in March, 1792 during the first session of the second Congress. The House established a select committee to investigate the defeat of General St. Clair by Native Americans in the Northwest Territory. President Washington recognized the Congressional authority to hold this investigation and was fairly cooperative. The investigation found that the late delivery of contracted for supplies, among other problems, laid the groundwork for the defeat.[102]

The Joint Committee on the Conduct of the War, established in 1861, investigated, among many other issues the cost of heavy ordnance purchased by the Army and the reasons why delivery on contracts was so slow.[103] While this committee has been seen as too partisan and as interfering in the conduct of the war, it has some success in examining contractual problems.

The Constitutional basis for the Congressional ability and power to conduct oversight was clearly decided in 1927. In *McGrain v. Daugherty*, a unanimous Supreme Court stated, "The power of inquiry with process to enforce it is an essential and appropriate auxiliary to the legislation function...." Unitary Executive theory notwithstanding, Congress clearly

---

101   (Waxman, The Waxman Report 2009) p.p. 151-152
102   A good description of this investigation may be found in (Schlesinger 1975).
103   (Schlesinger 1975) p. 88

has the power to investigate and provide oversight to executive agencies. In doing so it may compel persons to testify and to produce papers under threat of conviction for contempt of Congress, which is punishable by fine or imprisonment.

Fortunately, Chairman Davis was a moderate member of the Republican Party. He worked at maintaining a good relationship with Henry Waxman and the minority members of his committee. He was comfortable with holding a hearing on this topic, with Henry Waxman in the lead. However, he could not go beyond party constraints, such as allowing the Democrats subpoena power. Congressman Waxman wrote:

> Beginning in 2003, the Oversight Committee experienced a marked improvement when Tom Davis, a moderate Republican from northern Virginia, took over. Unlike Burton, Davis recognized the value of responsible oversight and tried, within the strictures imposed by Republican leadership, to reassert Congres's [sic] role.[104]

This hearing provided Congress with some useful information. At this time the Army was forthright in describing both the accomplishments of the LOGCAP contract and the major problems encountered. The Army did not have adequate control of the requirements process which was generating too many demands and constant changes. The DoD agencies with authority for oversight of the LOGCAP contract in Iraq, Afghanistan and Kuwait, Defense Contract Management Agency (DCMA) and the Defense Contract Audit Agency (DCAA), did not have enough specialists with the right skill set to do an adequate job. My own contracting office, which had the responsibility for awarding and managing LOGCAP was understaffed and behind on much of the administrative work.

Over the past few years most of these problems have been corrected, or at least significant improvement has been made. However, some of the basic problems with the Army's management have not been addressed. This is the situation despite over 25 hearings in the House and Senate, at least 20 GAO reports, congressionally initiated DoD Inspector General Investigations and the efforts of the Commission on Wartime Contracting. In many ways Congressional oversight of this massive Army program has been a failure. Understanding this failure provides insight into a general problem with the ability of Congress to perform effective oversight functions.

---

104   (Waxman, The Waxman Report 2009) p. 154

While the chief duty to provide oversight of the LOGCAP program falls to the Department of Defense, Congress should be a key part of this task. When I teach American Federal Government, I lecture on the oversight responsibilities of Congress. Congress authorizes the programs which Agencies such as DoD execute and, of course, provides the funds through appropriations. Congress has the responsibility to ensure that those programs are carried out in accordance with the authorizing legislation and that the funds are spent in an effective and efficient manner. Identification of problems by Congressional oversight may result in changes in the way agencies conduct business. We saw this when the Army initiated Project SAFE to correct electrical deficiencies in LOGCAP provided housing, described below. Oversight may also identify issues which require new legislation to resolve problems.

Oversight is also a means to keep citizens informed about how their government works. Many of the problems with LOGCAP would not have received media attention if the Congress had not held hearings concerning those issues. Woodrow Wilson considered this informative role to be a key legislative task:

> It is the proper duty of a representative body to look diligently into every affair of government and to talk about what it sees. It is meant to be the eyes and the voice, and to embody the wisdom and will of its constituents. Unless Congress have and use every means of acquainting itself with the acts and disposition of the administrative agents of government, the country must be helpless to learn how it is being served.... The informing function of Congress should be preferred even to the legislative function.[105]

Joel D. Aberbach identifies 14 ways in which Congress performs the function of oversight:

Senate Frequency of Use of Oversight Techniques, 95th Congress	
RANK	TECHNIQUE
1	Staff Communication
2	Amendment Hearings
3	Program Reauthorizations Hearings
4	Congressional support Agency program Evaluation
5	Oversight Hearings
6	Committee Staff Program Evaluation
7	Agency Reports
8	Analysis of Proposed Regulations

---

105   (W. Wilson 1913) p. 303

9	Member Communication
10	Staff Investigations and Field Studies
11	Agency Program Evaluations
12	"Outsiders" Program Evaluations
13	Review of Casework
14	Legislative Veto*

* *(Aberbach 1990) p. p. 138*

We shall see that many of these techniques have been applied to the LOGCAP contract. It is noteworthy that 2 and 3, which would involve the loss of money by the Army, are techniques that have not been applied. Oversight hearings (#5), Agency Reports (#7, mainly the DoD IG), Congressional Support Agency Program Evaluations (# 4, mainly the GAO but also the Congressional Budget office and the Congressional Research Service), Committee Staff Program Evaluations (# 6) and some Outsiders Program Evaluation (# 12, my testimony is an example) have been the main techniques.

The extensive oversight of the LOGCAP program, however, highlights the difficulties in effective Congressional oversight which results in substantive change. DoD and the Army have resisted most of the demands for change which this oversight has produced. An examination of this situation reveals changes which could improve the oversight of LOGCAP and other agency programs.

REP Henry Waxman and the House Committee on Oversight and Investigations

Congressman Henry Waxman, a Democrat, has represented California's 30th district for over 35 years. In 2003 he was the ranking minority member of the House Committee on Oversight and Reform. While each standing committee of Congress has oversight functions for their area of responsibility, the Committee on Oversight and Government Reform has broad authority to investigate problems in any area of Government.

The oversight responsibilities of the Committee are set forth in House Rule X, clauses 2, 3, and 4.

House Rule X, clause 2(b), provides that the Committee shall review and study on a continuing basis—

(A) the application, administration, execution, and effectiveness of laws and programs addressing subjects within its jurisdiction;

(B) the organization and operation of Federal agencies and entities having responsibilities for the administration and execution of laws and programs addressing subjects within its jurisdiction;

House Rule X, clause 3(i), provides that the Committee shall "review and study on a continuing basis the operation of Government activities at all levels with a view to determining their economy and efficiency."

House Rule X, clause 4(c)(1), provides that the Committee shall:

(A) receive and examine reports of the Comptroller General of the United States and submit to the House such recommendations as it considers necessary or desirable in connection with the subject matter of the reports;

And House Rule X, clause 4(c)(2), provides that the Committee "may at any time conduct investigations of any matter without regard to clause 1, 2, 3, or this clause [of House Rule X] conferring jurisdiction over the matter to another standing committee."

As noted above, in 2003 Representative Waxman was able to convince the Chairman to hold hearings on LOGCAP performance as some whistleblowers began to emerge on the public scene. When Representative Waxman became Chairman in 2007, he was able to increase the value of his oversight hearings on LOGCAP, as he now had control of the agenda and subpoena power if necessary. Overall Representative Waxman held six hearings fully devoted to LOGCAP.

Prior to that first hearing in 2003, I prepared a briefing book for the leaders who would testify. Since most Congressional hearings generally have senior agency leaders on the panel, preparing those leaders is important. The General Officers from the Army Materiel Command, whom I supported, had a very good command of the issues and facts involved. Since they could expect some detailed questions at such hearings, both generals received a large briefing book prior to the hearings. Their objective was to provide accurate and complete testimony.

While the hearing was useful, it brought home to me some of the fundamental flaws in Congressional oversight through such hearings. The process is followed by both the House and Senate committees. After opening statements from members and the panel, questions are asked by committee members alternating from the Republican side to the Democratic side (or the other way if Democrats are in the majority), starting with the Chairman. Each member usually has five minutes and often uses part of this time to make a point, rather than ask a question. Little follow-up is done. The issues under consideration change drastically as a new member begins her five minutes. Unlike some previous Congressional hearings, the Committee counsel, usually an expert on the issue does not ask questions on behalf of the committee. Now it is the members who are front and center, which is not always conducive to the oversight mission. During that first hearing I observed committee members, on both sides of the dais, who were not well informed on the issues.

Representative Waxman held hearings on electricity, transportation, security and other LOGCAP problems. The electricity hearings, along with the work of Senator Dorgan, described earlier and below, actually accomplished some reform, an unusual outcome for this oversight. REP Waxman was responsible for obtaining key documents from DoD which contradicted some of the positions taken by the Army and forced them to re-examine matters they had attempted to close. A new DoD Inspector General investigation was initiated in response to this hearing.

Another success occurred when, after the killing of four Blackwater personnel in Fallujah, the Committee held hearings on why Blackwater was providing security on a subcontract associated with the LOGCAP contract. The LOGCAP contract explicitly states that the U.S. Government will be responsible for security on LOGCAP. Most of this happens routinely, as LOGCAP operations of base camps are protected as part of the general protection of the camp. Other mission, such as transportation, requires the detailing of U.S. forces to provide guards for convoys. Costs for security are not allocable to the LOGCAP contract.

Yet the Blackwater group at Fallujah was protecting the movement of kitchen supplies associated with a KBR managed dining facility. KBR was responsible for notifying the Army of such missions and obtaining security for them. Instead, the subcontractor bought security and passed the costs along to the Army.

Representative Waxman's staff identified this discrepancy and the Congressman demanded an explanation. One day prior to the formal hearing on the matter, the Army sent KBR a letter requiring them to refund $19 million in costs associated with the Blackwater security. Representative Waxman stated, at the hearing, that he felt he had accomplished at least $19 million in value for the American taxpayer.

Other than these successes, the hearings obtained information, generated some publicity and little change.

SEN BYRON DORGAN AND THE SENATE DEMOCRATIC POLICY COMMITTEE

Without control of the Senate until 2007, the Democrats in the Senate could not achieve support for major oversight hearings. Senator Byron Dorgan of North Dakota was the Chairman of the Democratic Policy Committee. This committee was not a standing committee of the Senate; did not have subpoena power and often had a tough time finding an available hearing room. However, this body could hold hearings on issues of interest to the members of the party who wanted more oversight of the agencies.

One of the issues that concerned Senator Dorgan was the Army's management of LOGCAP. This contract was spending an exceptional amount of taxpayer funds and stories of problems with the contract were beginning to emerge. In 2004 his staff had learned that the Defense Contract Audit Agency (DCAA) considered unreasonable almost $1 billion in costs for which KBR had billed the Government. Whistleblowers were describing waste under the contract along with poorly performed work.

Senator Dorgan decided to use the DPC to hold a series of hearings on the LOGCAP program. These hearings would serve to publicize such problems, inform the Army of Congressional concerns and provide information which might become the basis for legislative action. This committee has held over sixteen hearings on LOGCAP and related contracting issues.

I left the LOGCAP program in 2004 due to those disputes with Army leadership concerning the management of the contract. After I retired in 2008, I testified before two of these hearing panels. Senators such as Senator Casey of Pennsylvania, Senator Whitehouse of New York, Senator Klobuchar of Minnesota, Senator McCaskill of Missouri, Senator Sanders of Vermont and of course Senator Dorgan were well informed on the issues and asked knowledgeable questions. Occasionally a question centered on Halliburton and Vice President Cheney, but most questions were non-political, aimed at improving Army support for troops.

After a hearing, the DPC staff would scan the cable news channels to see if the hearing generated media attention to the issue discussed. One of their main goals was to publicize issues in hopes of generating more information, more discussion and some pressure for change.

While the hearings explored many issues with LOGCAP, in only three cases were the hearings successful in generating what I would consider real change. Along with Representative Waxman's House committee, the DPC investigated the electrocution of a number of soldiers in KBR managed bases. The most egregious case was that of SSG Ryan Maseth, described in chapter 8. You will recall that SSG Maseth was a Special Forces soldier with an outstanding record. He was housed at the Radwaniyah Palace Complex, managed by KBR under LOGCAP, in the Baghdad area. On January 2, 2008 he was found by his comrades in the shower of his quarters, dead from electrocution. The Army assigned a number of different causes for this tragedy. None of them admitted a general problem, any KBR responsibility, or need for corrective action. The House Committee, however, through excellent staff work, unearthed documentation which indicated this was a case of negligence rather than an accident.

The committees were helped greatly by Ms. Cheryl Harris, SSG Maseth's mother. She put a compelling human face on the story. She exhibited proper outrage at the Army and KBR along with a dogged dedication to ensuring that other soldiers and their families should not go through this suffering. At the time she had two other sons serving their country in Iraq. Committees that can bring forward such witnesses have a much better chance of actually bringing about change in agency policies.

As a result of these hearings, the Army instituted Project SAFE to examine and repair other possible electrical problems in theater. Their investigations found numerous situations which endangered the lives of soldiers living in KBR-managed base camps. The corrective action may have saved soldiers lives.

The second success came after a follow on hearing on electrical problems. Senator Dorgan invited me to testify on the relation of such poor performance to the award fees which KBR was earning. I outlined the award fee process and the criteria for earning award fee. I noted that award fee was to be paid for performance over and above meeting the basic scope of work. The electrical failures did not meet this basic standard and should have eliminated award fee for the periods prior to correcting those defects. In my opinion the unnecessary death of a single soldier at a KBR-managed camp due to this failure should eliminate all award fees for that period.

In February 2010, KBR, in an SEC filing, took a charge of over $100 million against previously reported profits for 2008. They stated this was due to an Army decision to give them $0 award fee for periods in 2008. This decision by the Army was due to the electrical failures. I was told by one of my friends that KBR was blaming me for this decision.

We should be happy at the positive results of Project SAFE and the change in award fee evaluation. However, even this was not a complete success. KBR actually received additional work and profits to support Project SAFE. The Army has never indicated that KBR lost any cost payments because of the poor work they were paid to correct. Despite the information uncovered by the DPC, the Army has not changed its basic approach to managing LOGCAP, which often puts contractor interests ahead of the taxpayer and the troops.

The Senate DPC also had a positive impact through hearings on a KBR project under their Corps of Engineers RIO contract. They were tasked under the contract to repair the Qarmat Ali water treatment plant. This was not a drinking water treatment plant. Water was used to maintain pressure in an oil field to keep oil flowing to the surface. It is also used to maintain some pressure in the pipeline. The available water required treatment to prevent it from corroding the pipes. Although KBR started work in 2003, by August 2005 the plant was only operating at 33% capacity.

This failure to get the plant working, turned out not to be the main problem. The anti corrosion chemical the Iraqis used to treat the water was sodium dichromate. When KBR arrived, this substance was spread all over the plant area, perhaps on purpose. With KBR came units of the, who were replaced by a unit from the Washington. A few years later, soldiers from these units began experiencing extreme, often lethal illness.

The problem was known by KBR in 2003. In September of that year an Army Medical Directorate Environmental Monitoring Team had performed an assessment at Qarmat Ali.[106] The KBR safety people at the plant were contractually responsible for the health of their workers and the soldiers stationed at the plant to guard them. KBR failed to take proper care of these men. Senator Dorgan held a hearing on this issue, but more importantly, his staff worked tirelessly to obtain proper treatment for the affected soldiers. The testimony was heartbreaking, especially when Senator Dorgan expressed a desire to speak with a lieutenant colonel who had led one of the teams. He was informed that the officer was now in hospice care and would be unable to speak about this prior to his death.

Work by Senator Dorgan and Senator Byah ultimately resulted in the Army and VA taking responsibility for additional care for these soldiers.

---

106 (Army Medical Directorate 2003)

DPC hearings have the stigma of a Democratic committee and do not have the publicity potential of hearings conducted by a House or Senate standing committee. Reporters pay more attention to perceived non-partisan or bi-partisan investigations. Even though these issues were non-partisan, it was hard to get around the Democratic in DPC. These investigations could be, and were often, written off by the media as partisan in nature.

SEN CARL LEVIN AND THE SENATE ARMED SERVICES COMMITTEE (SASC)

The Senate Armed Services Committee is one of the major standing committees in the Senate. The SASC has subpoena power. The SASC also has great leverage with the military as the authorization committee for military programs and the confirmation authority for general officer promotions. SASC hearings are often bi-partisan, with both sides asking hard questions of the military.

However, the SASC has not proved to be an effective oversight body for the LOGCAP program. They have held two hearings on LOGCAP, one in 2004 and one in 2007. I attended the earlier hearing in which little of note was addressed. The hearing held on April 19, 2007 by the Senate Armed Services Committee to examine problems with the Army management of LOGCAP and KBR's performance is indicative of the problems with effective oversight. This was the one major SASC hearing on LOGCAP and the Army was determined to defend their management actions and KBR at all costs.

Senator Dorgan, who is not a member of the committee, provided testimony about the concerns he had which stemmed from the work of the Democratic Policy Committee. Unfortunately, as is mostly the case with standing committee hearings, the rest of the witnesses were the usual suspects from the Army; the Assistant Secretary of the Army for Acquisition, Logistics and Technology, the Commander of the Army Sustainment Command, the Auditor General for the Army, along with the Directors of the Defense Contract Management Agency (DCMA) and the DCAA. No dissenting view would be heard from the panel of witnesses.

Senator Levin began the hearing by noting that, "There has been a history of highly favorable treatment of this contractor throughout the contract." He mentioned the billing for un-served meals, the purchase of high priced living containers, and the overall high costs with little commensurate value.

Senator Dorgan then testified citing DCAA audits which took exception to hundreds of millions of dollars which Army negotiations did not sustain. He spoke to the water contamination at Ar Ramadi and to KBRs mishandling of transportation issues. He cited several whistleblowers who described problems with KBR's management of LOGCAP.

It soon became clear that Army leaders considered their mission was to support KBR against the claims described by Senators Levin and Dorgan and defend Army management of the program. Their message was that all was well with the program and getting better. They inadvertently confirmed Senator Levin's charge of favorable treatment of KBR by providing inaccurate and misleading testimony at many parts of the hearing in order to defend KBR.

Following the hearing the Army issued a formal correction to the testimony of the Commander, Army Sustainment Command concerning payments for containerized housing which DCAA had disputed as unreasonable. He had testified that KBR had not been paid for these items, when in fact; they had been paid by his contracting office. Such a correction was a very unusual event for such testimony. This was not the only problem with Army testimony.

Senator Dorgan had heard testimony from former KBR employees of problems with the water KBR supplied to Camp Ar Ramadi (chapter 7.) He brought up this issue during his testimony. The issued was followed up by questions from Senator Warner. Senator Warner and Senator Mc-Cain brought a bipartisan sense to this hearing by asking probing and critical questions. At this point the transcript of the hearing is useful.

From the transcript:

MG Johnson:

Sir, we've looked into the water-power problem at Al [sic] Ramadi, and a couple of issues. One, during the time of the allegation, KBR was not operating the water site. I was operated by an Army unit doing road fuel operations.

WARNER:

So KBR was not involved in the water?

MG Johnson:

Not during the time that the allegation was made. KBR assumed control of the operation about two months later. Additionally DoD...

(Crosstalk)

WARNER:

Wait a minute, whoa, whoa, whoa. We've got to get this straight. So at the time of the allegations KBR did not have a responsibility. That responsibility rested entirely with, what, the Corps of Engineers?

MG Johnson:

It was an Army water unit that had the capability to produce water using an Army RO pure—reverse osmosis.

WARNER:

But so, in any event, the responsibility for the potability and safety of that water rested with the Army as opposed to any LOGCAP contractor?

MG Johnson:

At that time.

As discussed in Chapter 7, the Commander of the Sustainment Command's assertion that the Army was responsible for the bad water at Ar Ramadi was an incorrect interpretation of the contractual relationship between KBR and the Government. The KBR contract states that, "IAW applicable Army Regulations, the contractor shall provide, install, operate and maintain potable and non-potable water systems, to include plumbing, sewage, gray/black water separation, and gray/black water disposal, to facilitate the operation of facilities provided or operated by the contractor, previously designated by the government or as directed by the ACO for new requirements." Both the Government and the contractor understood that this clause places full responsibility for potable and non-potable water at the camp on KBR.

The provision of non-potable water at Ar Ramadi involved removing water from the Euphrates River, running it through a Reverse Osmosis Water Purification Unit (ROWPU), putting the water into tank trucks and moving it to the main base water system tanks and distributing it through that system. When the incident in March 2005, a KBR ROWPU unit was not yet operational and an Army unit was providing this part of the service. The Army had to provide this service because KBR had failed to implement its' own ROWPU unit in a timely manner. The contract called for this service within sixty days of start of work. Over a year after start of work KBR was not providing this part of the water service.

KBR was also responsible for the proper transfer of water to the tank trucks. KBR was responsible for testing the water at every necessary stage of the operation. They were also responsible for chlorinating the water if necessary. KBR internal documents, in the possession of the House Committee on Oversight and Government Reform recognize these responsibilities, which were based upon applicable Army regulations.

Senator Dorgan writes about this in his book, *RECKLESS!* In a chapter on his investigations and testimony he states:

> Even in the face of facts that proved the opposite, an army general came to the Senate Armed Services Committee hearing to specifically deny the charges that had been leveled at Halliburton for providing contaminated water to military bases in Iraq. That general denied the entire incident even though the Pentagon Inspector General had informed the Pentagon prior to the general's testimony that the allegations were true.

> ...we know that statements by Halliburton and testimony by the Pentagon officials deceived Congress and the American people on this matter. As of this publication, the matter was under investigation as a result of my request to the Secretary of Defense.

> But that is what happened.[107]

During the entire hearing, Army leaders give the impression that KBR performed in a quality manner and earned the fees and profit paid. Their answers concerning the cost of meals, award fees, and contract negotiations provide a misleading impression of the operation of the LOGCAP contract. This testimony is not supported by DoD IG reviews, DCAA audits and other documentation which various committees obtained after the hearing. As he noted, Senator Dorgan has asked the DoD to investigate the testimony provided at this hearing. As I write the DoD has not released the results of such an investigation. However, the general in question has retired, which usually signifies no consequences will ensue.

If one of the major functions of Congress is oversight of the management of programs authorized and funded by legislation, then his oversight is only possible if the Agencies provide Congress with accurate and complete testimony regarding that management. The testimony presented by the Army at this hearing is quite troubling as it appears to fail in being either accurate or complete. If committees do not receive accurate testimony, they are unable to fully understand the problems and press for resolution through agency action. They also cannot formulate any appropriate legislative action to correct problems.

The result of the SASC hearing is that nothing has changed. In fact there may be an adverse effect on future oversight hearings. The military appears to be willing to back general officers and officials who mislead

---

107   (B. L. Dorgan 2009) p. 172

Congress. Future panel members will have an incentive to also mislead in ways which defend their actions, without fear of consequences if they are caught.

REP Andrews and the House Armed Services Committee

The House Armed Services Subcommittee on Defense Acquisition Reform, chaired by REP Robert Andrews of New Jersey, has also held hearings on the LOGCAP contract. These hearings have not been particularly useful in providing Congress or the public with helpful information. The usual suspects, such as the Executive Director, Army Contracting Command, are brought in to appear on the panel. They do not admit to many errors and claim those that may possibly have existed are now corrected. The Committee members show some deference to these leaders and do not ask many hard questions.

The committee members are also hampered by a lack of knowledge of the intricacies of these contractual issues. In framing a question during a hearing on July 16, 2009, a committee member mentioned the term "negotiation." This is a term of art in Government contracts which applies to a situation where the price is undetermined at the beginning of work and is only "definitized" later in the process. The member appears to think that the term refers to negotiating a more definitive statement of the work to be performed, missing the financial application of the term.

Overall, the House Armed Services Committee has shown little interest in probing into the problems of the LOGCAP contract and holding the Army accountable for effective and efficient management of over $40 billion in taxpayer dollars. With the responsibility for military authorization legislation and subpoena power, this committee could be an effective oversight body for issues such as LOGCAP.

SEN Claire McCaskill and the Subcommittee on Contracting Oversight (SOCO)

Senator McCaskill is one of the most knowledgeable and aggressive members of the Senate concerned with Government accountability. She is inclined to ask, when apprised of a major failure of the process, whether anyone has been fired over this matter. This subcommittee is designed to do the work of oversight which is obviously of interest to Senator McCaskill. The subcommittee website asks anyone with knowledge of these contracting issues to inform the committee of their concerns. She and her Republican counterpart, Senator Susan Collins, appeared to work well together.

When the SASC investigated a particularly bad government contract with a firm called AEY, the Senator was outraged. AEY was hired to provide non Army standard ammunition (such as 7.76mm AK-47 ammunition) to the Army of Afghanistan. When the ammunition arrived in Afghanistan in paper bags and appeared to be old and possibly unusable, the Army and the Press began to look at AEY. The company was run by a teenage Israeli citizen and the VP was a former masseuse. They had no creditable experience which would justify awarding this contract. In fact, a pre-award review by DCMA had suggested no award be made, but was over-ridden by the contracting officer. The contract was eventually terminated and the AEY principals were convicted of fraud.

The Army Contracting Command found nothing particularly wrong with this contract. According to the Civilian Executive Director, everything was done correctly; it just didn't turn out well. Again, SENATOR McCaskill questioned why nobody was fired over this. The Army had no answer at this time, but later demonstrated their imperviousness to oversight. The contracting officer, who awarded the contract despite a recommendation from the pre-award review not to do so, was promoted to a position of additional contracting leadership duties.

The major SOCO hearing which concerns LOGCAP was a hearing titled *Afghanistan Contracts: An Overview* held on Thursday, December 17, 2009. The Army participants were, again. among the usual suspects; the Executive Director Army Contracting Command and the Deputy Assistant Secretary of the Army (Procurement). By labeling them the usual suspects I do not want to question their integrity in these hearings. These Army leaders a classic example of "where you stand depends on where you sit." Their job is to defend the Army and convince the Congress that all is well. Unless the Congress member is skilled in drawing out the information, or already possesses it, they will find it difficult to obtain pertinent facts on possibly poor performance of both the contractor and the Army.

This hearing elicited a commitment that things would be different in Afghanistan. New processes were in place along with new contractors under LOGCAP IV. What the hearing failed to obtain was any real recognition of past problems with root cause analysis on real change.

Senators McCaskill and Collins have also attempted to prod the military into reclaiming money from KBR which was improperly earned when their employees accepted bribes in return for high subcontract prices. James Glanz reported, "The Pentagon has done little to collect at least $100 million in overcharges paid in deals arranged by corrupt former officials of Kellogg Brown & Root, the defense contractor, even though the officials admitted much of the wrongdoing years ago, two Senators have complained in a letter to Defense Secretary Robert M. Gates. The letter also said that the Army had almost completely failed to move away from the monopolistic nature of the logistics contract that has paid the contractor, now called KBR, $31.3 billion for logistics operations in Iraq, Kuwait and Afghanistan."[108]

While the government has instituted a number of such bribery cases, as described in chapter 6, there has been no action to recover the costs for improperly inflated subcontracts. For example, in the contracts awarded by, Stephen Lowell Seamans, who pleaded guilty to bribery and conspiracy in March 2006, Pentagon auditors quickly found potential excess profits by a Kuwaiti subcontractor of $49.8 million, or 76 percent.[109] Total costs to be recovered appear to be in the $100 million rang. If the SOCO under Senator McCaskill can force the Army to take back this money, they will have earned their keep. Given Senator McCaskill's determination and knowledge of contracting, their remains some hope of some real action by this subcommittee. So far, however, this hope has not been realized

The Congressional Research Service (CRS)

The CRS provides Congress with the analytical support it needs to address the most complex public policy issues facing the nation. Its work incorporates program and legislative expertise, quantitative methodologies, and legal and economic analysis.

In 1914, Congress passed legislation to establish a separate department within the Library of Congress. President Woodrow Wilson signed the bill into law, and CRS, then called the Legislative Reference Service, was born to serve the legislative needs of the Congress.

With the Legislative Reorganization Act of 1970, Congress renamed the agency the Congressional Research Service and significantly expanded its statutory obligations. The services provided today by CRS are a direct result of congressional directives and guidance.

---

108 (Glanz 2009) p.1
109 (Glanz 2009) p. 1

CRS has nearly 700 employees. This team, working in Washington, D.C., includes more than 450 policy analysts, attorneys, information professionals and experts in a variety of disciplines.

The Congressional Research Service has provided Congress, and the public, with a great deal of information on LOGCAP. Examples are:

- Iraq: Frequently Asked Questions About Contracting, Updated March 18, 2005
- Defense Contracting in Iraq: Issues and Options for Congress, January 26, 2007
- Defense Logistical Support Contracts in Iraq and Afghanistan: Issues for Congress, June 24, 2009
- Department of Defense Contractors in Iraq and Afghanistan: Background and Analysis, December 14, 2009
- The reports provide information which can inform Congressional hearings and provide the public with this same information. The reports are, however, only as effective as the hearings or publicity which they generate. Given the military response to oversight, their impact appears to be negligible.

THE CONGRESSIONAL BUDGET OFFICE (CBO)

On its web page the CBO describes its mandate as "to provide the Congress with objective, nonpartisan, and timely analyses to aid in economic and budgetary decisions on the wide array of programs covered by the federal budget and the information and estimates required for the Congressional budget process. " Congress has utilized the CBO to examine some of the issues associated with LOGCAP and contingency contracting in general.

In October, 2005 the CBO issued a study entitled *Logistics Support for Deployed Military Forces.* This study is the most comprehensive analysis of the risks, costs and benefits of using contractors instead of organic military units to provide logistics support. The study uses data from LOGCAP Task Order 59 to compare with the calculated costs of the Army units which would be needed to provide the same support. Using Army planned rotation policy, the CBO finds a significant cost advantage to using LOGCAP rather than organic support. I will discuss this study in some detail in the next chapter.

The CBO has provided valuable financial analysis on the costs of LOGCAP to Congress. Their mandate does not extend to waste, fraud and abuse. Their analysis is beneficial to the extent Congress uses it to support conclusions regarding LOGCAP oversight issues.

THE GOVERNMENT ACCOUNTABILITY OFFICE (GAO)

The Government Accountability Office (GAO) also performs investigations and prepares reports of their findings. The GAO was established by the Budget and Accounting Act in 1921. The act states that the Comptroller General [Head of the GAO], "shall investigate, at the seat of government or elsewhere, all matters relating to the receipt, disbursement and application of government funds." (Section 312) Joseph Harris describes the auditing authority of GAO in this manner:

With some limited exceptions specified by statue, the auditing authority of the GAO extends to all activities, financial transactions, and accounts of the federal government. It includes the records of contractors having contracts negotiated without advertising, their subcontractors' records, and the records of certain recipients of federal assistance in the form of loans, advances, grants, or contributions. All officers of the government are required by law to make their records available and to cooperate with the GAO.[110]

Then named the Government Accounting Agency, the Comptroller General and the GAO have accumulated a number of functions. One known to all contracting personnel is to settle protests by unsuccessful offerors during the award process. To some degree the GAO acts as the external auditor for government agencies, just as private companies hire outside auditors to review their financial statements and management processes.[111]

The GAO describes their mission and work in this manner:

Our Mission is to support the Congress in meeting its constitutional responsibilities and to help improve the performance and ensure the accountability of the federal government for the benefit of the American people. We provide Congress with timely information that is objective, fact-based, nonpartisan, non-ideological, fair, and balanced. Our Work is done at the request of congressional committees or subcommittees or is mandated by public laws or committee reports. We also undertake research under the authority of the Comptroller General. We support congressional oversight by auditing agency operations to determine whether federal funds are being spent efficiently and effectively; investigating allegations of illegal and improper activities; reporting on how well gov-

---

110   (Harris 1964) p. 139
111   (Pois 1979) p. 18

ernment programs and policies are meeting their objectives; performing policy analyses and outlining options for congressional consideration; and issuing legal decisions and opinions, such as bid protest rulings and reports on agency rules.

We advise Congress and the heads of executive agencies about ways to make government more efficient, effective, ethical, equitable and responsive.

The GAO has been quite active in monitoring the LOGCAP program. They have issued specific reports on improving LOGCAP program management and improper payments under the contract. More general reports have examined the use of award fee contracts, unpriced contracts, service contracts and use of contractors for soldier support; all of which are applicable to the LOGCAP program.

These reports are also only effective if they result in action on the part of the military. This only occurs with effective hearings and publicity. GAO reports are a useful tool of Congressional oversight with the proper follow up. They can result in improvement, when Congress presses and the military is willing to listen.

In the fall of 2009 the GAO released reports on the Defense Contract Audit Agency (DCAA). These reports were highly critical of audit quality and general management at DCAA. With Congress asking additional questions as a result of these reports, the Department of Defense did take action. The Director of DCAA was replaced and a new director was appointed with a mandate to improve matters. This is the type of action which DoD has not taken with LOGCAP, even with much more extensive oversight.

REQUESTING AN INVESTIGATION

As noted above, Congress will occasionally request that an Agency investigate a certain issue and report to Congress. This is usually done by the Inspector General of that Agency. In the case of LOGCAP, the DoD IG has performed several investigations of the LOGCAP contract. These investigations have included electrocutions, congressional testimony, water problems, Government contractual oversight and transition between LOGCAP contracts.

Agency IGs have a responsibility both to their agency and to Congress. Eleanor Hill, former DoD IG, is quoted in the Project on Government Oversight guide to Congressional Oversight as explaining, "Although (Inspectors General) are in the Executive Branch and they are statutorily operating under general control and supervision of the head of their agency, they have a statutory responsibility to report to Congress and to keep Congress fully and currently informed."[112]

Unfortunately, the DoD IG currently appears to take the agency responsibilities more seriously than those it has to Congress. IG investigations spurred by Congressional requests appear to take longer and reach conclusions that are protective of DoD. Investigations are narrowly circumscribed by the Congressional request and do not look for additional context.

These reports on LOGCAP issues follow a general pattern. Some problems are identified and the Army provides a plan for corrective actions. The problems are often not the root cause of the specific issue, which often involves negligence or poor decision making. No individuals are held accountable for any decisions or inaction. KBR is generally relieved of some of their responsibility, making accountability difficult.

The DoD IG report on electrocutions formed the basis for the Army Criminal Investigations Division to drop any prosecution effort in the death of SSG Maseth. The report spreads blame around, identifies no individual failures and somewhat clouds the matter of who did what on this issue. The IG mentions some problems with the contracting effort, but does not follow those through to root cause or real corrective action. In October of 2010 KBR asked a court to dismiss the wrongful death suit by SSG Maseth's parents, specifically citing these IG reports.

The DoD IG water report, while generally a good report, appears to conclude that all problems are corrected and it is time to move on with increased oversight. Again, accountability is lost in the report. The report appears to be ignorant of the contractual language which makes KBR fully responsible for the water at the bases examined.

The DoD issued a report on the 15 percent withhold, requested by the SASC which included my removal and that of my lead contracting officer among the questions. Again, this report followed the usual course, restricting the scope of the report, finding some problems for which the recommended changes to policy and training, and finding insufficient evidence to hold anyone personally accountable.

The IG found that my removal and that of my lead contracting officer were not related to our attempt to enforce the 15 percent withhold. While in both cases they followed immediately after we were overturned, this was considered a coincidence. They also found that the manner of

---

112 (Project on Government Oversight 2009) p. 26

our removal was not in accordance with policies and regulations and rec-ommended a training course for the Command, as if this was accidental.

If the DoD IG will not be an agent of accountability, when Congress identifies problems, then this tool of oversight becomes impotent. One of the key problems with the Army's management of LOGCAP is the complete lack of personal accountability for poor decisions which have negatively affected the supported troops. In looking at the Army's total treatment of KBR, only three people have had negative impacts on their careers. Ms. Bunnatine Greenhouse was demoted from an SES position at the Army Corps of Engineers because she opposed non-competitive awards to KBR for the Restore Iraqi Oil project. My lead contracting officer and I were removed from our positions and ultimately demoted because we fought to hold KBR to the provisions of the contract which they signed and to conserve precious resources for soldier support and the U.S. taxpayer.

THE COMMISSION ON WARTIME CONTRACTING

Congress, in the Defense Authorization Act for Fiscal Year 2008, cre-ated a Commission on Wartime Contracting. Senator Dorgan had early on pushed for this commission. Senator Claire McCaskill and Senator James Webb of Virginia were the main sponsors of this legislation. The commission was to be modeled on the 1941 Senate Special Committee to Investigate the National Defense Program, known as the Truman Com-mittee. However, President Bush included a signing statement when he assigned the 2008 Authorization Act that said of the Wartime Commis-sion provision, among other provision of the Act, "... [These provisions] purport to impose requirements that could inhibit the president's ability to carry out his constitutional obligations to take care that the laws be faithfully executed, to protect national security, to supervise the execu-tive branch, and to execute his authority as commander in chief. The executive branch shall construe such provisions in a manner consistent with the constitutional authority of the president." [113]

Senator Webb of Virginia immediately denounced the signing state-ment from the floor of the Senate. He stated, "We don't quite know what the Administration intends with this sort of language, but I want all my colleagues to be aware of it and to be aware that it potentially is an im-pingement on the rights of this legislative body—in effect saying that the

---

113 (D. Rasor, Bush Fears that the New Truman Commission Could Be a Threat to National Security 2008) p. 1

President has the authority to ignore a law that is now passed, a law that he has now signed. We are going to go forward with this Commission. We are going to work with the Administration, we hope, to set it up. We are going to move as rapidly as we can, because the clock is ticking in terms of the statute of limitations on some of the charges that might be filed."[114]

The Commission was given the mandate to investigate logistics support contracting, private security contracting and reconstruction contracting in Iraq and Afghanistan. LOGCAP is the major logistics support contract. I have spoken with Commission members and staff on several occasions concerning the LOGCAP contract. These are very experienced and bright people with a good understanding of the issues. The commission was given the power to hold hearings, issue reports and refer any violation of law to the Attorney General.

The Truman Committee is often considered to be a model of a successful congressional investigatory body. The standard estimate for savings resulting from the committee's work is $15 billion in 1945 dollars.[115] In addition, thousands of lives were saved as the committee prevented the delivery of defective war supplies. They operated during World War II without being the kind of impediment to the war effort that the Civil War era Joint Committee on the Conduct of the War. (Robert E. Lee is purported to have said that that committee was worth two divisions to the South). Truman was determined to not encroach on the conduct of the war and investigate issues which could enhance wartime efforts. SR71, 1941 gave the Committee authority to investigate aspects of contracting programs, among other interests:

- types and terms of contracts awarded;
- the methods by which contracts are awarded and contractors selected;
- the performance of contracts and the accountings required of contracts;
- benefits accruing to contractors with respect to amortization for purposes of taxation or otherwise;
- practices of management or labor and prices, fees and charges which interfere with or unduly increase the costs of the program.[116]

---

114 (Webb 2008) p. 1147
115 (Schlesinger 1975) p. 339
116 (Riddle 1964) p.15

The Truman Committee had subpoena power for witnesses and doc-umentation necessary for the committees work. In 1946 the Committee received the authority to examine Federal income tax returns of individ-uals and corporations. The Commission on Wartime contracting does not have any subpoena power; let alone the authority to look at income tax returns.

The Truman Committee was originally comprised of seven Senators, later increased to ten. At all times the Democratic Senators outnumbered the Republicans. In this structure there was always a clear decision au-thority and the Committee recorded no tie votes to hamper an investiga-tion. The Commission on Wartime Contracting has an even number of members, half appointed by each party. Decision making stalemates are a real possibility.

A major difference between the Truman Committee and the Commis-sion on Wartime Contracting is the difference between a committee and a commission. Comprised of U.S. Senators, the Truman Committee had major contacts and lines of communication with the rest of Congress. Truman Committee members were also members of other Senate stand-ing committees, which "strengthened the Truman Committee's position with other committees and facilitated its coverage of such a broad and complex subject as mobilization."[117] Each Committee member had power and authority connected with the position of a Senator. Truman's ability to utilize this network of power and communication greatly enhanced the work of the Committee. Truman remained interested in procurement reform as President. He was personally responsible for the development of the procurement regulations in the Armed Services Procurement Act of 1947.[118]

The members of the Commission on Wartime Contracting do not have this power and authority. The do have the connections associated with an ex-congressman or a former DoD Comptroller, for example. Yet these connections offer little power which may be brought to bear for committee needs. It may be difficult to quantify this difference, but is certainly a real one. A minor but telling point is that the Commission on Wartime Contracting operates out of rented offices across the Potomac from Washington. The Truman Committee operated from Congressio-nal offices, especially Truman's "Doghouse" office.

---

117 (Riddle 1964) p.33
118 (Fox, Arming America 1974) p. 110

The Truman Committee investigation which could most closely re-semble an inquiry into LOGCAP was the Curtis-Wright Inspection Case. Curtis-Wright made several variations of air-cooled engine used on a large number of military aircraft. A number of inspectors at the plant, both Government and contractor complained that improper inspection at the Lockland plant was resulting in the delivery of defective engines to the Army Air Force. Both the Army and the company sent represen-tatives to testify that these charges were groundless. The Army found nothing wrong with inspections or plant management.

The Committee then held hearings which developed 1,286 pages of sworn testimony and found the company was delivering defective en-gines by:

- falsification of test results;
- destruction of records'
- forging reports
- numerous other illegal activities[119]

Committee reports and hearings forced Curtis-Wright to reform the engine inspection process and forced the Army to increase oversight. Several hundred engines which were ready for shipment were recalled, found to be defective and repaired; possibly saving the lives of air crew members. Curtis Wright refunded several millions to the Army. An Army general went to jail.[120]

Two problems the Committee identified in these hearings were the re-luctance of the Army to admit mistakes and the perception that the con-tractor and the Army were allies against a common enemy, Congress![121] Of course we have seen these same problems repeatedly in the Congres-sional oversight of LOGCAP.

One of the best members of the Commission has resigned her position. Ms. Linda J. Gustitus was a Staff Director of several oversight subcom-mittees in the Senate for more than 20 years, including the Permanent Subcommittee on Investigations (PSI). When I spoke with her prior to leaving for Washington and the assignment, she expressed her concerns at the lack of subpoena power and equal number of members. Given the lack of progress for the Commission, her concerns appear justified.

Subpoena power is critical to a full and complete investigation. Elise Bean, who was Chief Counsel to the PSI, is quoted by POGO concerning

---

119 (Riddle 1964) pp123-124
120 (Jarecki 2008) p.145
121 (Riddle 1964) p.35

subpoenas as follows, "We use a lot of subpoenas. On a lot of subcommittees it's harder for them to arrange mostly because they have never thought of the rules and changed the rules in such a way that would make it easier to use subpoenas. We wish a lot of committees would correct the rules, so they would have the option of issuing a subpoena."[122] We noted earlier how Republicans prevented Henry Waxman from using subpoenas when they were in the House majority. Lack of this authority definitely hampers the Wartime Commission from getting at the truth of crucial contracting issues.

What Has the Commission Actually Done?

The Commission issued its final report in August of 2011. The above described differences between the Truman Committee and the Commission on Wartime Contracting highlight effect constraints on the Commission's efforts. One example was seen when the Commission handled the issue of poor KBR business systems. This problem hampered LOGCAP contract administration throughout most of the KBR contract. The Defense Contract Audit Agency (DCAA) has continually examined KBR estimating, cost accounting, labor-hour reporting and procurement systems and found them deficient. This leaves the Army, which relies on such systems under a cost type contract, with untrustworthy data. The Commission developed two points during their hearings; the Government did not withhold any payments as incentive to improve these systems and the Army, the defense Contract Management Agency (DCMA) and DCAA did not work effectively together.

The Commission directed the representatives from Army, DCAA and DCMA to return with a plan to play better together. The Commission took no notice of the fact that the Army had the authority to withhold payments, was required by the contract to do so under certain circumstances, knew they had that authority and made a decision not to do so in 2004. After August 2004 the Army opposed most efforts by DCAA to force KBR to improve their business systems. By the time of the Commission hearings, most of these systems were still deficient.

Commission hearings settled into a routine. Army and other Agencies officials were invited to discuss a certain issues, such as subcontracting or security contracting. Some problems were identified and occasionally the Agencies actual admitted to the problems. The problems were then attributed to a lack of resources, organizations which should be restruc-

---

122 (Project on Government Oversight 2009) p.

tured, lack of emphasis on the Acquisition career field in the military, poor communications or poor laws and regulations. No individual ever was identified as having done something wrong.

Occasionally contractor executives were invited to hearings. They, for some reason, never admitted wrong doing and offered to give back money to the Government. The Commission certainly did not pursue those kinds of problems. At one hearing, some outside experts were invited to testify. They also generally found a lack of resources, poor communication and a need for some new laws, regulations and guidance.

So the Commission, in its final report, has not held any DoD agencies or individual decision makers accountable. They have made no attempt to recover any money negligently paid to contractors and have announced no criminal referrals. Senator Webb should not have been concerned about the expiration of the statue of limitations for offenses the Committee would discover, as they have apparently found none! This Congressional creation appears to be a pale shade of the Truman Committee, which is unlikely to further the goal of effective oversight of the LOGCAP program along with other contingency support contracts. While testimony has generated useful information, there has not been direct follow through.

One of the best members of the Commission resigned her position early in the process. Ms. Linda J. Gustitus was a Staff Director of several oversight subcommittees in the Senate for more than 20 years, including the Permanent Subcommittee on Investigations (PSI). When I spoke with her prior to leaving for Washington and the assignment, she expressed her concerns at the lack of subpoena power and equal number of members. Given the lack of progress for the Commission, her concerns appear justified.

My general sense when I read the Commission recommendations is that a good acquisition conference of two weeks could have identified all of these proposed improvements. Consider that the Commission found in Chapter 2 that "Inherently governmental' rules do not guide appropriate use of contractors in contingencies."[123] In February of this year, the Defense Science Board found, after an approximately one year review of service contracts, that, among many other findings "Up-to-date guidance to *define inherently-government functions* is a particular need."[124]

---

123 (Commission on Wartime Contracting, 2011) p. 28
124 (Defense Science Board, 2011) p. 11

MISSED OPPORTUNITIES IN A TARGET RICH ENVIRONMENT

Contracts with which I am familiar, the LOGCAP contract, the Restore Iraqi Oil contract and the Prime Vendor Food contract, offered ample opportunity to explore personal responsibility for decisions favorable to contractors, but not favorable to the taxpayer and troops. These and other contracts offered opportunities to recover unjustified costs, as the Truman Committee did. These contracts were worth, collectively, over $50 billion. The Commission passed on any such investigations.

The most pointed testimony criticizing the way which the Army managed the LOGCAP contract (after I left the program) was given at a hearing by the then Director of the Defense Contract Audit Agency, Ms. April Stephenson. In her testimony she raised several important issues. They were:

(1) FAR 52.216-26, *Payments of Allowable Costs before Definitization*

> Ms. Stephenson notes that the Army included this clause, which requires withholding of 15% of all payments prior to the negotiation of a final cost base, in LOGCAP III. The Army anticipated that in contingency operations, Task Orders would be implemented within 48 hours, based on a Rough Order of Magnitude (ROM) estimate of costs and a Technical Proposal (TEP). This would result in an Un-priced Contractual Action (UCA), which would require submission of a cost proposal suitable for audit and a negotiated definitization of the estimated cost. (Sorry for the contracting jargon.)

> The 15% withhold of vouchered costs during the period prior to definitization was designed to incentivize the contractor to quickly submit an auditable proposal, as Ms. Stephenson stated. She is correct in her analysis that this is an important tool for the PCO to manage the definitization process. Early definitization is a critical cost control measure. When I managed this program I proposed the other tool which a PCO has, unilateral definitization. This was rejected by senior leadership. DCAA strongly recommended the implementation of this withhold, but Army leadership rejected this in August 2004.

(2) *Subcontracting by KBR under LOGCAP*

> Ms. Stephenson's testimony was quite correct: KBR purchasing in the AOR was a mess. I visited the KBR purchasing operation in Kuwait in 2003 and personally say the disarray of the purchasing operation. Lack of a sound purchasing system, collecting the proper data was a prime problem in negotiation of KBR task orders.

The Dining Facilities (DFAC) problem with the first year of LOGCAP III, as described by Ms. Stephenson, was the major example of this problem (though purchasing of trucks, other vehicles, housing containers and ice plants also illustrate these problems). My understanding is that KBR subcontracts guaranteed the DFAC operator revenue at a specific level of meals served, even if the contractor served significantly fewer meals. This problem was exacerbated by KBR's inability to accurately track the number of meals served. (KBR disputes that they were required to do this.) As Ms. Stephenson points out, while fighting the questioned costs under the first year of DFACs, KBR incorporated the DCAA recommendations into the next round of subcontracts, producing more efficient results. In 2005 the Army negotiated the costs for the first year of DFACs. The Army accepted almost all of the costs which DCAA had questioned. The Army then made an incredible move. The first year of DFACs were converted to fixed price contracts with a profit of 3%, the maximum fee they could have earned under a cost type contract. By converting these contracts to fixed price, DCAA could not perform a post contract audit of costs, rejecting those that were not allowable or were unreasonably incurred. This move probably saved KBR one quarter of a billion dollars. An Army Memorandum states that this was done specifically to preclude DCAA from performing such an audit.

(3) Force Protection

Ms. Stephenson pointed out that knowledge of the $19.7 million charge for private force protection only came about through the unfortunate death of four Blackwater employees who were escorting some kitchen equipment to a DFAC site. Despite initial denials, we soon learned that the Blackwater employees worked for a KBR subcontractor and KBR was passing these costs along to the Army. As Ms. Stephenson points out, the contract did not allow this. The issue saw daylight due to Congressman Henry Waxman's work on these issues.

(4) Award Fee

This was absolutely the most dismaying part of Ms. Stephenson's testimony. I left management prior to the establishment of Award Fee Boards. When, during 2005, I saw the high level of fees I was disappointed in the way the boards were working. During these periods KBR's accounting, estimating and purchasing systems remained unapproved. They were an integral part of the contract requirements and key management tools for the Army. Without the ability to trust this data, the Army was unable to manage the cost of these services. Since the Army was placed on a budget to manage the war in late 2003, cost management was vital to providing the troops all of the services and equipment they needed.

Ms. Stephenson states that these all of these issues were presented to the Award Fee Board Chairman. It appears that these boards were managed to achieve an outcome decided in advance and not based upon actual performance. To do so was incredibly harmful to the program and the troops. Money was wasted on excess award fee, which could have been spent on body armor or up-armored vehicles, possibly saving lives. In addition, KBR was provided no incentive to control performance. If you get the fee anyway, why work toward positive outcomes which will just raise expectations. It is not surprising that KBR systems, which Ms. Stephenson discusses, were not really fixed until 2008.

Ms. Stephenson's testimony indicates that early in the contract they were in a position which should have reduced award fees to the 30 percent or less area. Total failure on 70 percent of the criteria would not lead you to the 82 percent level, which KBR received in the early award fee boards. There is a strong disconnect between Ms. Stephenson's testimony and the Army testimony in a Senate Armed Services Committee hearing 2007.

Following her testimony, Ms. Stephenson was removed from her position as director of DCAA. She was replaced by the head of the Army Audit Agency. Since then no one at DCAA has been publicly critical of the Army. The Commission's final report shows no curiosity about this situation. You will find no mention of the award fee problems, the Army's extreme favoritism towards KBR or Ms. Stephenson's dismissal.

SUMMING UP THE COMMISSION ON WARTIME CONTRACTING

I could mention many other missed opportunities of the Commission. While there are worthwhile aspects of the final report, the need to eliminate contracting out inherently governmental functions and the need to grow organic capabilities for example, these are not sufficient for improved performance in the next contingency operation. All in all, the Commission missed an opportunity to address some root causes of poor wartime contracting.

The nexus of retired general officers and civilian political appointees in influencing decision was never discussed. There may have been a very good reason for this. After the Commission released its disappointing report in August of 2010, Michael Thibault, one of the co-chairmen, took a job with DynCorp, one of the contractors who contributed to the waste in wartime contracting. [125] Since the Commission had established itself as not a threat to contractors, Mr. Thibault qualified for a lucrative position.

Contractors were never confronted with their poor work, cooked books and failure to cooperate with the government. The Agencies were never confronted with their cooperation with this looting of the treasury and denial of efficient support to the troops. These confrontations should have been followed by demands to give the money back and get rid of the malefactors. That is what Harry Truman did, and it worked!

CONCLUSIONS

The LOGCAP contract has received extensive oversight actions from the Congress. However, not much has changed in the Army's management of the contract. The Army has not admitted obvious problems and runs the risk of repeating problems on the new LOGCAP contracts in Afghanistan, Kuwait and Iraq. This failure of oversight is replicated in other oversight missions of Congress.

Christopher Foreman describes oversight as, "the efforts to gather information about what agencies are doing and to dictate or signal to agencies regarding the preferred behavior or policy."[126] Congress has gathered significant information on LOGCAP and certainly signaled to the Army some changes which are desired. However, the Army has not responded in a positive way. Perhaps it is time for the "dictate" phase.

In order to make Congressional oversight more effective, there are some significant changes which could be made:

- During hearings the committee counsel should be given a period to ask questions of the witness panel. While this would cut into member time, it would make the hearings more effective. This has been done by previous committees, an example being the Pujo Committee, 1912.[127]
- While Congressional time is a precious commodity, more questioning time in hearings would help. Five minutes is too short to develop questions and probe for answers. If a second round is held, continuity suffers.
- The committees should use their leverage powers to obtain timely and accurate information. For example, the Senate Armed Services Committee could hold up the promotion

---

125 (Gordon, 2012) p. 1
126 (Foreman 1988) p. 13
127 (Schlesinger 1975)p. 174

of some three star generals until the needed information is provided.

- The must be consequences of misleading testimony. When the military is asked to investigate one of its officers, the results will generally be slow in coming and lack accountability. Congress has the authority to refer such matters to the Department of Justice, directly.
- Since agencies may send panel members determined to defend the agency and contractors at all costs, committees must call other witnesses. Experts in the field, whistleblowers and others may have a better perspective and more information than the agencies' representatives.
- Congressional commissions, such as the Commission on Wartime Contracting, must have a majority leadership which can force action and subpoena power to compel documents and testimony. At this point the Wartime Commission should be given this power and more time to work its mission or should be replaced by a Congressional Select Committee with subpoena power.
- The current push to reduce the resources and capacity of the CRS, CBO and GAO must be stopped. These organizations provide vital data which is necessary for members of Congress to perform their jobs and also necessary for citizens to understand their government.

Congressmen and Senators are already overwhelmed with hearings, committee work, floor actions and constituent relations (not to mention fund raising). When issues such as the financial collapse, healthcare reform and unemployment dominate for over a year, time for oversight is necessarily cut. It is amazing that as much time as has been devoted to one issue, LOGCAP, has been found.

However, Congressional oversight of the LOGCAP Program, and of other Agency programs, is vital to the national interest. The need to protect the taxpayers from overcharging by defense contractors, such as KBR, has not changed since the Truman Committee. Neither has the networks of DoD military and civilians with their former colleagues, now in the defense business, changed. Waste in one area costs needed resources in other areas. Waste in LOGCAP deprived military leadership of funds for more body armor, armor for vehicles and other vital support. Waste costs the taxpayer the value they expect to receive for their money.

Strong Congressional oversight is necessary to avoid these costs of waste and inefficiency in Government programs.

Both parties should realize that the strong oversight of Federal Agencies, as advocated by Representative Waxman and Senator Dorgan, is generally concerned with non-partisan issues. Such oversight can improve the outcomes of agency programs and protect the American taxpayer. Along the way members of Congress may receive deserved credit for accomplishing these public goals. Sounds like a classic win-win situation.

CHAPTER 11. THE USE OF CONTRACTORS FOR COMBAT SERVICE SUPPORT

GEN Anthony Zinni is a former Commander in Chief (a title no longer used) of the U.S. Central Command. He said, "If I had to revamp how we do things, I would start with what should be contracted out and what should not."[128] In this chapter I will examine the decision to outsource combat support/combat service support under the LOGCAP contract. I believe there is good reason to call for a reversal of this decision.

The use of Private Military Contractors (PMCs) is a controversial issue with many complications. One of these is distinguishing exactly what we are talking about. P. W. Singer categorizes PMCs according to their function.[129]

- Military provider firms are those which may participate directly in combat situations.
- Military consulting firms aid a government in developing their military capabilities, which may include studies, organizational guidance and training.
- Military support firms contribute non-combat services such as maintenance and combat service support (LOGCAP).

LOGCAP is clearly a military support contract. Private security contractors, such as Blackwater are more than military support contractors but not quite military provider firms, as our State Department uses them.

---

128 (Stanger 2009) p.29
129 (Singer, Corporate Warriors 2003) p. 91

Another complicated issue is evaluating the costs and the benefits of using PMCs. Deborah Kidwell, an Assistant Professor of Military History at the U.S. Army Command and General Staff College provides a clear account of these complications.

> Political and military leaders have yet to establish clearly the cost-efficiency of PMCs in their current roles. Numerous studies by government agencies, journalists, and congressional inquiries document cost overruns and unexpected indirect costs, such as corruption, increased security needs, and nonperformance. Furthermore, the consequences of the extensive privatization of military services to future U.S. overall military effectiveness and mission capability remains unknown — and for now largely ignored. Americans may find that the indirect costs to society — potential loss of employment, education and training opportunities, as well as the ever-widening gulf between the military and civilian communities — that result from the extensive use of PMCs may be more than the country, is willing to accept.[130]

A number of the indirect costs to society center on the concept of sovereignty. Does the use of PMCs transfer critical governmental functions to the private sector? As more functions are outsourced, the government appears to lose even the ability to oversee and manage the private firms. One possible solution to this problem has been to outsource the management and oversight function, even though these would appear to be inherently governmental. LOGCAP has seen the assignment of what appear to be oversight functions to a private firm, SERCO. Though the Army denies that SERCO performs inherently governmental functions, we saw that they, and their predecessor firm RCI, effectively replaced the Defense Contract Audit Agency in providing financial analysis of contractor performance to the Army.

With the experience of extensive LOGCAP support for Operations Enduring Freedom and Iraqi Freedom, the Army has the opportunity to re-evaluate decisions to use contractors for combat service support. Such a review can evaluate the additional risks posed by contractors on the battlefield, based on over eight years of experience. Unlike previous reviews, there is now experience regarding the problematic legal status of contractor personnel. Issues such as Defense Base Act Insurance were previously not understood in context. Finally, we have new cost data to make a much better cost/benefit evaluation comparing contractors to troops.

---

130   (Kidwell 2009) pp. 4-5

OUTSOURCING

Outsourcing of government services was institutionalized as early as 1955, when the then Bureau of the Budget issued a directive which discouraged the agencies of the government from producing any item or service they could procure from a commercial vendor.[131] The successor to the Bureau of the Budget, the Office of Management and Budget (OMB) later, in 1968, issued the government bible of outsourcing, Circular A-76.

Thus, the Army's decision to create the LOGCAP program as a means of using contractors for combat services support did not happen in a vacuum. In the 1990s outsourcing was a popular business concept. A firm should concentrate on its core competencies and purchase other services from firms who had that service as a core capability. A furniture store, whose business is to sell furniture, should hire a company to store and then, deliver the furniture. They would contract with a firm in the warehousing and delivery sector, which could perform that function in a more efficient and less expensive manner.

It is interesting that many of the frequently outsourced services resemble those services under the LOGCAP contract:

- Transportation and distribution of supplies,
- Janitorial services.
- Cafeteria, coffee and water for the offices,
- Personnel support.

Outsourcing these functions has allowed some firms to reduce their management overhead, cut costs and obtain a higher quality service. This only happens if they maintain a capability to purchase the service effectively and conduct oversight of the contractor's performance.

Certainly, outsourcing will only be done if there is a real cost savings to the firm. The firm must take into account all factors which impact profits. If our furniture store receives too many complaints about the delivery process, they will probably lose business in the long run. This is not an acceptable risk and may lead to performing the delivery service with in-house personnel who are committed to company goals.

Following the industry paradigm, most defense analysts recommended outsourcing of logistics efforts. As an example, Jacques Gansler provided a list of defense reform recommendations in 1995. Number 9 on the list was "Shift logistics support to industry (from organic), and use "lean"

---

131 (Donahue 1989) p. 4

(just in time) concepts."[132] Unlike 1995, we now have substantial experience in the use of outsourced logistics support.

In this chapter I will look at the use of LOGCAP to provide combat service support in the same general way. I will make some "back of the envelope" calculations and add some assessments of risk based upon my personal observations. This analysis is designed to provide a model for a more thorough and complete analysis which the Army could perform. However, I am rather comfortable with the conclusions I reach.

You will recall that the LOGCAP program was initiated based upon the KBR study under Secretary of Defense Richard Cheney I mentioned in chapter 2. The later LMI study used the limited experience in Bosnia, along with other constraints to reach a conclusion that contractors were less expensive than soldiers. The major study since that time was performed by the congressional Budget Office in 2005.[133] This was in the first two years of combat in Iraq and had significant data to evaluate. In the following, I will discuss the CBO analysis in detail.

RISK ANALYSIS

First we need to establish the risks associated with possible strategies for providing support to our troops. I would suggest we look at three possible alternative strategies:

1. The status quo, with LOGCAP providing the set of services currently provided in Iraq, Afghanistan and Kuwait. The services include:

- Air Terminal and Air Field Operations
- Ammunition storage and supply
- Camp Operations
- Communications and Information
- Equipment Maintenance[134]
- Firefighting Services
- Morale, Welfare and recreation
- Property management
- Transportation

---

132 (Gansler, Defense Conversion 1995) p.232

133 (Congressional Budget Office 2005)

134 Maintenance of major systems is normally not provided by LOGCAP. Contractor Logistics Support (CLS) for tanks, Bradley Fighting Vehicles, Apaches, etc. is normally provided by the manufacturing contractor. While these contractors have the experience to do the job, you can see the number of contractors in theater multiplies, creating command and control issues.

2. A reduced footprint for LOGCAP and increased organic support. Selective support missions, such as Air Terminal operations and transportation, for example, would return to organic support.

3. Full organic support. Army units would perform all of the above stated LOGCAP missions.

RISKS OF USING CONTRACTORS

Each of these Courses of Action (COAs in Army terminology) will present a different set of risks for the Army in accomplishing missions. Basically the third COA will mitigate all of the risks of using contractors. The first COA will generate the most risk. Some form of the second COA will have reduced risk, compared to the first COA. They will also have a different set of costs and benefits, which I will discuss, below.

There is general agreement on the risks associated with using contractors on the battlefield.[135] The first risk is an agent and principal problem. The classic statement of this problem is Stephen Ross' paper The Economic Theory of Agency: The Principal's Problem.[136] We can restate the problem as:

The agent and the principal have different goals for the contract (independent utility functions, in economic terms.) The Government wants the scope of work accomplished in the most effective and efficient manner. The managers of the contractor have a fiduciary responsibility to shareholders to maximize profits, or minimize losses. This may conflict with providing the Army exactly what they want or need, when the contract is ambiguous about the requirement.

The vehicle for aligning these independent goals is the fee schedule. In the LOGCAP III contract the fee schedule was a base fee of 1% of estimated costs and an award fee of up to 2% of estimated costs. Ross points out that, "A market-imposed minimum expected fee or expected utility of fee by the agent would be one economically sensible constraint."

The contract is impacted by uncertain variations in the state of nature. For LOGCAP III this was generally the changing combat environment resulting in changes to the Government's needs.

The agent will have superior knowledge concerning his capabilities with relationship to the scope of work. We theoretically hired KBR to perform the LOGCAP III Scope of work as a better alternative to organic support. Under a performance scope of work we do not tell the contrac-

---

135 (Camm 2005) Appendix B
136 (Ross 1973) p. 134-139

tor how to perform. In addition, as military and civilian oversight person-nel rotate in and out, contractor employees on the ground become the effective experts at any location.

Ross concludes that, "In general, though, it is clear that the solution to the principal's problem will not be Pareto-efficient." Any given fee schedule is unlikely to motivate the contractor to perform in the way the Government wants.

A way to move closer to the principal's desired outcome is to monitor the agent's actions. Of course we know that such oversight was impos-sible for the Government to perform under LOGCAP III.

Contract law, including the Federal Acquisition Regulation and the contract itself govern the behavior of the contractor. The contractor must perform according to the scope of work in the contract and not in accordance with the commander's directions. This relationship is out-side of the Army command and control structure. Problems may manifest in several ways.

Use of a contractor will not ensure that that the military commander gets the performance he wants in the same manner as placing an organic army unit under his control. The military commander cannot directly order the contractor to perform some service. Only the warranted con-tracting officer can give such direction. The commander must provide the contracting officer with a description of the task and money to pay for it. This sub-optimizes the commanders' ability to quickly respond to changing situations. The first year of LOGCAP in Iraq was subject to sev-en major scope modifications and over one thousand change directions issued by a contracting officer. Each of these represented new direction from the combatant commander, which went through the contracting chain.

This risk is especially critical during the build up phase and then dur-ing the draw down phase. As I write, the Army is drawing down forces in Iraq. While the Army develops plans for managing this process, the contractor must respond through contract direction. The Government expects the contractor to prepare plans for their operations, but these must work with the military's plans. We have seen a changing military and political situation in Iraq, with consequent changes to the military plans and the contractor plans. It is difficult for a contracting process to coordinate with the Combatant Commander's responses to this con-stantly changing situation.

Part of this risk is that the contractor will retain excess capacity to re-spond to possible changed situations. In Iraq we see that the contractor personnel are not reducing at the same rate as the military draw down. This is the result of a number of factors, but DCAA has identified excess capacity maintained by KBR in Iraq, amounting to over $100 million in early 2010.

These problems increase when the contractor utilizes subcontractors for certain tasks. The Government does not have "privity of contract" with the subcontractor. This means the Government can only deal with the subcontractor through the prime contractor, not directly. One of the problems with LOGCAP III was the Army's expectation, based upon KBR's proposal, that KBR would self-perform most contract tasks. Instead, many tasks such as operation of dining facilities were completely subcontracted. The Agent/Principal problem was thus doubled.

Experience under LOGCAP III in Iraq, Kuwait and Afghanistan revealed the second major risk area. With contractor support requirements tend to increase beyond those which organic support would have provided. Organic military units provide support in strict compliance with military regulations and guidance. During Phases I and II of operations, where military commanders were not constrained by a budget, they continually added more support to their requirements. The increased costs for LOGCAP support during these phases were substantially driven by increased requirements.

My experience suggests that camp services, such as dining facilities and living arrangements, would not have been as elaborate under an organic support concept. When I visited Camp Arifjan in Kuwait, for example, I saw a steady increase in the level of services in both these areas. The serving line ended up with a pastry section that included various cakes and pies. It looked like a fairly nice bakery in the states. I believe that an organic DFAC would have been somewhat more austere than the ones I observed. Troops would still have received a variety of food choices, but at a lower cost.

Once these services are provided at this level, it is extremely hard to reduce them. The commander must take into account the impact on morale which such a reduction must entail. When the Army went into phase III in 2004, a budget was imposed on conduct of the war. When I met with GEN Casey, as he prepared to leave for Iraq, one of his concerns was reducing the number of entrees in DFAC serving lines to save money. He understood that any extra funds expended on LOGCAP were lost to him for providing other needed support to troops.

The third major risk to be dealt with concerns continuity of support. Use of contractors for military services has experienced this problem for a long time. Machiavelli wrote in 1513, "...they [contracted military] have no love or other motive to keep them in the field beyond a trifling wage, which is not enough to make them die for you."[137] Once the Army develops a force structure, with units to perform support functions, they have assurance of continued provision of the services. While there will be planned rotations, any unit can be ordered to stay until a relief unit is available. Units will not cease support and will perform as ordered. As contractors are added to the mix, the risk of lost continuity of support will increase.

Lacking a Congressional declaration of war, which we have not had for any military operation since World War II, the military cannot force a contractor to remain on the battlefield. When an Army officer was killed in the "tree cutting incident" on the demilitarized zone in Korea in 1976, our defense condition was upgraded to level three. As a result hundreds of civilian s requested immediate transportation out of the Korean theater.[138]

As we have seen in the preceding discussion, KBR, at least threatened to cause support to cease because of the threatened 15% withhold issue. I did not believe that KBR would actually do this, but the Army has stated they believed this. While I believed KBR would stay, this does not mean that every contractor would do so. Other companies, without the Halliburton guarantee, for example, may get into financial difficulty and not be able to continue performance. Certainly any company, KBR included, might cease performance if they suffered significant casualties within their workforce. Any analysis of risk must take into account an increased risk to continuity of support with civilian contractors.

The fourth major risk area is the legal status of civilian contractor personnel and their companies. Military units, Government civilians and contractor personnel appear to all have a different legal status when operating in a combat theater. Control of these individuals is a mixed affair of the Combatant Commander, the supervisory chain and the contractor's management. Some of the important questions are:

- Is each of these categories a legitimate military targets for enemy forces?
- Will the personnel receive prisoner-of-war status, if captured?
- Are the personnel subject to the Uniform Code of Military Justice (UCMJ)?

---

137 (Machiavelli 1950) p. 45
138 (Croft 2001) p. 21

- Are the personnel subject to prosecution by non-U.S. authorities for acts committed in support of U.S. forces (war crimes)?
- Are the personnel subject to criminal prosecution by non-U.S. authorities for personnel criminal acts, not in support of U.S. forces?

While the answer to these questions for military forces is not always clear, it is certainly much more defined than for contractor personnel. The uncertainty to those answers creates a risk for the Combatant Commander. Contractor personnel may feel free to behave in ways which do not support the U.S. mission due to perceived or actual immunity from prosecution. We have seen such actions in Iraq on several occasions, especially with regard to private security forces, such as Blackwater.

There have been efforts to clarify some of these issues. In 2000 the Congress passed the Military Extraterritorial Jurisdiction Act (18 U.S.C. 3261-3267). This law provides for trail in federal court for criminal acts by civilians accompanying the force. The law applies only if the UCMJ or host nation legal systems have not tried the case. This law was little used by 2004.[139] However, there have been a few prosecutions in recent years. For example, Aaron Langston, a KBR contractor, was indicted in federal court under MEJA for assaulting a fellow contractor.[140] The Commission on Wartime Contracting recommends clarification of the U.S. criminal jurisdiction over contractors overseas.[141]

A fifth major risk area is the Government's current lack of ability to provide effective oversight of contractor work. One of the lessons of this book is that effective oversight of work was not conducted for LOGCAP III. The GAO has reported that, "Challenges in providing an adequate number of contract oversight and management personnel in deployed locations are likely to continue to hinder DOD's oversight of contractors."[142] The lack of oversight will inevitably increase the costs of contractor support and reduce the quality of contractor performance. That is the experience of LOGCAP III. In addition, the lack of oversight has a negative effect on the integrity of the Government contracting system. Writing contracts, without the ability to oversee and enforce them, will reduce the trust which citizens have in effective government.

---

139 (Singer, War, Profits, and the Vaccum of Law: Privitazed Military Firms and International Law 2004) p. 537

140 (Dickinson 2011) p. 55

141 (Commission on Wartime Contracting 2011) p. 5

142 (GAO 2010) p. 6

Soldiers and civilians who provide this oversight are on rotational schedules which reduce the effectiveness of their work. Soldiers are on a one year assignment. Air Force and Navy officers assigned to the Defense Contract Management Agency appeared to be on six month assignments. Civilians are on a maximum of one year assignments and often on six month assignments. When some skill in doing this job is attained, the personnel changes and the process begin again. The contractor often has the most experience at any given location and can skew directions in his favor.

This risk is a matter of contractor support. Organic military units have their own established command and control systems which governs the work of soldiers. The cost for this oversight is built into the unit costs which include headquarters and staff personnel who perform the management tasks.

The sixth risk area is divided responsibility. As we saw in the water chapter it was unclear, at least to some senior leaders who was responsible for providing water at some camps. While the contract held KBR responsible, military units were actually taking water from the Tigris and Euphrates rivers and sunning it through their purification units. Senior Army leaders, seeing these operations, assumed the Army was thus responsible for the water. They were, in fact wrong, but KBR was in a position to use this divided responsibility perception to their advantage.

Contract oversight was also a divided responsibility. My contracting officers worked with the Defense Contract Management Agency's Administrative Contracting Officers, the Defense Contract Audit Agency's auditors and technical Representatives from the supported unit. This is the way contract oversight is currently designed by the military and will be the way it will operate in the next contingency operation.

Army units operate under a unified chain of command, which removes the possibility of divided responsibility for oversight of work. My experience was that KBR would routinely try to play off of this issue. Since ACOs and technical Representatives rotated on a six month or yearly basis, they could often take advantage of the "new guy" coming in. The Commission on Wartime Contracting, after extensive research in theater, identified this problem as a significant issue:

> When Federal personnel rotate in and out of theater too quickly and when long-serving contractors become the local resident experts, reliance on contractor support becomes a detriment to effective government management and oversight of contractors.[143]

---

143   (Commission on Wartime Contracting 2011) p. 15

This would not happen with organic Army units.

The next risk area is a very sensitive risk area involves our evaluation of contractor casualties as opposed to military casualties. Contractor service support personnel have a much lower fatality rate than military service support personnel.[144] This is certainly because the military support operates much closer to the combat troops. One may speculate that military units, performing the same LOGCAP work, would have the same or possibly lower fatality rate because they are authorized to carry weapons and defend themselves.

The data also indicates that some contractor personnel, such as truck drivers, are taking on jobs that are much more hazardous than the equivalent jobs within the U.S. Between September 2001 and December 2010, at least 2,200 contractor employees have died and 49,800 were injured, according to Department of Labor, Defense Base Act Insurance claims.[145] (This number included all contracts in theater, not just LOGCAP.) Driving a truck in the United States is a fairly hazardous occupation, with a fatality rate of 17.5 per 100,000 employees. For LOGCAP employees overall, CBO found the fatality rate was 40.3 per 100,000 employees. The rate for KBR truck drivers was even higher, based on my observation of where fatalities occurred, but this was not calculated by the CBO. The overall fatality rate for workers in the United States is about 4 per 100,000 workers.

From these numbers we can conclude that LOGCAP contractor personnel are subject to risks significantly higher than their counterparts in the United States workforce. But we place a different value on military and civilian casualties. Soldiers sign up knowing they may be ordered to go in harm's way. Soldiers carry weapons and may defend themselves. They are trained to do so. They are expected to accept the risk of sustaining casualties in combat. We do not have similar expectations concerning civilians.

Civilian workers, although they may be apprised of the risks, do not have the same obligations and expectations as soldiers. They are not combat-trained and are forbidden to use weapons. They must rely on someone else to protect them in dangerous situations. LOGCAP was designed with the intent that civilian workers would be "behind the lines." In Iraq and Afghanistan, there is no "behind the lines." Civilian contrac-

---

144   (Congressional Budget Office 2005) p. 13
145   (Commission on Wartime Contracting 2011) p. 8

tors now work in what are essentially low-intensity combat zones. This was an unanticipated risk of LOGCAP support.

In the first Gulf War the single deadliest incident occurred when an Iraqi Scud missile hit a barracks housing an Army Reserve water purification unit, far from the actual front.[146] Today, that water purification function is assigned to the LOGCAP contractor. Those deaths would have been civilians, rather than military.

There is also an operational risk from using civilians instead of troops. Every soldier, even those operating the dining facility, carry weapons and are trained to use them. In the event of an attack on the unit, they can aid in the defense. Contractor personnel do not carry weapons. In the event of attack, they cannot help and must be defended. An additional burden is placed on the troops, along with a loss of available combat power. Machiavelli noted this when he wrote, "As to the levelers [road construction workers], which is your second question, I would have my own soldiers do this office, both because in the ancient military it was so done, and also that there may be fewer un-armed people and fewer impediments in the army."[147]

Rear Admiral Henry R. Eccles described this risk in terms of the flexibility of the force. He wrote:

> The composition and disposition of military forces and of logistics reserves are important consideration in the development of flexibility. Thus, if a force is designed to do one task only, great effectiveness in that particular task may be achieved. The flexibility of the force will be small. On the other hand, a force whose combat elements are so balanced as to be able to fight a variety of actions gains greatly in its tactical flexibility.

> When such a force includes a built-in or attached logistics support element, great strategic and tactical flexibility are attained. This particularly true if there is uncommitted reserves of combat and logistics resources available for selective augmentation of the operating forces as the situation develops.[148]

Suppose the Army in Iraq, instead of 130,000 contractor personnel, requiring protection, had a mix of 100,000 contractors and 30,000 soldiers performing CS/CSS functions. The 30,000 soldiers would be armed and trained for combat operations. At times, they could have proved a ready reserve force to support specific operations. Army logistical units are considered capable of dealing with up to a Level 2 threat — company

---

146 (Zamparelli 1999) p. 37
147 (Machaivelli 2003) pp. 107-108
148 (Eccles 1959) p. 120

and below sized enemy formations.[149] This would have provided additional flexibility in operations and additional security for bases where they were located.

With the great use of contractors the Commander must devote some of the available combat power, not to operations, but to the protection of the contractor force. In Iraq this was not a particularly important issue at the major base camps. The security of the camp protected soldiers and civilians alike. Transportation operations, in contrast, required a heavy use of combat support to protect civilian truckers. Contractor support of the smaller forward operating bases (FOBS) also required military protection.

We have, in fact, seen contractors pick up weapons and participate in defensive actions. This creates problems with the Command and Control under the rules of engagement and international law. These civilians may have actually become "unlawful enemy combatants" since they are not in uniform and part of the U.S. combat forces.

The behavior of contractors in theater poses a significant risk to the ultimate U.S. goals in the area of operations. We have seen the instances of private security forces, such as those of Blackwater firing on, killing and wounding civilians in Iraq and Afghanistan. These cases were a real setback to our initiatives to "win the hearts and minds" of the local populations. I occasionally rode on military planes with some of these "cowboys." They were usually armed to the teeth with weapons not available to soldiers. Their standard comportment was a swagger that said get out of my way, or else. I always felt little good would come of having these folks in country.

Other contractor personnel can just be rude and obnoxious, often with alcohol involved. In an article entitled "More Examples of Contractor Headaches at a Glance", the AP reported in the Washington Post on December 19, 2010 of, "previously undisclosed offenses committed by more than 200 contract employees of the State Department in Afghanistan, Iraq and other countries between 2004 and 2008."[150] Contractor employees may sometimes live off base and have more interaction with local people. While the contract may have requirements concerning contractor employee behavior, the incidents still happen resulting in the firing of individuals, but seemingly no new controls on employees.[151]

---

149 (Croft 2001) p. 37

150 (Associated Press 2010) p. 1

151 A number of KBR employee memoirs of work in Iraq provide anecdotal evidence of the poor behavior of KBR personnel. An example is Rick D. Cleland's

Contractor behavior may also have an adverse effect on the morale of our troops. Laura Dickinson reports on her discussions with military lawyers:

> Nevertheless, even in this relatively benign context [base camp support], the lawyers worried that the lack of adequate disciplinary controls over contractors undermined soldiers' conduct and morale. For example, the judge advocates noted that if contractors drank or used drugs and troops joined in and got caught, the soldiers would be punished because these actions violated military discipline, while the contractors would not be subject to the same rules. Furthermore, when logistics contractors some-times did commit crimes, the failure of the system to provide adequate accountability for them was galling.[152]

It is quite obvious that soldiers are under more discipline and greater restrictions than contractor employees. They live on the base and gener-ally in Iraq and Afghanistan only left the base for mission related activi-ties. They receive training in how to behave. Perhaps of most importance, their access to alcohol is virtually non-existent.

By outsourcing these functions, the Army loses skills which may be needed at a future time. Organic support units are always in a cycle that includes training. As some soldiers leave the service, they may stay in a reserve unit, continuing to make those skills available and receiving ad-ditional training. Keeping a supply of new recruits, we keep a pipeline of trained specialists in support tasks. Since contractors only hire when they have a contract, they will not support such a cycle of trained person-nel. They generally try to hire personnel trained by the Army, but soon there will be no more Army-trained resources.

The Army will also find itself in circumstances where contractor sup-port is unavailable. At this point they must retain some organic skills. Lack of these skills will result in a very inefficient use of resources. David Scholes describes the situation he encountered with the British Army, where a Camp had to be built in a location in Afghanistan where contrac-tors could not go immediately:

> Building the camp, which would consist of about eight individual tem-porary deployable accommodation camps, a hospital and quarters for the contractors, had been an enormous undertaking and was not one that the Army was properly trained to carry out. The British government's policy of out sourcing so much of the practical work to contractors such as KBR had ensured that the Army had lost or failed to acquire the vital skills

---

Working for KBR in Iraq: An Exercise in Frustration (Cleland 2007) pp. 17-18
152 (Dickinson 2011) p. 176

needed. The royal engineers working on Camp Bastion had never built temporary deployable accommodations before. [153]

Another area of risk is more controversial. The use of contractor support appears to obviate what has been called the Abrams' Doctrine. General Creighton Abrams restructured military forces to closely integrate the reserve and guard components with regular Army units. For example, a combat division could not deploy and operate without a reserve transportation unit to move their supplies and a reserve water unit to produce and transport water. There is speculation that Abrams intended this linkage to force leadership to realize that any use of combat forces would require broad support as reserve and guard units were mobilized. Replacing these reserve units with contractors may create a moral hazard in that a President can now commit troops to war without calling up significant reserve and guard units.

The use of civilian contractors may create an additional risk of combat operations, unsupported by the citizens of the United States. However, some may consider this a good aspect of contractors, as it gives the President more leeway in protecting the United States. Since this is controversial and hard to quantify, I will not use it as a risk factor in this analysis. I mention it because it does concern me, since I believe the use of military force should be a considered decision which includes the support of the citizens.

Finally, the use of contractors for these support services creates a constituency which will profit from war. It may seem cynical to think that people would advocate for war, with the resulting deaths and injuries of our troops, their troops and civilians (always in other countries) along with the general destruction; because some money is to be made. My sense of human nature and observation as to who tends to fund the organizations which advocate military action, indicates this is all too possible. Certainly we do not really need more people who will suffer no consequences of war and reap financial benefits.

ADVANTAGES OF USING CIVILIAN CONTRACTORS

Use of civilian contractors may offer the Army some advantages in accomplishing mission such as Operations Iraqi Freedom. There is a large pool of former military enlisted personnel who have combat service support skills and abilities learned in the Army. Having served in the military and either finished that service or retired, they are not ready to

---

153 (Scholes 2008) p. 196

re-enlist when a conflict is imminent. Contractors have access to this pool of skilled personnel.

When I worked in the private sector after retirement, I worked for a company that provided skilled maintenance and training personnel for Army howitzer programs. Our workforce pool was 90% former military personnel, who had received extensive training and experience in these areas. We did this in peace time and were ready, when called on, to deploy some of these former military to provide unit maintenance support in Afghanistan and Iraq. LOGCAP contractors will utilize this same pool to provide trained employees for troop support needs.

However, much LOGCAP work does not require these skills. The heavy use of foreign subcontractors and third country nationals indicates the ability to staff most LOGCAP jobs without relying on this pool. Truck drivers, electricians, carpenters and other skills were hired without regard to military training. In fact, the maintenance and repair work is the prime venue for ex-military workers and that is mainly done through CLS contracts, not LOGCAP. Since I am concerned with LOGCAP in this book, I will not address the comparison of organic support to CLS support for maintenance and repair. However, A. G. Metheny has written an informative and entertaining account of his work in Afghanistan and Iraq as a CLS contractor. His book, *Baghdad F. T. U.*[154] (Field Technical Unit) is the work of a great American, determined to support our troops, and he is a very good story teller.

This advantage is also mitigated by the eventual loss of these skills acquired through military training. If the skills are mission essential and provided by contractors, the Army will cease training soldiers and giving them the necessary experience. If contractors provide all of this support, the pool of military trained professionals will evaporate.

Using contractor support also provides the Army with a flexible work force. Contractors can increase and decrease the size of their work force with greater ease than the military. Military enlistments are for a specific period and usually offer the ability to re-enlist regardless of whether operations are ongoing or drawing down. If a soldier makes promotion progress they may stay until their 20 year retirement.

Contractor employees are usually hired as "employees at will." This legal designation means they do not have a contract and may be removed at will. The cost to the contractor is unemployment insurance payouts, which are allowable costs to the contract. When a mission terminates,

---

154 (Metheny 2009)

a contractor may downsize the workforce quicker and more efficiently than the military.

Our experience with LOGCAP suggests that the government is not achieving this advantage. During the draw down DCAA identified a situation in which KBR was not reducing personnel at the same rate as the military. DCAA recommended that KBR achieve additional savings by reducing staff at an increased rate. The Army placed a personnel limit on KBR which did not result in the increased rate of drawn down.

This advantage is also somewhat mitigated by the employee at will doctrine. Employees may also resign at will. They are not under a contractual obligation to stay. We have seen a turnover of workers in a combat zone when employees realize what they have actually taken on with this job. Soldiers do not have this option.

Use of LOGCAP for support functions allows the military to concentrate on combat training and readiness. This is the "Tooth to tail" issue we examined in chapter 2. Often Congressional limitations or Status of Forces Agreements restrict the number of military personnel who may be deployed in a specific theater. The use of contractors allows the Army to augment the force, without breaching these limitations.

In low intensity situations, such as peacekeeping duties, the use of contractors can allow the military to reduce the apparent military profile. The Army can encourage the contractor to hire local nationals rather than use soldiers for certain duties. Often this will have positive diplomatic mission benefits.

These advantages somewhat offset the risks identified, above. An analysis of the use of contractors for combat services must take these advantages into account. On the whole it would seem that introducing contractors onto the battlefield to provide mission essential support functions introduces significant risk for the commander.

Cost Analysis

Having identified the mission risks, we must now consider the comparative costs of using contractors or soldiers for support services. The analysis must ask the key question regarding the incremental cost of using organic forces instead of LOGCAP to provide the combat support functions identified, above. The CBO compared Task Order 59 on the LOGCAP III contract, which provided support to Joint Task Force Seven (CJTF-7) the initial designation of troop units in Iraq. Task Order 59 accounted for over fifty percent of LOGCAP costs during the two years it was in effect.

The CBO estimated the number of Army units necessary to carry out the full range of tasks which Task Order 59 provided for JTF-7. They determined that "177 units of 38 distinct types, populated by 12,067 soldiers"[155] would be required. They took into account units already in the military force structure, but unavailable because they are assigned to other missions, such as Korea. They assumed a twenty year period with two contingency operations and two periods of peacetime, in which units were trained and reconstituted. They calculated the cost per soldier, with the average length of service and the accumulation of veterans and retirement benefits. Unlike previous studies, the CBO understood the different costs of reserve and regular army units.

The comparison would be with LOGCAP support during operations. During peacetime, LOGCAP would perform some program management and planning functions at a minimal cost of several million dollars per year. LOGCAP costs also do not include any post retirement benefits, as these are included in the cost base for operations, usually contributions to 401K accounts. While LOGCAP supports contractor program offices during peacetime, there is little training cost during these periods.

Based on these calculations the LOGCAP costs are approximately $41.4 billion for twenty years compared to organic support of $78.4 billion for the twenty year period. The costs are portrayed graphically in the following table. [156]

Figure 3-3.

Comparison of Cumulative Incremental Costs for Providing Logistics Support to Deployed Army Forces Using Two Approaches

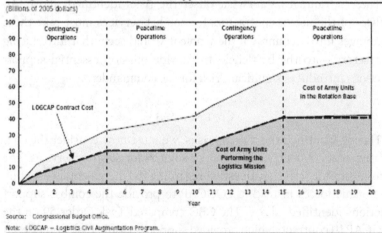

Source: Congressional Budget Office.

Note: LOGCAP = Logistics Civil Augmentation Program.

---

155 (Congressional Budget Office 2005) p.28
156 (Congressional Budget Office 2005) p.37

As can be seen, the military cost curve is steep at the beginning as new units are created. While the contractor cost curve is almost flat during peacetime, the military will continue to incur costs for those units.

The makeup of the costs is contained in the following table, provided by the CBO.[157]

TABLE 3-4. COMPARISON OF INCREMENTAL COSTS FOR TWO APPROACHES TO PROVIDING LOGISTICS SUPPORT TO DEPLOYED ARMY UNITS

(BILLIONS OF 2005 DOLLARS)

	One-time Costs[a]	Periodic Annual Contingency Costs[b]	Contingency Costs[c]	Annual Routine Operating Costs[d]	20 Year Total
Logistics Support Provided By LOGCAP Contractor					
Non-recurring	n.a.	2.7	n.a.	n.a.	5.4
Recurring	n.a.	n.a.	3.6	*	36.0
Total	n.a.	2.7	3.6	*	41.4
Logistics Support Provided By Army Units					
Costs to Perform Mission					
Contingency Operations Costs (Existing units)	n.a.	0.7	1.7	n.a	18.5
Acquisition cost (Additional units)	0.7	n.a.	n.a	n.a	0.7
Routine Operations Costs (Additional units)	n.a.	n.a.	n.a	0.3	5.9
Contingency Operations Costs (Additional units)	n.a.	0.6	1.6	n.a	17.6
Subtotal	0.7	1.3	3.4	0.3	42.7
Costs to Provide Rotation Base					
Acquisition cost (Additional units)	5.0	n.a	n.a	n.a	5.0
Routine Operations Costs (Additional Units)	n.a	n.a	n.a	1.5	30.7
Subtotal	5.0	n.a	n.a	1.5	35.7
TOTAL	5.7	1.3	3.4	1.8	78.4

Source Congressional Budget Office
*Note: LOGCAP = Logistics Augmentation Program; n.a = not applicable; * = less than $50 million per year*

157 (Congressional Budget Office 2005) p. 38

1.   One-time costs include the hiring and training of personnel and the acquisition of equipment for additional Army units. These costs would be incurred only in the first year when the Army decided to provide logistics in house.CBO assumed that existing units would already be fully equipped and there would be no acquisition costs for those units. Equipment replacement is included under annual contingency and routine operating costs.

2.   Periodic contingency costs occur in the first year of each contingency operation and include the costs to procure equipment and procure facilities needed specifically for that operation.

3.   Annual contingency costs occur in each year of a contingency operation or for 10 years during the period of this analysis.

4.   Routine operating costs occur each year or 20 times during the period of this analysis. Routine operating costs for the LOGCAP contract are only a few million dollars each year. Half of the routine operating costs for each additional unit would be incurred during periods of contingency operations. Funding for these routine operating costs could be used to pay for a portion of the costs of contingency operations.

Based upon the CBO calculations, the cost differential over a twenty year period would be $37 billion, in 2005 dollars. Organic support costs approximately 90% more than using contractors.

The CBO study examined a variety of operational scenarios, differing lengths for missions and peacetime, and found that the cost differential was not sensitive to these variations. Of course the study is extremely sensitive to a major assumption of the analysis, the Army's rotation schedule. A major assumption of the CBO study was the Army's unit rotation policy. The Army policy is for a three year rotational schedule. One year is spent performing a mission, followed by a year of reconstitution and a year of training for the next mission. Given this schedule, each unit created to replace the LOGCAP contract must have two other similar units to complete the rotation cycle. If the Army could live with a two year rotational schedule, the cost differential between organic support and LOGCAP would be significantly reduced.

While a three year rotation schedule may be necessary for some units, it is not clearly required for all units. For example, water purification units. These units are a necessity at the beginning of operations, but as major bases were established at existing locations, the possibility of rehabbing the base water system allowed decreased use of purification units. This could result in a different rotation schedule during operations and the CBO twenty year timeframe.

Transportation units may be able to operate on a two year rotation schedule. This puts additional pressure on the soldiers. However, their training requirements may not be as extensive as those of other units. Building up a force of truck drivers can be done rather quickly and does not require as much re-training.

During the years of combat in Iraq and Afghanistan we have seen a number of units rotate quicker than the standard three year schedule. Any new study of the costs and benefits of contractor support instead of organic support should examine this assumption. It should take into account the actual; rotation schedules we have imposed upon troops to maintain these two wars.

ADJUSTMENTS TO THE CBO STUDY

This CBO report is the most complete study of the costs of using LOGCAP prepared. However, there is room for improvement. The CBO study was based upon costs for Task Order 59 as they were understood in 2004. Since that time we have additional experience with the price under Task Order 59 and the follow-on Task Orders for the same services, TOs 89, 139 and 159. This additional experience indicates a somewhat higher cost and some additional expectations for the tasks performed. The chart in figure 3-3, above, indicates an average per year cost of greater than $4 billion for LOGCAP during a contingency operation. Our experience to date would indicate that cost should be approximately $4.5 billion. This would add another $5 billion to the LOGCAP twenty year cost.

Based upon the experience of LOGCAP in Iraq, Afghanistan and Kuwait beyond the 2005 date of the CBO report, there are important costs of using LOGCAP which the CBO did not take into account. It became clear in 2004 that the DoD was not able to manage the LOGCAP contract with the resources they had on hand. Had these resources been available, the cost and quality of LOGCAP performance could expect to be improved. The resources were located in five organizational sectors:

- Army Contracting Command required more contracting positions to manage the LOGCAP contract.
- Army Sustainment Command required more resources to work the LOGCAP Program office, including the reserve component known as the LOGCAP Support Unit.

- Defense Contract Management Agency (DCMA) required more resources to administer the LOGCAP contract on site and at headquarters units.
- Defense Contract Audit Agency (DCAA) required more resources to audit the contractor work under cost type contracts.
- Supported Units required resources to provide Contracting Officer Technical Representatives (COTRs).

If the CBO analysis had the data from increases in military oversight resources, they would have considered these additional costs of a sound LOGCAP program, offset by any cost improvement they would achieve. Army testimony before the House Armed Services committee and the Commission on Wartime Contracting indicates that all of these sectors have seen a buildup of resources since 2004. The cost of establishing a permanent structure for these five organizations which can support use of LOGCAP in contingency operations must be added to the LOGCAP comparison costs. These will be full time positions for both military and civilians and will accrue costs in peacetime and during a contingency. Sectors 1 and 4 will be mainly civilian. Sectors 2 and 3 will be a mix of civilian and military, while sector 5 will be military personnel. Post-retirement benefits for military and benefit costs for civilians must be included.

The Army Contracting Command has increased the number of contracting personnel managing the LOGCAP contract from the two individuals I started with to approximately forty. This includes additional legal and administrative support. The contract with SERCO provides an additional thirty positions to support this program.

Globally, the Army Contracting Command has proposed to add 617 military and 1,635 civilian positions to support the expeditionary Army.[158] This increase is not entirely devoted to supporting the LOGCAP program. Use of contractors for Iraq, Kuwait and Afghanistan is supported by contracting offices in these locations and by newly established Contracting Brigades which deploy with the forces. This does provide an indication of the increases required when programs such as LOGCAP jump from $60 million per year to $5 billion per year.

The LOGCAP Program office, located at Rock Island in the Army Sustainment Command has established deputy program manager offices in Kuwait, Iraq and Afghanistan. In addition the program office at Rock Island has grown. This increase would add another twenty positions to manage the program. While the offices in theater would not be active

---

158   (Parsons 2008)p.7

during peacetime, we know the government does not flex its workforce as well as contractors. These positions would be needed in a new operation and would remain, in some form, during peacetime.

DCMA has significantly increased the administrative personnel devoted to LOGCAP. Even after seven years in Iraq, they still do not have sufficient personnel for adequate contracting oversight. In 2009 Mr. Charlie E. Williams, Director of DCMA, testified before the Commission on wartime Contracting.

> In late 2007 and early 2008, in an effort to support the expanded need for additional contractor oversight to the LOGCAP III contract, as well as other theater-wide contract activities, DCMA deployed an additional 100 personnel into Iraq and Afghanistan. These personnel perform the full range of DCMA core competencies, including administrative contracting, property administration, and quality assurance. We have approximately 275 personnel now in theater overseeing the LOGCAP and other Department of Defense contracts. However, as delegations increase in Afghanistan and transition from LOGCAP III to LOGCAP IV occurs, we will see an increase to our manning requirements.[159]

While, once again, DCMA increases made and planned will support contracting efforts other than LOGCAP, we can make some rough calculations, based upon the relative cost and prevalence of in theater contracts. Task Order 59, the order used by the CBO for comparison purposes, operates all of the major troop bases in Iraq and most of the minor ones maintained by the Multinational Force. A large proportion of DCMA Administrative Contracting Officers, Quality Assurance Specialists and Property Accountability specialists are assigned to these 82 locations.

DCAA has also had a significant increase in workload to support the use of contractors in Iraq, Kuwait and Afghanistan. Mr. William Reed, then the Director of DCAA described this increase before the House Committee on Investigations and Government Reform in 2007:

> Based on the inventory of auditable contracts as of September 30, 2006, DCAA is responsible for auditing contracts at 93 contractors. These contractors hold more than 175 prime contracts with contract ceiling amounts of $51.8 billion, of which $38.5 billion had been funded at the end of fiscal year 2006. DCAA audits of cost reimbursable contracts represent a continuous effort from evaluation of proposed prices to final closeout and payment. Initial audits of contractor business system internal controls and preliminary testing of contract costs are carried out to provide a basis for provisional approval of contractor interim payments

---

159 (Williams 2008) p.

and early detection of deficiencies. Comprehensive contract cost audits are performed annually throughout the life of the contract and are used by the contracting activity to adjust provisionally approved interim payments and ultimately to negotiate final payment to the contractor. To carry out these audit requirements, DCAA did open an Iraq Branch Office in May 2003 and implemented planning and coordination procedures to effectively integrate audit work between that office and more than 50 DCAA CONUS Audit Offices with cognizance of companies performing contracts in Iraq. Through fiscal year 2006, DCAA has issued more than 1,800 reports on Iraq-related contracts. We estimate issuing another 600 reports in fiscal year 2007.[160]

Some of this increased workload was not attributable to LOGCAP. DCAA audited other contracts let in Iraq for reconstruction work and for local purchases. At the end of 2006 LOGCAP appeared to make up about half of this workload. Translating this workload in to equivalent positions is not easy. DCMA has used reassignments from other work while they increased personnel strength.

The GAO has reported that in 2009 DCMA required 1,828 COTRs for Iraq and Afghanistan.[161] Mr. Williams, in the testimony cited above, stated that they still needed 697 more COTRs and 57 additional Subject Matter Experts to be drawn from army units. While these individuals may often perform COTR duties as extra duties, they can and should be full time duties at major installations. Failure to fill these kinds of positions has led to events such as the electrocution of soldiers by faulty contractor installed wiring.

Supported units must recruit, staff, and train soldiers to perform these duties. The numbers required are equivalent to six Combat Heavy Equipment Transport Companies. As with other military calculations, the required support is tripled; therefore 18 equivalent companies are required to provide this COTR support. This number will be mitigated by the part-time nature of the assignment, but full support will require some full-time equivalent positions.

I have done some calculations for the purposes of this analysis. These are meant to indicate the rough order of magnitude of the adjustment needed to account for the increase in contract management and oversight required by the LOGCAP program. It is indicative of the cost analysis which should be preformed to provide a full comparison between LOGCAP and organic support.

---

160   (Reed 2007) p. 2
161   (GAO 2010) p. 8

Additional Resources Needed for full LOGCAP Support					
	DoD Civilians	Active Army	Reserve Army	Total	Twenty Year Cost (millions, 2005 dollars)
Contracting Personnel	70			70	196
LOGCAP Program Personnel	10		10	20	40
DCMA Personnel	350	75	75	500	979
DCAA Personnel	90	10	10	110	273.2
Supported Unit Personnel		500	300	800	820
Total	320	585	395	1,300	2,308

Combining the adjusted cost of support, based upon additional data from follow-on task orders with these costs of management and oversight, we would add $7.3 billion to the cost of LOGCAP support during a twenty year period. These adjusted numbers would reduce the cost differential to $29.7 billion for the twenty year period.

A more difficult cost to quantify is the macro-impact which use of LOGCAP has had in theater. LOGCAP is generally first on the spot and performs a significant amount of subcontracting and hiring. A significant portion of the approximately $5 billion per year LOGCAP costs went to subcontractors. The regional market for non-tactical vehicles, food services, gravel, plywood and other commodities saw a significant increase in demand. Following LOGCAP into theater, the Corps of Engineers, USAID and the State Department commenced contracting for new construction and reconstruction. They bought many of the same services as LOGCAP, but at inflated prices.

Similarly, the cost of labor acquired through labor brokers or on the local economies saw an increase in wages. When the reconstruction contracts were awarded, KBR experienced numerous attempts to hire their general managers and engineers for the new projects. Each attempt resulted in a ratcheting effect on the wages of ex-pats in certain labor categories. Some of these costs were felt by the LOGCAP program while others were transferred to State and AID contracts.

I have not seen any economic analysis of how this may have affected the costs of US contracts in theater. However, it is obvious that organic support would significantly dampen these costs. Centralized acquisition of supplies and services in theater would also have a significant cost control effect.

Again we can make some back of the envelope calculations. With total yearly spending in Iraq on all contracts escalating to significantly, and the assumption of a fairly inelastic supply of people and materials, the additional cost could be in the range of $500 million to $1 billion per year, during operations. Over the CBO twenty year period, the cost would be in the range of $7.5 billion. This would reduce the twenty year cost differential, between LOGCAP and organic support to $22.2 billion.

The GAO did not take into account the cost of money for using LOG-CAP. The Government may be assumed to finance LOGCAP through borrowing. Currently, the Government's cost of money is near zero, at least less than 1%. However, using LOGCAP then entails that the contractor borrow money to finance the gap between incurring a cost under the contract and receiving payment from the Government. At times KBR was floating in excess of $600 million in financing under the contract. This cost impacted the Government in two ways. When it grew so large, it threatened to impact the contractor's ability to perform under the contract. It is also a cost that contractor's took into account in bidding under LOGCAP IV, resulting in the higher fee structure for all LOGCAP IV contractors.

Because of the timing of the GAO analysis, they were also unable to capture the costs of litigation which have resulted from the use of contractors rather than soldiers. Both the Army and the contractor are currently in litigation over many aspects of the LOGCAP program. Former employees of KBR have asserted claims to additional compensation, which may be owed to them. Should they prevail, these costs would be allowable under the contract.

The Army is incurring litigation costs concerning costs claimed by KBR which have been disallowed by the contracting officers and fraud cases involving the LOGCAP contract. Litigation is a costly process which involves the labor of contracting personnel and lawyers, both with the Army and the Department of Justice (DOJ). Contracting personnel must devote time to preparing case files and providing documents and testimony to the lawyers. The DOJ has a fairly large group of attorneys in Rock Island, Illinois who develop and prosecute fraud cases concerning LOGCAP. All of this represents additional costs of using contractors.

We have also seen an impact from LOGCAP on other contracting in the theater of operations. LOGCAP contractors come into theater and hire subcontractors, materials and labor. They also hire experienced U.S.

workers for various jobs. In each case they tend to bid up the price of these materials and services. Other contracts then pay the price. Sometimes the introduction of new contracting initiatives, in turn, drives up LOGCAP prices. When Iraqi reconstruction contracts were let, we saw a bidding war for experienced managers and for supplies in Iraq.

An added problem is the possibility of a general inflation of prices in the affected area. This is often not a desired effect for the national building component of the operation. While an organic force would also purchase labor and materials in theater, they would have a better chance of aligning this activity with other contracting and nation building activities. As with most parts of warfare, this is an old problem. Byzantine operations in the Middle East during the fourth century disrupted prices and the civilian economy around Antioch.[162]

Finally, as noted above, the fee structures under LOGCAP IV are significantly higher than the LOGCAP III contract analyzed by GAO in 2005. Taking these higher fees, which are in the normal range for cost type contracts, the costs for contractor support used by GAO should be increased by another 6%.

Adjusting for cost of money, litigation, area inflation and increased fees under LOGCAP IV reduces the cost differential to approximately $20 billion over 20 years. I use this estimate for ease of calculation. Again, these are back of the envelope calculations which could be improved upon in a more detailed study.

A final thought on cost is that some of the cost advantage comes from the current situation where many of the skilled support personnel sent to theater by contractors are those who have been trained by the Army and other services. As the Army has eliminated these positions, they are no longer training these personnel. At some time this supply of trained personnel may run out, as the contractors have no incentive to train during peace time. Rolf Uesseler, writing about all of the NATO countries as they move to outsourcing stated:

> The first difference in cost structure applies to personnel. What makes a regular soldier in intelligence, logistical, or technical areas so expensive is not his or her salary. It is the cost to the government of finding the correct individual for the job amidst a mass of personnel. State armies recruit hundreds of thousands of soldiers, check their suitability, form them through more or less lengthy training regimens, and test the quality of skills they have acquired in diverse sets of circumstances. All of this is to be paid for. The PMCs have no such costs. They exploit the time and money states

---

162 (Lynn 1993) p. 46

have spent in t4raining specialists, simply luring them away from the national armies with lucrative offers. If the PMCs were required to compensate the state for the training of their employees, they would be no longer able to balance the cost-benefit equation. [163]

COST/BENEFIT ANALYSIS

In testimony before the House on March 11, 2010, Under Secretary of Defense for Acquisition, Technology & Logistics, Dr. Ashton B. Carter stated that, "All studies show that that [organic support] is more expensive than contractors and a distraction from military functions for military people."[164] While this agrees with our analysis, above, it does not address the full criteria for determining whether contractor support is a good buy. We need to ask, "Is $20 billion, over a twenty year period, worth the risk reduction achieved by using organic support rather than relying on LOGCAP?" The answer will depend upon how you evaluate the risks outlined, above.

The Army has a standard procedure for assessing risk.[165] Risks are evaluated in accordance with a matrix which combines the severity of the risk to mission with the probability that that risk would occur. Field Manual 3-100-12, for example contains the following matrix.

SEVERITY	PROBABILITY				
Low	Substantial	Extreme	Occasional	Seldom	Unlikely
Catastrophic	Extremely High Risk	Extremely High Risk	High Risk	High Risk	Moderate Risk
Critical	Extremely High Risk	High Risk	High Risk	Moderate Risk	Low Risk
Marginal	High Risk	Moderate Risk	Moderate Risk	Low Risk	Low Risk
Negligible	Moderate Risk	Low Risk	Low Risk	Low Risk	Low Risk

The next step would be to assign a risk evaluation to each of the areas of risk associated with using LOGCAP for combat service support to

---

163 (Uesseler 2008) p. 48

164 (Carter 2010) I do not quite understand how a soldier assigned to logistics duties is "distracted" from military functions. If we use organic support for logistics, then this is his or her military function. Since this soldier is also available for combat functions, unlike contractors. There is some improvement in the Army's combat capability.

165 The 2005 Rand study by Frank Camm and Victoria Greenfield entitled, *How Should the Army Use Contractors on the Battlefield?*, provides a detailed elaboration of this type of risk analysis.

troops. Mitigation factors would be taken into account in this evaluation process. For example, should all of the contract oversight requirements, identified above be filled, then the risk associated with oversight would take on a lower value.

One way to do this would be to assemble a team of officers with experience during the current operations. Discussions would be held to evaluate the residual risk after mitigation policies are implemented. We might obtain something like the following:

RISK AREA	EVALUATED RISK
Agent Principle	High Risk
Requirements increase	Moderate Risk
Continuity of Support	High Risk
Legal Status	Low Risk
Oversight	Low Risk
Contractor Safety	High Risk
Operational Risk	High Risk
Litigation Risk	High Risk

Continuity of Support is assigned a high risk since we have an actual instance of the Army claiming to react to this possibility by shifting resources away from troops to the contractor. The operational risk is high since there are no mitigations strategies for having unarmed non-combatants who require Army protection and do not contribute any combat power. Oversight is given a low risk rating, based upon the assumption that the resources discussed above, are actually provided to the Army, DCMA and DCAA. Similar considerations would establish the other risk evaluations.

Are these risks acceptable to save $20 billion over twenty years? After looking at the risks of contractor support, I believe $1 billion per year is worth the avoidance of the risks outlined above. I am, however skeptical that we can move forward with a full re-establishment of organic support units.

ARMY OFFICERS EXAMINE THE RISKS OF LOGCAP

In my years of service I worked with many soldiers, mainly field grade officers. I came to the conclusion that, in general, Army officers are better read in their profession than managers in the private sector. They study the literature on the many issues with which they will eventually work. In the middle of their career they attend the Army War College, the Command and General Staff College or the Industrial College of the Armed Forces and study, analyze and write about significant topics in military management. Because of this we already have the work of some of these officers on LOGCAP and the issue of contractors on the battlefield.

Mark Cancian, a retired Colonel, published an article in the U.S. Army War College journal Parameters in 2008, entitled *Contractors: The New Element of the Military Force Structure*. Col (Ret) Cancian is convinced that using contractors for CS/CSS is the correct solution. He bases this analysis on two findings:

1. The use of contractors is less expensive than the use of organic forces. This conclusion is based on the CBO study discussed above.

2. We do not have the ability to replace civilian contractors with military personnel. He writes, "With the Army struggling to meet the more modest target of its current expansion, an increase of 65,000 active-duty soldiers, such a large expansion [the approximately 25,000 the CBO estimated] would appear impossible without reconstituting the draft."[166]

My earlier analysis of the CBO study addresses point 1. As to point 2, I do not believe a draft is necessary to reconstitute the organic capability of the Army to provide CS/CSS. In the past, through the all volunteer army instituted in the 1970s, we have been able to recruit and train a larger Army to support cold war missions in Europe and Korea, along with a large force stationed in the United States. Many new immigrants to the United States would readily join the Armed Forces if this was a faster track to full citizenship. With unemployment at a very high rate, approaching 10 % as I write, military service could have a strong attraction.

To accomplish this change we need to end the two wars in Iraq and Afghanistan, with their endless assignments abroad. A military that was on a peace-time footing and ready to respond to real national emergencies would be a much more attractive career. Once the support forces are reconstituted, they would be easier to maintain. In 1985 we were able to support an Army with 18 active duty divisions and 16 reserve and National Guard divisions. Each of these divisions was composed of 3–5 combat brigades (around 111 combat brigades in 1989) with the associated organic support.[167] Now we have 33 Combat Brigades with little organic support. With the population increase in the last 26 years, it is hard to believe we could not recruit and train these organic support troops.

COL (Ret) Cancian doesn't seem to place much importance on the fact that the military made a conscious decision to outsource these activities, not based upon the lack of recruits but on a wish to show a de-

---

166 (Cancian 2008) p. 73
167 (Kaufmann 1984) p. 26

cline in the visible Army without reducing combat effectiveness. There was an attempt to solve a really non-existent "tooth to tail" problem, as I discussed in Chapter 2. Some thought that this approach would save money in the long run. There is not an inability of the United States to recruit, train and maintain an effective Army.

A different approach is taken by Major Christopher Croft in a monograph written for the Army Command and General Staff College entitled, *Contractors on the Battlefield: Has the Military Accepted too much Risk?* Writing in Early 2001, Major Croft asked whether the Army was accepting too much risk by contracting out core logistical capabilities. Noting many of the risks I discussed above, Major Croft also recognized the trend to using more contractors on the battlefield. He concludes, "The presence of contractors is a foregone conclusion. The real question is how the military decides to embrace the increased mission reliance on contractors and create the future."[168] He believes the military can mitigate the above mentioned risks through planning, training and doctrine.

Having watched the military grapple with the lack of training and planning which included the extensive use of contractors in Afghanistan and Iraq, I am somewhat skeptical. Use of contractors was an afterthought, until they appeared in great numbers on the battlefield. Commanders were unable to keep tight control of requirements in the first two years of combat operations. Doctrine was still being revised during the course of the war. The legal status of contractor personnel is still not completely resolved.

In the short term, the Army could consider immediately instituting the second course of action, reducing the amount of LOGCAP support. By looking at LOGCAP support functions which (when reviewed individually) could have catastrophic consequences or have the highest risk of contractor safety, we may determine a better mix of LOGCAP and organic support is advisable. The Army might analyze the following scenario:

- Provide transportation services by organic units. Transportation of supplies is a mission critical service which also has the highest safety risk of all services under LOGCAP. Movement of ammunition, fuel, water and food has to happen on a regular basis. Having armed soldiers as drivers would provide better defensive capability to convoys. This service can be located in Reserve units, and training and doctrine are readily available.

---

168 (Croft 2001) p. 50

- Provide potable water to bases with organic units. The failure of KBR to get their Reverse Osmosis Water Purification Units (ROWPU) up and running caused significant problems for the troops. I do not believe we yet understand the number of troops who were incapacitated due to illness caused by bad water. Since ROWPU operations are performed "outside the wire" at most camps, there is also a contractor safety issue which can be resolved. To avoid responsibility conflicts, the Army should perform the full range of potable water services at the bases.

- Provide airfield operations by organic units. This function appears to be a stretch for the LOGCAP mission. One of the major concerns is that contractor personnel would become involved in inherently governmental and military decisions. With contractors providing information and analysis on weather conditions, incoming and outgoing schedules and operating control towers; it would be a small step to deciding whether missions take place or not. The military should have total ownership of this process.

LOGCAP should be a last resort for any tactical equipment maintenance. The CLS contractors along with the Army's GMASS contract provide sufficient contractor maintenance capabilities. Prior to using LOGCAP, the Army's Pre-positioned Stock storage and maintenance contracts should be considered. The DoD IG report on Tactical equipment Maintenance at Balad indicates that this use of LOGCAP is also open to incredible waste.[169]

Analysis of contracted-out services, provided by Paul Verkuil, suggests that the major base camp support functions performed by LOGCAP are those with the least risk of involving the contractor in inherently governmental functions and are now, due to force structure decisions, essential to military operations.[170] The second COA would leave these missions with LOGCAP, unless additional analysis of the total cost of the LOGCAP program suggested full organic support was the most efficient course of action.

If the Army removed these missions from the LOGCAP contract and established organic units to perform them, then we could achieve a considerable risk reduction at a comparatively small cost. A joint analysis by

---

169 (DoD Inspector General 2010) p. 4
170 (Verkuil 2007)p.129

the CBO and the Army Audit Agency, with support from experienced soldiers could decide whether this is a wise course.

Such action may be necessary to bring the LOGCAP program into compliance with Congressional direction. The FY2009 National Defense Authorization Act (P.L. 110-417) Section 832 offers a "Sense of Congress" provision that operations in "uncontrolled or unpredictable high-threat environments" should be performed by the military forces; that private security contractors should not perform inherently governmental functions in the area of combat operations, but that it should be in the "sole discretion of the commander of the relevant combatant command" to determine whether such activities should be delegated to individuals not in the chain of command. It is not clear that this section applies beyond private security contracts, however performance in a high threat environment and the use of individuals not in the chain of command are aspects of current LOGCAP performance. Following this reasoning, there should be a preference for organic support.

The Commission on Wartime Contracting, in their second interim report came to the same general conclusion. Their first recommendation was to "grow agencies' organic capacity."[171] They also advocate a risk-based assessment to determine the organic resources which are required to preserve core capacity and generate the right mix of contractors and soldiers.

CONCLUSION

The additional risks which we have incurred from the use of contractors for LOGCAP support appear to greatly outweigh the relatively small cost savings from the use of organic support. As a country of 300 million citizens, we do have the capability of fielding a military, sized for our current threats, which can provide for itself during combat operations. The move to privatize this support was initiated in secret, based upon minimal cost benefit analysis, sold with a slogan of reducing the rather unimportant "tooth to tail" ratio, and of benefit to substantial private interests.

Reversing this situation will take time and careful planning. As new units are established, money will be shifted from contractor support to these units. At times this will show as an increased military cost and be attacked in the name of budget cutting. Over the long run, however there will be a cost savings which must be explained. The risks, identi-

---

171   (Commission on Wartime Contracting 2011) p. 15

fied above, equate to additional costs, as any insurance actuary will demonstrate. Perseverance will be necessary to restore a complete organic military support structure.

Those of us who see the increased influence of private interests on the military, and such important decisions as going to war, see this as an important step in reclaiming such decisions from these private interests. When, as Janine R. Wedel points out, a private contractor wrote the Army field Manual, "Contractors on the Battlefield,"[172] privatization has gone way too far. The United States will be better off through this change.

---

172   (Wedel 2008) p. 117

Chapter 12. Use of Contractors to Oversee Other Contractors

The Problem of Contracting Out Oversight of Contractors

As I discussed above, one of the principle problems with management of the LOGCAP contract was the initial lack of resources in my organization, DCMA and DCAA. Because of the immediate growth of the contract we were not able to provide the contract oversight necessary for fully successful outcomes. In a time when outsourcing government work was in vogue, finding contractors to do some of this work was considered a possible solution. In my opinion this was a great mistake.

This problem was not restricted to LOGCAP and continues today. A recent GAO report cites an Army study which found that 2,357 contractor employees were performing jobs which are inherently governmental. Another 1,877 contractor employees were providing unauthorized personal services that federal employees should have been performing. Finally, 45,934 contractor employees were working in areas, including contract management, which may be inherently governmental areas.[173]

A quick check of my friends in government contracting indicates that the use of contractors to provide oversight of other contractors has been on the increase. Logically, this appears a bit odd. If I hire contractor B to provide oversight of contractor A, then I would need contractor C to provide oversight of contractor B and so on. At some point I need

---

173 (Brodsky 2011) p. 1

to step up and obtain government oversight of some contractor, so why not start with contractor A.

Unfortunately there are some peculiar governmental aspects which cause contracting personnel to look for contractor solutions to oversight. The current political situation, calling for the general reduction in government, may lead agencies to reduce full time employees and to rely on more contracting out of oversight. During a build-up in work, it is difficult to increase full time employees in an agency and contracts provide an immediate solution to the need for more oversight. Additionally, the different types of government funds often make funds available for contracts, where no funds are available to hire employees. Contracts may also provide skill sets which are not available in government agencies.

The use of contractors to provide oversight of other contractors, however, creates a number of problems for the government. The chain of problems begins with the outsourcing of inherently governmental functions.

What Are Inherently Governmental Functions?

The concept of an inherently governmental function stems directly from the Constitution. Article II, Section 3 states that the President, "shall Commission all the Officers of the United States." By officers the document refers to government officials, not just military officers. This is made clear in Section 4 which states, "The President, Vice President and all civil Officers of the United States, shall be removed from Office on Impeachment for, and Conviction of, Treason, Bribery, or other high Crimes and Misdemeanors."

Immediately, two distinctions are made between government officials and employees of contractors. Government officials derive their authority from a Presidential commission; often delegated in the case of civil servants. When I began my government employment I swore an oath of office, accepting that commission. Contractor employees do not do so. Civil officers of the United States are also subject to removal for various reasons stemming from the Constitution and implementing legislation. Contractor employees are not necessarily under this constraint.

Civil officers of the government are required, by the Constitution, to provide the President with "the Opinion, in writing of the Principle Officer in each of the Executive Departments." Should critical functions of the department be in the hands of private contractors, it may be hard for even the Secretary to provide an informed opinion. We should also note that the Freedom of Information Act does not apply to private contractors, reducing transparency if they are providing critical services.

There is an interesting tradition of legal decisions which attempt to come to terms with the scope of "officer", as opposed to an employee. In *Buckley v. Valeo* the Supreme Court dueled that the authority of "officers" could not be delegated outside the government. Officers had significant authority, tenure in office and permanent responsibilities; as opposed to employees with insignificant authority. Clearly every officer of a company or the government is an employee, but not every employee is an officer (following Chief Justice Marshall). Among my titles when I worked for the Army was "Contracting Officer." I had a signed warrant which gave me authority to execute and approve contracts on behalf of the United States. No contractor should have that or similar authority.

Acting as a contracting officer along with certain other government functions are reserved for government officials. These are the inherently governmental functions that are intimately related to the public interest. Inherently governmental functions include activities that require the exercise of discretion in applying government authority, exercising decision making authority on behalf of the government, or the making of value judgments on behalf of the government.

According to the Federal Acquisition Regulation (FAR) Subpart 7.503, examples of inherently governmental functions include:

- Awarding contracts and approving contractual documents;
- administering contracts;
- determining whether contract costs are allowable, allocable, and reasonable;
- determining what supplies or services are to be acquired by the Government; and
- determining the disposal of Government property.[174]

How do we tell if a function is inherently governmental?

The FAR Subpart 2.101 provides a definition of inherently governmental as it relates to government contracting, our concern here. "Definitions," defines an inherently governmental function as a function that is so intimately related to the public interest as to mandate performance by Government employees. These functions include activities that require either discretion in applying Government authority or judgment in making decisions for the Government.

---

174   (US Government 2011) p.374

What is the possible harm of contractors performing inherently gov-ernmental functions?

1. The situation is illegal. As noted above certain government actions are reserved for government officials by law, regulation and judicial decisions. Violations of these laws and regulations diminish the integrity of the procurement system.

2. Contractors performing inherently governmental functions can increase the government's exposure to fraud and other malfeasance. Some possibilities are:

3. Contractors accepting poor work, providing high performance evaluations and accepting improper costs in order to keep a good working relationship with another contractor,

4. Contractors obtaining proprietary information about possible competitors,

5. Contractors producing results desired by the contracting office (known as the customer) which are not warranted by the facts.

6. The Government loses the advantages of utilizing government employees. As Paul Verkuil notes, "A government appointment creates a public servant who, whether through the oath, the security clearance, the desire to achieve public goals, or the physic income of public service, is different from those in the private sector."[175]

A CASE STUDY — REVIEWING THE LOGCAP SUPPORT CONTRACT

In 2004, the Army Sustainment Command (ASC) issued a non-com-petitive delivery order to Resource Consultants, Inc. (RCI) for work on the LOGCAP program. At first they were only tasked with performing administrative actions which eased the burden on a strained contracting office. The RCI employees collated documents, created a filing system, created an electronic document repository and prepared binders on spe-cific topics. They did not exercise any discretion, provide any recommen-dations or prepare any decision documents. Later, however, their role significantly increased, to include oversight actions, including financial oversight.

In August of 2004, the ASC received new leadership, and so did my group: my top staff and I were replaced. The new leadership team imme-diately took actions to negotiate currently undefinitized costs on LOG-CAP Task Orders.

---

175 (Verkuil 2007) p.1

My contracting team had not negotiated these costs because numerous DCAA audits found that KBR business systems (such as cost estimating, procurement and cost accounting) were inadequate. DCAA, in their audits of individual KBR proposals to definitize task orders, had taken over $1 billion in exceptions.

After KBR had failed to provide sound proposals in accordance with a definitization plan instituted in February 2004, I advised KBR that my contracting officers would unilaterally definitize the cost bases for these task orders, at the DCAA recommendations. KBR could either provide us with the data to modify these settlements or provide that data in court.

Under new leadership, this move to unilaterally definitize task orders was stopped. Instead, a new plan to negotiate was devised. Appropriately, though somewhat late in the game, significant additional resources were provided to LOGCAP contracting for these negotiations. Special Cost Analysis Teams (SCATs) were set up to negotiate the two largest task orders (59 and 43). The major issue on both task orders was questioned DFAC costs, though there were other questioned costs.

RCI (now SERCO) was issued a sole source contract (at the direction of MG Johnson) to, in effect, duplicate the DCAA audits, but with a different outcome. RCI appears to have taken suspect KBR financial data, performed simple linear regression analysis and projected estimates to complete work. They found that most of the KBR costs were justified! The ASC leaders then directed the negotiations which, if I am interpreting briefing charts correctly, allowed most of the questioned costs.

A briefing provided to the Deputy for Procurement to the Assistant Secretary of the Army for Acquisition, Logistics & Technology (DASA (P)) on 25 March 2005 notes on page 10 that the Government position is only a decrement of $25 million out of $6 billion in proposed costs. Page 12 notes that cost positions on the DFAC issue are based upon regression analysis, estimates at completion and KBR proposals, not the DCAA audit position. Chart 13 notes the pursuit of a fixed price settlement. The DASA (P) was continually briefed on the progress of these actions, approved decisions and provided some guidance. It was clear at this point that the LOGCAP program was overseen and managed by high level Army leadership.

Another briefing to DASA (P), on 30 March 2005 provides a summary of DCAA questioned costs on chart 11. DCAA found $264 million in questioned costs for DFACs and an additional $189 million in questioned costs on Task Order 59, alone. Task Order 59 was the major Base Camp in Iraq Task Order. Chart 12 shows that of the $264 million in

DCAA questioned DFAC costs on Task Order 59, the government position based upon the RCI analysis was to question only $57 million. The Post-Negotiation Memorandum for Task Order 59 makes it clear that reliance was placed upon the RCI analysis and the DCAA audit exceptions were ignored.

In response to a Senate resolution, the DoD IG conducted an investigation into several issues involving the Army's management of LOGCAP. I was interviewed by the DoD IG for this report. Although their results were fairly standard IG results, some wrong things happened, nobody was responsible and some additional training should take care of the problem, there was one rather interesting part of the report.

The DoD IG report (Report on Review of Army Decision Not to Withhold Funds on the Logistics Civil Augmentation Program III Contract; Report No. D-2010-6-001) was issued in February 2010. The report included a review of the Army's use RCI on the LOGCAP program. The IG found that:

As of September 2004, the Army Sustainment Command had awarded two contracts worth $6 million to Resource Consultants, Inc. (RCI), to perform cost analysis services. They stated that "Our preliminary review of the Army's use of RCI disclosed concerns that we will address in our ongoing review of contracting officer actions on incurred cost audit reports involving Iraq reconstruction activities."[176]

Later the IG states:

Based on our preliminary review, we identified the following concerns:

- The type of services provided by RCI may qualify as accounting and auditing services covered under DoD Directive 7600.2, *Audit Policies* (Version dated March 20, 2004), which requires prior approval by the DoD Assistant Inspector General for Audit Policy and Oversight. The Army Sustainment Command did not obtain approval in accordance with DoD Directive 7600.2 before utilizing the services.

- The negotiation memorandum for the dining facilities cost, which comprised a large portion of total costs, indicates that the Army solely used estimates prepared by RCI as a baseline to settle the cost. The negotiation memorandum does not address the DCAA questioned costs or explain the fundamental differences between the DCAA and RCI positions. DoD Instruction 7640.02, Enclosure 3, paragraph 3.b., requires that

---

176 (DoD Inspector General 2010) p.1

the contracting officer document his or her rationale for any disagreement with the auditor. While DCAA had questioned $360 million in dining facility costs, ASC had only negotiated a downward adjustment of $55 million.

- The type of services provided by RCI may be inherently governmental and potentially violate DFARS 237.102 and DoD Directive 4205.2 (enclosure 2.1.9). Use of a contractor to perform cost analysis services deviates from the norm. In most cases, a Government price analyst performs these services.

- The LOGCAP III contract file did not contain any final report issued by RCI as the contract terms required. Without a final report, the Army has no detailed written record of the services provided.[177]

These are serious concerns regarding the use of RCI by the Army to provide financial analysis of another contractor. My observation of the RCI work was that they provided the customer with exactly the results they wanted. DCAA, on the other hand had taken significant exceptions to KBR proposed and accrued costs. DCAA found the KBR business systems unreliable and the proposal data not adequate for an audit. As noted above, I ignored these problems and basically took KBR data and calculated an estimate at completion. Of course the old maxim, "Garbage In/ Garbage Out" applies in this case.

This experience with RCI illustrates one of the major problems with utilizing contractor oversight of other contractors. If the customer wants a good report, they will generally get one whether it is justified or not. During Mr. Smith's 31 years of experience in defense contracting he found that the independent reviews by DCAA and DCMA would provide unbiased, accurate and thorough analysis. He often received reports he was not hoping for and had to deal with it.

Finally, the IG promised an additional report on these issues. So far, this additional report has not been issued.

SOME ADDITIONAL BACKGROUND INFORMATION

The last action I took on the LOGCAP program for the Army was to create the strategy for LOGCAP IV. The LOGCAP IV team explored a number of possibilities, including regional contracts, which was the preferred position of the Army G4. However, this strategy would have resulted in a single contractor responsible for Southwest Asia, which is

---

177 (DoD Inspector General 2010) p.2

that we had under LOGCAP III. The team rejected this strategy in favor of three contractors, each with global responsibility, who would compete for work when feasible.

This strategy created a problem for the planning function of LOGCAP. The LOGCAP program embeds logistics planners with the regional commands to develop regional and operational plans, along with a worldwide plan for utilizing the LOGCAP contract. Should these planners have been from one of the three contractors, the plans would have probably favored that contractor's approach and inhibited competition. For this reason the team proposed a fourth contract to perform the planning function alone. They would work with the operating contractors to understand their general mode of performance and capabilities. The planning contractor would develop generic performance plans which could be performed by any of the three operations contractors. They would not have access to operations contractor financial data. The planning contractor could not be an operations contractor nor could they partner with one of the operations contractors.

So far so good!

Unfortunately the Army changed the scope of work for the LOGCAP Planning Contract into the LOGCAP Support Contract. They added additional duties, including some that have placed this contractor in a position of providing oversight on the operational contractors. This oversight includes financial analysis of contractor proposals and business systems. It also appears to include evaluation of contractor performance. These are functions which are performed by the Defense Contract Audit Agency (DCAA) and the Defense Contract Management Agency (DCMA). These two agencies were established, by law, specifically to perform these oversight functions.

The LOGCAP IV Support Contract, Contract Line Item (CLIN) 004, Program Support Subpart 2.3.1 — Proposal Evaluation, Negotiation and Closeout, has the following requirements:

***

Support LOGCAP Director with proposal evaluation, negotiation, and closeout functions for twenty-five operational LOGCAP contingency task orders annually to include qualifying cost proposal, basis of estimate (BOE), rough order of magnitude (ROM) cost estimate, technical analysis, labor mix proposal, contractor assumptions, and PWS.

Subpart 2.3.2 – Technical and Financial Services Support has the following requirements:

Support LOGCAP Director with technical and financial services to include:
Cost Monitoring
Financial & Technical Analysis of Cost and Performance
Incredibly, Subpart 2.3.4 – Federal Fiscal Law Support has the following requirement:

Alert LOGCAP Program Director and PCO of federal fiscal law concerns that arise during program planning, estimating, execution. Recommend corrective actions.

SERCO fulfills these requirements by providing:

For Subpart 2.3.1 – Proposal Evaluation, Negotiation and Closeout:

Embed technical/financial support personnel with Government teams to provide life cycle support for contract actions
Assist Government team to evaluate Performance Contractor proposals, analyze BOE/ROMS
Assist with PWS requirements definition
Coordination with event support and liaison officers embedded with COCOM and ASCC commands
Provide continuous logistics intelligence analysis and feedback to LOGCAP PM to ensure timely operational decisions

For Subpart 2.3.2 – Technical and Financial Services Support:

Embed technical/financial support personnel with Government teams to provide technical and financial services support
Provide cost report monitoring and analysis using the Funding and Expenditure Tracking System (FETS) Model
Monitor Performance Contractor cost and performance metrics
For Subpart 2.3.4 – Federal Fiscal Law Support:
Assist ASC General Counsel (GC) with legal reviews
Augment ASC GC staff to conduct legal research
Serco will provide support from our General Counsel's office.

***

SERCO is not only the Army's technical and financial analysis organization for LOGCAP, rather than DCMA and DCAA; they are also the Army's legal office! It is hard to contemplate the assignment of more inherently governmental functions to a contractor.

After the issues of 2004–2005 RCI, was acquired by SERCO, a British company. They were one of two bidders on the LOGCAP Support contract, and the only one with a significant chance of winning. Other potential bidders, SAIC for example, either did not participate or partnered with SERCO. The word appeared to be out that SERCO would win. They had good reason for this belief, as RCI/SERCO had hired a number of influential retired employees of the Army sustainment Command. They hired a retired Colonel who had been the head of LOGCAP operations until his retirement. He became the assistant program manager stationed at Rock Island. They also hired a former Deputy Director of Contracting with strong connections to the ASC contracting leadership. Finally, they hired a number of retired logistics managers from ASC.

Contractors deciding not to compete with SERCO for this lucrative business included:

- SAIC, who performed planning for DynCorp on LOGCAP III
- Booz, Allen, Hamilton
- MPRI
- LSI

During market research the Army had identified these contractors as likely possible competitors. However, they all chose to join the SERCO team, rather than compete.

WHAT WENT WRONG THIS TIME?

The Army's use of SERCO rather than DCAA has resulted in problems for the Army. When the Army competed the first operational task order on LOGCAP IV, for the support work in Kuwait, SERCO, rather than DCAA, performed a financial analysis of the proposals. These awards are competitive, but include an evaluation of the technical proposal, the contractor's past performance and a cost reasonableness analysis. This type of award requires both a technical evaluation, and a financial analysis of the proposed costs to determine if the reasonably accord with the scope of work and the contractor's technical plan. DCAA has the authority to review contractor financial data and the skill set to determine of proposed costs are reasonable.

Award was made to DynCorp on this basis. DynCorp has since submitted a Request for Equitable Adjustment, seeking to increase the price of the contract by approximately 90%. Their basis is that they significantly underestimated the labor costs, and cannot perform at the award price. The DynCorp proposed cost was certainly not reasonable. Unfortunately, SERCO did not catch any problem with the proposal. This appears to be another case of the contractor providing results they thought the Army wanted.

SERCO also appears to be intimately involved in the financial management of task orders after they are awarded. Operating contractors are now providing their cost reports to SERCO. Cost management evaluations for award fee must now be provided by SERCO as they are the only entity with the immediate access to the data.

In January 2011, the DoD IG released a report of their examination of the issues with the Army's use of SERCO (Logistics Civil Augmentation Program Support Contract Needs to Comply With Acquisition Rules; Report No. D-2011-032, January 7, 2011). This report identifies a number of significant issues with the Army Contracting Command management of the SERCO contract.

> The IG finds that the SERCO contract created a situation of:
>
> Potential organizational conflicts of interest
>
> The LOGCAP support contractor's inappropriate access to other contractors' proprietary information while supporting the non-LOGCAP contracts.[178]

It is surprising that this report ignores the major issued raised in the earlier IG report. All of the issues regarding the performance of inherently governmental functions, poor support to negotiations, lack of justification of negotiated costs and violations of regulations disappeared. These were the most significant issues with the Army's use of SERCO for financial analysis and oversight of KBR, and we are unlikely ever to see a full investigation of those problems.

It is clear that using the LOGCAP support contract for financial and performance oversight of the LOGCAP operational contracts has failed the Army and cost the taxpayer money. It is also clear from the DoD IG report that the Army has had difficulty with oversight of the SERCO contract, which may be, in turn, providing faulty oversight of the LOGCAP operations contractors.

THIS PROBLEM IS NOT RESTRICTED TO DoD CONTRACTING

According to the Project on Government Oversight the General Services Administration (GSA) hired CACI, Inc to Process Suspension and Debarment Cases. Scott Amey at the Project on Government Oversight (POGO) reports that:

> Senior government employees with knowledge of CACI's work told POGO that the outsourcing of these functions caused them concern. Turning this work over to CACI has potentially placed it in the extraordinary position of having unfair access to Sensitive data from its competi-

---

178   (DoD Inspector General 2011) p.4

tors as well as providing the company the opportunity to undermine the standing of future competitors for government contracts.[179]

Apparently, the GSA had outsourced suspension and debarment work to CACI because there was a shortage of qualified employees within the agency. I noted above that this is one of the classic reasons for outsourcing this type of work.

Suspension and debarment is serious government decision. It certainly meets the criteria for an inherently governmental function of the FAR and acknowledged by GAS. However, a GSA e-mail, which the POGO article quotes, indicates that CACI was tasked with reviewing files and drafting proposed decisions for signature. GAS appears to have knowingly assigned inherently governmental functions to CACI. As is usually the case, a GSA IG report decided the actions of CACI were not inherently governmental, exonerating the agency. They reached this conclusion because a government official signed the decision letter. Note the fine line between analyzing and preparing the decision, which will have great influence on the signature authority and actually signing the decision.

The GSA IG apparently was aware of this problem. In the report the IG did state, "In addition, while we concluded that CACI did not perform inherently governmental work, due to the serious nature of suspension and debarment sanctions, it may not be prudent for GSA to utilize contractors in support of this function."[180]

Aside from the inherently governmental issue, the situation creates opportunities for fraud and other malfeasance. In performing their work CACI obtained information about problems with the actions of other contractors, serious enough to warrant potential suspension or debarment. While there is no indication that CACI improperly used this information, this is information which should be protected and limited to government officers.

A final problem here is that the contract was awarded without competition to CACI, which had no particular expertise in this area. According to POGO, CACI was solicited for the work via an email Sent from GSA on June 12, 2006, and was subsequently awarded the contract on a GSA consulting services schedule. This kind of favored relationship between the customer and the contractor, similar to the relationship between RCI/SERCO and the Army, may, as noted above, lead to results which please the customer, but are not warranted by the facts.

---

179   (Amey 2007) p.1
180   (Amey 2007) p.1

In 2007 the Department of Homeland Security (DHS) hired contractor Booz, Allen to help oversee the Homeland Security Department's $8 billion Secure Border Initiative Network surveillance system. Boeing Co. was awarded a contract for the initial segment in Arizona in September 2006. At the time Booz Allen had significant subcontracts with Boeing.

In a letter to Henry Waxman, DHS provided a list of 50 contractor personnel involved in contract oversight and management, including employees of Booz Allen, Acquisition Solutions Inc., Oakton, Va.; Mitre Corp., McLean, Va.; Organizational Strategies Inc., Arlington, Va.; Performance Management Consulting Inc., Alexandria, Va.; Robbins-Gioia LLC of Alexandria, Va.; and Contracting Strategies Inc., Washington.[181]

Even if one were to conclude these functions are not inherently governmental, they create opportunities of fraud and other types of contract malfeasance. In the words of the GSA IG, "...it may not be prudent for GSA (the Government) to utilize contractors in support of this function." Fortunately the fix for this situation is not difficult. I will discuss this in my recommendations.

In September of 2006 U.S. Senators Byron Dorgan (D-N.D.) and Ron Wyden (D-Ore.) and U.S. Representatives Henry A. Waxman (D-Calif.) and John Dingell (D-Mich.) Sent a letter to the Secretary of Defense calling on DoD to stop outsourcing the oversight of large Iraq reconstruction contracts to private companies. The letter cited potential conflicts of interest and opportunities for significant additional waste and fraud in the use of taxpayer dollars. They identified over $100 million in spending on reconstruction oversight contracts for seven private contractors. Scopes of work for the contracts included "being asked to carry out essential government oversight functions, including defining and prioritizing project requirements and actually overseeing the work of construction contractors."[182]

For a time it appeared that the trend would shift to ins-source these functions. The GAO, in a report released in January, 2011, describes the impact of new guidance:

> In 2008, Congress amended this provision in section 807 of the National Defense Authorization Act for Fiscal Year 2008 to add a requirement for the Secretary of Defense to submit an annual inventory of the activities performed pursuant to contracts for services for or on behalf of DOD during the preceding fiscal year.12 The inventory is to include a number of specific data elements for each identified activity, including:

---

181 (Lipowicz 2008) p.1
182 (Office of Senator Ron Wyden 2006) p.1

- the function and missions performed by the contractor;
- the contracting organization, the component of DOD administering the contract, and the organization whose requirements are being met through contractor performance of the function;
- the funding source for the contract by appropriation and operating agency;
- the fiscal year the activity first appeared on an inventory; the number of full-time contractor employees (or its equivalent) paid for performance of the activity;
- a determination of whether the contract pursuant to which the activity is performed is a personal services contract;
- and a summary of the information required to be collected for the activity under 10 U.S.C. § 2330a (a).

Once compiled, the inventory is to be made public and, within 90 days of the date on which the inventory is submitted to Congress, the Secretary of the military department or head of the defense agency responsible for activities in the inventory is to review the contracts and activities for which they are responsible and ensure that any personal services contract included in the inventory was properly entered into and is being performed appropriately; that the activities in the inventory do not include inherently governmental functions; and to the maximum extent practicable, activities on the list do not include any functions closely associated with inherently governmental functions.

In April 2009, the Secretary of Defense announced his intent to reduce the department's reliance on contractors and increase funding for new civilian authorizations. More recently, in August 2010, the Secretary of Defense announced plans to reduce funding for service support contractors by 10 percent per year from fiscal years 2011 to 2013.[183]

By complying with the statutory requirements, and looking at lessons learned from use of contractors for oversight, the DoD is in a position to in-source activities such as contractor oversight which are now performed by contractors.

Unfortunately, Marjorie Censer reports in the February 7, 2011, edition of Capital Business that the Army is putting in-sourcing decisions on hold. Ms. Censer reports that, "In a Feb. 1 memo, Army Secretary John M. McHugh suspended any already approved insourcing actions and said he will personally authorize any new proposals."[184] While the stated reason is that earlier efforts did not save much money, there has obvi-

---

183 (GAO 2011) p. 5-8
184 (Censer 2011) p. 1

ously been significant contractor pressure to keep these lucrative efforts outsourced to business.

Further, Secretary McHugh's action does not deal with the issues identified by the GAO regarding the use of contractors to perform inherently governmental functions, personal services and functions which may be inherently governmental. The Army's inventory of service contracts identified over 50,000 contractor employees who fall into these categories. Saving money should not be a requirement for insourcing inherently governmental functions.

Another step in changing this situation would be to implement a training program to supplement the guidance. For example organizations would receive training on how to fill the government positions. Given the current economy it should not be hard to find qualified candidates for contracting related positions. My old former command was able to staff a rapid buildup of the contracting organization by hiring candidates with business degrees with a minimum 3.5 GPA. Often the applicants already had achieved an MBA.

The final step would be to conduct internal compliance audits to ensure that the policy is being followed. Organizational leaders must have compliance as part of their scorecard. Such audits are already a standard part of government work; this would just add a new category for review.

Conclusion

This problem of contracting out contracting functions is especially serious in a contingency environment. The incentives for contractors to please the customer rather than provide objective assessments along with the possibility of conflicts of interest can have magnified consequences in a conflict environment. This is why the Commission on Wartime Contracting found that:

> Contracting out acquisition and security functions introduces especially high risk to a contingency mission. Contractors performing acquisition management functions may commit the government to a certain course of action and usurp the government's discretion. . .

Even when the risk of turning too much control for acquisition decisions over to contractors is recognized, safeguards have been ineffective e or non-existent. On one of the largest contingency support contracts, LOGCAP IV, the DoD Inspector General found the contracting officer failed to establish appropriate firewalls for a support contractor who was assigned responsibility for developing contract requirements valued at approximately $1 billion.[185]

185   (Commission on Wartime Contracting 2011) p. 16

Chapter 13. Lessons Learned

The Army has not performed any serious review of the management of LOGCAP III, especially a critical evaluation of what went wrong. As we saw in the chapter 10, Army leadership denied that any problems occurred or blamed poor outcomes on soldiers or Government employees. If you do not recognize a problem, then you are quite likely to repeat that problem in the future.

Has the Army learned anything from the experiences of LOGCAP III? The answer is yes, but not enough.

LOGCAP IV

DOD Instruction 3020.37 *Essential Services Planning Procedures* requires an annual evaluation of the performance risk inherent in contracts providing essential services. In 2005 we analyzed the risks associated with one LOGCAP contractor providing almost all Combat Support/ Combat Service Support for troops engaged in Operation Enduring Freedom (OEF) and Operation Iraqi Freedom (OIF). Our analysis has determined that the risk of having one contractor perform the essential LOGCAP functions is unacceptable.

We identified risks such as:

- The failure of the contractor to effectively perform some tasks in a timely manner. Such failures generally require a decision by the Procuring contracting Officer whether to terminate the contract and re-solicit the requirement. Given the nature of the requirement and the time to re-solicit LOGCAP, this is almost a completely impractical course of action.

- The abandonment of the contract by the contractor due to conditions of performance. In Iraq our LOGCAP contractor incurred significant loss of life by employees engaged in performance. The contractor also had some strong disagreements with Government management of the contract. On several occasions the operating contractor indicated that abandonment of the contract was considered

- The abandonment of the contract due to financial problems. When the LOGCAP contract grew to approximately $7 billion dollars per year, the contractor experienced significant cash flow and cash management problems. The contractor had to finance approximately $800 million of costs incurred which were awaiting Government reimbursement on a continual basis. This financial burden was seen as endangering the ability of the contractor to continue.

- The abandonment of the contract due to corporate considerations. The LOGCAP operating contractor's performance was endangered by corporate issues involving settlement of outstanding lawsuits. Any contractor may have problems with corporate re-structuring, sale of business units or re-orientation of business strategy. Any of these could endanger performance.

- Inability of the contractor to take on new missions. The single LOGCAP contractor has utilized their available leadership and technical assets, along with financing and support operations to handle OEF/OIF. An extensive new mission, in PACOM for example, could present problems in performance.

From August 2004 through August 2005 I led a team which developed a strategy for LOGCAP IV. This contract would be similar to LOGCAP III but have three contractors instead of the single contractor under LOGCAP III. Provisions for competing the work among the three contractors and for replacing one of the contractors on a task would be incorporated into the solicitation and resultant contract. This approach met our four objectives of reducing program risk, increasing capacity, reducing costs through competition and providing an incentive for superior contract performance. Multiple contractors reduce the risk that accompanies a single source of support. Should one LOGCAP IV contactor fail, go bankrupt, or become otherwise unable to support the program, other LOGCAP IV contractors would be available to pick up the work rapidly. Multiple contractors also prevent the possibility that additional operational support would exceed the capacity of a single LOGCAP contractor. Finally, as each LOGCAP IV contractor executes support requirements, they are more motivated to maintain high quality and control costs as other capable contractors could more readily replace them.

Introducing competition into the program was a prime goal. While LOGCAPs I through III were all awarded as the result of competition, task orders were not. With three contractors prepared to do the work, there would be opportunity to compete for work. Jacques Gansler has pointed out that, "An additional aspect of the Defense market's uniqueness is the dramatic shift that takes place in relative bargaining power of industry and government once a commitment to a single supplier has been made."[186] The follow-on task orders for work in Kuwait and Afghanistan have been competed among the LOGCAP IV contractors.

Early in the LOGCAP III we realized that the greatly expanded scope of operations by U.S. military forces and the resulting surge in LOGCAP support in Southwest Asia has placed challenging and resource intensive requirements on the current single LOGCAP contractor. It could be very difficult for that same contractor to provide a high level of troop support at the same time in another part of the world, if required. This growing concern for future support led to a change in acquisition strategy from a single LOGCAP contractor, to a strategy to award multiple contracts available to support future operations. LOGCAP II had demonstrated the risk of supporting extensive operations with only one contractor. The significant growth in the number and scope of both current and future LOGCAP actions, and the continuing growth in the reliance on contractors to provide combat support and combat service support (CS/CSS) previously provided by soldiers would increase these risks in the future.

With multiple contractors the Army would be able to compete most of the work. This competition would reduce the overall costs to the Army and should improve the range of solutions offered for competed tasks. While there may still be some tasks which are awarded without competition, due to the urgency of the requirement, an expedited process for competing task orders will allow a significant amount of competition in the program.

Multiple contractors would provide back up for possible failure of one contractor to be able to complete an assigned task. Security, financial

---

186   (Gansler, The Defense Industry 1980) p.78

and managerial issues arose under LOGCAP III which threatened continuity of performance on several occasions. Without other contractors
as part of the program, we had to rely on bringing in soldiers to perform
that work or a much expedited competition for a replacement contractor.
Neither of these was considered an adequate course of action.

Multiple contractors would also be available to take on new contingencies which might arise during a conflict. We were always apprehensive about the possibility of the need to utilize LOGCAP in Korea, Africa
or another area while KBR was fully engaged in SWA. Given the problems with current operations it seemed highly unlikely that KBR could
effectively support a new operation.

The LOGCAP IV contract, which I designed along with a great team,
is a significant improvement over LOGCAP III. It provides three prequalified contractors who can take on task orders for work in the AOR.
These contractors compete for orders, which should reduce the costs to
the Army.

On July 26, 2005, HQ AFSC conducted a LOGCAP IV Industry Day.
There were Representatives from 44 companies (33 large businesses, 11
small businesses). We met with 23 companies in individual meetings to
discuss questions they had on different acquisition strategy alternatives
presented. Subsequently we received written comments and recommendations from 11 companies. Due to the size of the program, small businesses were looking for teaming or subcontract opportunities. There was
extensive industry interest in forming teams to propose on the solicitation upon its release. Some of the concerns were: (1) how new contracts
would synchronize with the current contract to maintain logistics support, (2) how and when work would transition off the current LOGCAP
contract, (3) how non-U.S. companies could participate, (4) opportunities for small business, (5) how task orders would be awarded under
multiple contracts, and (6) whether LOGCAP IV would be awarded as
global or regional contracts.

The principal objective of LOGCAP is to provide CS/CSS augmentation to Combatant Commanders (COCOMs) and Army Service Component Commanders (ASCCs) throughout the full range of military operations. LOGCAP services are also available to support military services,
coalition and/or multi-national forces, and other governmental/non-governmental agencies. A second objective is to provide worldwide and regional planning. Under LOGCAP I, II and III the single contract provided
both planning and operational support. Three contractors presented a

difficulty. Should they each develop their own plans? Should one contractor develop plans which another would execute?

On October 17, 2005, HQ AFSC posted an additional possible acquisition strategy for Industry input. It asked for comment on possibly awarding multiple LOGCAP IV contracts, with all contractors working jointly in developing LOGCAP plans and sharing work on large logistics support actions, and competing on smaller task orders. Of the 11 companies who responded, two felt it might be a feasible approach, while nine said it created significant challenges to share information while protecting proprietary information, and then later competing for work against the joint planner for requirements based on those plans. Essentially, requiring them to work together and then later compete for work was a disincentive to optimal joint actions.

Solving this problem in a manner which satisfied all stake holders was difficult. The combatant commanders wanted one planning contractor to work with and preferred that contractor to then execute the operations. This contractor would be integrated in their war planning and be a part of the commander's staff. They suggested that each contractor under LOGCAP IV would work with a different regional command. This would have a contractor for Europe, one for SWA, one for the Pacific region and won for continental United States. This approach, unfortunately, placed us right where we were. While it mitigated the risk of new work in a different region, it would have left us with only one contractor in SWA, like LOGCAP III. There still could be too much work for a single contractor and little competition in the program.

We decided to award multiple LOGCAP IV execution contracts, and a separate LOGCAP planning/support contract. To preclude any perception of improper competitive advantage, the execution contractors and planning/support contractor could not have any business relationship (teaming, partnering, subcontracting) or financial interests in each other. Each contract would require the contractor to have employee agreements that specify limitations on the kind of information employees would make available to their new employer and adequate company policies to protect Sensitive or proprietary information. The planning contractor would be part of the combatant commander's staff and develop plans executable by any of the three other contractors. Naturally, the planning contractor could not also be an execution contractor.

The Army G4 signed off on this approach which allowed us to go ahead with the LOGCAP IV contract. By having multiple contractors under LOGCAP IV, we have considerably improved the Army's ability to manage this program in a successful manner. However, this ability must be utilized. There is already evidence that the Army's failure to learn the lessons of LOGCAP III is causing problems in the management of LOG-CAP IV.

The Army has also rescued KBR from the full impact of LOGCAP IV. The Army prepared a decision paper for Mr. Shay Assad, then the Defense Deputy for Acquisition and Policy (DPAP). This classified paper evidently recommended that the Army remain with LOGCAP III in Iraq, probably citing the Army's desire not to switch contractors during the drawdown. This is a rather odd conclusion, because the Army successfully switched contractors in Afghanistan during a more difficult build-up of troops. The success here is the Army's own conclusion.

This decision has had a significant positive impact on KBR. Their latest quarterly report notes that, while revenue is down due to the loss of work in Afghanistan, profit margins are up due to the steady flow of award fees from Iraq. These fees are for work, for which they did not have to compete. They continue to receive high award fees, even though problems with business systems and some work have continued.

This not the only favor Mr. Assad has done for KBR. He has set up a panel to review all DCAA issued Form 1s under LOGCAP III with KBR. DCAA auditors issue Form 1 documents when they encounter discrepancies so great that the recommend the Government withhold payments until these issues are resolved. The contracting officer usually decides whether to comply with the Form 1 and usually does so. This panel usurps the contracting officer's authority in these matters. The panel also appears to favor KBR in their decisions. A meeting was held on October 1, 2010 with DCAA and the panel to review pending decisions on four Form 1s. DCAA left the meeting feeling that the panel was ignoring the auditors and deciding in KBR's favor. As we saw before, the Army has consistently ignored DCAA auditors on LOGCAP III and provided unearned money to KBR.

This leads to another problem with LOGCAP IV; the Army continues to ignore DCAA when awarding new contracts. The first award for work under LOGCAP IV was for Kuwait. DynCorp received the award with a bid of $70 million dollars for a performance year. The Army did not have DCAA examine the proposals, even though they had promised the Commission on Wartime Contracting that they would. Shortly after the award DynCorp submitted a Request for Equitable Adjustment (REA). They requested an additional $50 million per year to perform the work. Evidently they had assumed they would hire many former KBR employees at lower salaries, among other mistakes. When this basis of providing the proposal did not pan out, they expected the Army to bail them out. After all, the Army had always done so on LOGCAP III with KBR. I have confidence that a DCAA review of the proposals would have identified this large a discrepancy and required additional competitive negotiations. The Army may have awarded this task order somewhere between the DynCorp initial proposal and their new request for an over 40% increase. This is an instance of a more general problem of using contractors to provide oversight of other contractors

In addition to the award of the LOGCAP IV contract, the Army has made other improvements in the LOGCAP program.

IMPROVED REQUIREMENTS CONTROL

The Army has also improved their approach to troop support by refining and expanding the specification of requirements for operation and maintenance of base camps. The Statement of Work (SOW) for the first task order (59) was 53 pages. The successor SOW to this task order (89) was 73 pages and the SOW for Task Order 139, the next base camp support task order, was 131 pages. Unfortunately, not all of the changes were productive, but there was a recognition that more needed to be done to ensure proper support to the troops.

The Army has established LOGCAP Deputy Program Manager Offices which are located in the AOR. At this time there are offices in Kuwait, Iraq and Afghanistan. The combatant commander receives support in identifying requirements which LOGCAP can fulfill and turning these requirements into viable scopes of work. These offices have helped the combatant commander's staff scrub the requirements, eliminating some that are unnecessary and thus reducing costs to the Army. Unfortunately, they also added contracting officer responsibilities in these offices.

ADDITIONAL CONTRACT OVERSIGHT RESOURCES

Of course the Army Contracting Command, DCMA and DCAA have all worked to increase the resources (money and people) available to support the LOGCAP contract. From the Gansler Report, through GAO studies to the Commission on Wartime Contracting, lack of people to provide appropriate oversight has been identified as a major problem. I completely agree with this finding and applaud the initiatives to provide proper oversight.

It is natural for any Agency to see growth as a positive benefit to the institution. As span of control increases, career paths improve, authority and power grow and visibility increases. We have understood this as a characteristic of bureaucracy since the studies of Max Weber. Still, this is an important improvement for the LOGCAP program.

IMPROVED ELECTRICAL SAFETY

Thanks to the tireless work of Cheryl Harris and the support of Senators Casey and Dorgan along with Representative Waxman, the Army has admitted a problem with electrical work in theater. They have initiated Project SAFE to identify and fix unsafe conditions. While I would like to see this project work on a larger scale and shorter timeframe, it is still a major accomplishment and will provide better conditions for our troops.

WE CAN DO BETTER

The Army, however, has not taken the opportunity to thoroughly examine the experience of LOGCAP III and look for additional improvements. The major issue is the Army's extreme reluctance to admit that any mistakes have been made. Lack of resources was a pre-existing situation that has been corrected. If it was a mistake not to foresee this need for more oversight personnel, that was based on decisions made long ago. A single contractor for LOGCAP III was a valid decision, based upon the facts at the time. LOGCAP IV was a proper response which corrected that problem.

The only real mistake which has been admitted is the electrical problems. As we saw in Chapter 8, the Army was dragged kicking and screaming into that admission. The initial response was to deny any problem, support KBR and attack any assertion that something was wrong. Only the weight of documentation and testimony gathered by Congressional oversight forced the admission and remedial action. This was not a shining hour for the Army.

This has been the Army approach to all other problems identified on LOGCAP. Water problems? Not the contractors fault and the really did not exist anyway. Were there DFAC problems? Well, it was wartime so anything the contractor did, any cost incurred was correct. Did KBR have poor business systems? Wartime, give them a pass and they were okay after five years. We had to give KBR all that money or they would have left the battlefield.

Time and again Army officials have appeared before congress and assured Senators and Representatives that KBR performance was wonderful and no problems really exist. These officials have included the then Assistant Secretary of the Army for Acquisition, Technology and Logistics, his deputy for Procurement and Policy, the Major General Commanding the Army Sustainment Command and the Civilian Executive of the Army Contracting Command. Move along folks, nothing to see here.

If you do not gather all of the relevant information concerning performance, then you will not be able to properly asses that performance and identify problem areas to correct in the future. If you do not admit problems, then you will never correct them. Battlefield commanders know that after any operation you must perform a thorough "lessons learned" after action report. Soldiers lives are at stake and the next operation must incorporate those lessons. As we have seen actions to provide proper LOGCAP support may also put soldier's lives at risk. The same need for lessons learned exists, yet the Army's basic position has been that of denial.

I have tried to understand the events which took place from August 2004 through 2005. This was from the time the decision to implement the 15% withhold to provide an incentive for KBR to improve their business systems was overturned through the negotiation of the cost base for approximately $% billion in task orders and the initial award fee boards. Based on my observations of meetings and briefings during this time period I understand that Army decisions were driven by MG Jerome Johnson, The deputy to the Assistant Secretary of the Army (ALT) Ms. Tina Ballard and the Assistant Secretary of the Army (ALT) Claude Bolton. I do not know what was in their minds when they made these decisions. I only know the decisions which were made and the effects on the contract and overall support to troops.

One technique for understanding this was suggested by Nobel Prize winning economist Joseph Stiglitz in his book *Globalization and Its Discontents*. He is trying to understand the decisions of the IMF which seem to benefit the financial sector in the developed world more than the developing countries the bank is supposed to help. He also does not know what was in the minds of IMF leadership when they made those decisions. He asks, however, that we think as if the leaders did intend to help the developed countries and their financial institutions. Would that be a sound explanation of their actions?[187]

---

187   (Stiglitz, Globalization and Its Discontents 2003)pp 207-213

Suppose we ask ourselves to think as if Army leadership was more concerned to help KBR than the American taxpayer and the troops. Would this offer a coherent explanation of the actions which they took?

The first action was to overturn the withhold decision. This certainly helped KB and Halliburton.

Halliburton stock rose as KBR was seen to have a more profitable future. The Sense that the Government would enforce all aspects of the contract was lost, providing an incentive for KBR to challenge other parts of the contract they signed. Money which would have provided other support for the troops was, instead paid out to KBR.

The Army has argued that they were afraid KBR would walk away from our troops. Perhaps this is true, though I suggested in chapter 4 that I do not feel this was a credible threat. So maybe the Army did succumb to blackmail. Let us consider this a wash in explanatory power.

Next the Army removed me and later the lead contracting officer. We were both determined to enforce the contract provisions. We were exploring unilateral negotiation of the cost bases for the task orders using DCAA analysis. Though we both strove to accommodate the real concerns of KBR and listen to their suggestions, we must have been seen as a thorn in the company's side. Removing us was a significant accommodation to KBR.

There may be a simpler reason here. The Army leadership had evidently decided on a course of action with respect to LOGCAP. This was a set of actions which I would have certainly opposed and would have found impossible to carry out. At some point I had to leave. Maybe this is a wash also.

At this point the Army had satisfied KBR's threat to leave the troops hanging and should have been in a position to act strongly in the negotiation of the task orders. Instead the Army ignored the DCAA audits and hired RCI/SERCO to provide the desired financial input to negotiations. Given KBR's current high rate of spending, estimates at completion were calculated and KBR received most of the costs the proposed. These very high costs bases would then result in much higher fees than KBR deserved.

The Army has claimed that RCI had skills which DCAA did not have, but we know from chapter 5 that this was at best disingenuous and basically not true. These actions cost the taxpayers additional wasted money. The troops lost funds from the current operational budget for Iraq which could have been used for better body armor and vehicle armor, saving lives. The only way I can reasonably explain this is that the actions are as if the Army was concerned to support KBR.

At this point the military did have a fallback position. For these cost type contracts DCAA would perform an audit of incurred costs after performance was over. If DCAA found costs that were not allowable under the Cost Accounting Standards or were not allocable to the LOGCAP contract they could disallow them. The greater threat was that DCAA would conclude that some costs were unreasonably incurred and disallow those. KBR would owe the money back. To fight for the money they would have to go to court and produce the facts which DCAA was not able to obtain from their business systems.

However, Army leadership decided to relieve KBR of this threat for over $1 billion in dining facility costs. By this time DCAA audits had found these costs unreasonable and would surely disallow them in the post contract audit. During negotiations the Army converted these costs to a fixed price basis, ending the threat of further audit. They gave KBR the highest available profit on these costs, even though they were the most unreasonable costs DCAA found.

Why would the Army do this? It cost the taxpayer and the troops more money. Since all of the costs were incurred having a fixed price provided KBR no incentive to control costs, the traditional value of a fixed price contract. Analyzing this decision as if the Army leadership was concerned to help KBR rather than taxpayers and the troops will provide a rational explanation for this action.

At least at this point the Army was in a position to use the award fee boards to inform KBR of the better performance they valued. Receiving less than 50% of the fee pool based upon faulty business systems and other performance difficulties would send this message. Given the lack of the withhold and the high cost bases, along with the removed threat of DCAA disallowing first year DFAC costs, KBR would withstand the lower award fee easily. The Army would provide KBR a clear path to improvement and the incentive to earn a better fee.

Instead, the Army gave KBR award fees amounting to 90% or more of the fee pool. They sent KBR a clear message that award fee was not related to performance. This message was followed by water problems, continuing transportation problems and the electrocution of U.S. troops. KBR business systems remained poor and appear to still be a problem as I write this book. The Army created a moral hazard where KBR did not pay a price for contract failure. Why on earth would the Army do this?

Looking at this as if the Army was committed to protecting KBR and not troops provides a rational explanation. I can think of no other.

The results of this kind of treatment have been known for years. Fredric M. Scherer wrote in 1964, "...if government agencies have in the past consistently rewarded good performance and penalized poor performance, defense contractors have a historical basis for expecting a similar correlation in the future."[188] Of course, the obverse is also true. If poor performance is rewarded, this is the performance which may be expected.

Unless the military seriously reviews what happened during this period they are very likely to repeat this performance. We now have two more LOGCAP contractors, with their retired generals and retired civilian leaders working LOGCAP. Will they be able to convince Army leaders that their best interests are to support the contractor, not the troops?

Unfortunately, there is also good reason to believe that the Army is making some of the same mistakes of LOGCAP III with LOGCAP IV during continued operations in Iraq, Kuwait and Afghanistan. LOGCAP IV was designed to add competitive incentives to the contractual program. Three contractors were chosen. They are each eligible for any task order. Competition for task orders provides an incentive for lower costs and superior performance, both evaluation criteria. The existence of two other contractors was supposed to provide an incentive to avoid poor performance, as this could cost future awards and provided the military an alternative should they terminate a task order.

However, this does not appear to be they way the Army is managing LOGCAP IV. Task orders have been spread around to all three contractors. DynCorp received Kuwait and part of Afghanistan. Fluor has received part of Afghanistan and Haiti support. Now KBR has received Iraq, even after the decision to award no fee for performance in 2008 which resulted in the death of a soldier due to poor electrical work. Even worse, KBR will receive a higher profit margin on work in Iraq under LOGCAP IV, than they received under LOGCAP III.

Meanwhile, the Army continues to shove the Defense Contract Audit Agency (DCAA) aside in evaluation of costs and prices under LOGCAP IV. The Army committed to the Commission on Wartime Contracting that they would change this practice, and then had to come back and admit they were still using a private contractor (SERCO) and not DCAA.

In 2008, James Risen reported the Army's plans to split awards, provide higher fees and use a private contractor for oversight. He wrote, "Yet

---

188 (Scherer 1964) p. 6

even as the Pentagon begins to pull apart the enormous KBR contract, critics warn that the new three-company deal could actually result in higher costs for American taxpayers and weak oversight by the military. In fact, under the new deal, KBR and the two other companies could actually make more than three times as much as KBR has been paid each year since the war began."[189] Unfortunately, this assessment is turning out to be quite accurate.

One of my reasons for writing this book is to both point out problems and suggest solutions. In some cases I believe that more information needs to be gathered for a full understanding of where things went wrong. I do not do this to attack the Army, an institution I served for over 31 years. I do this to continue to serve the soldiers, who deserve better support than they have received from the LOGCAP contract. I believe that most leaders in the Army share this concern for providing the best possible support to deployed troops in an effective and efficient manner. Unfortunately, some leaders have assumed a "protect my a__" posture which inhibits improvements.

RECOMMENDATIONS

What do I recommend? (Other writers have made similar recommendations worthy of consideration.)[190] Military contracting, especially during combat operations, must become more transparent. Contracts should be available to the press, independent organizations, such as the Project on Government Oversight (POGO) and the general public. These documents usually do not contain proprietary information of the contractor nor do they have classified information. In the few cases they do, this information may be redacted. Laura Dickinson pointed out that, "Moreover, members of Congress could not scrutinize many of the contract terms, because they were not publicly available. And of course there was no scrutiny by the general public at all."[191]

The classification issue will require careful Congressional oversight. The Corps of Engineers inserted an indemnification clause into the Restore Iraqi Oil contract, which may protect KBR from some of the consequences of their actions. The Corps then classified the clause, so that even Congress has not seen it. This is not a security issue, but rather one of hiding public actions. Allison Stanger has written, "Not surprisingly,

---

189 (Risen 2008) p. 1
190 For example see (Dickinson 2011) pp 191-195
191 (Dickinson 2011) p. 9

outsourcing as presently practiced is scandalous, a common result when the work of government takes place beyond the public eye."[192]

A change to the Army's general way of approaching service contracts is required. The new rules, cited in Chapter 12, requiring an inventory of service contracts and the presentation of this data in budget documents is definitely a step in the right direction. The Commission on Wartime Contracting noted that the Agency's culture is not one that place contracting at the forefront.[193] This results in poor planning, resourcing and management of these contracts.

The administration needs to appoint acquisition officials who are dedicated to supporting the troops through good contracting, contractor political pressure notwithstanding. These officials must have the highest ethical standards, with an appreciation of the past problems and current issues with LOGCAP. Given the size of this program and the criticality of the services provided, any candidates must understand the issues involved. Congress should examine the candidates to determine their dedication to reform which will benefit the troops and the taxpayers.

A re-establishment of the lessons learned approach to contracting would obviously help. I have been preaching this simple change for several years. This means you look at what worked and, especially, what did not did not work. Instead, the Army has been very defensive about LOGCAP III and unwilling to look at the way the contract was managed. The Army must review what happened in 2004–2005, understand the problem and take corrective action.

The Army must issue new guidance on Award Fee Boards. These boards must operate as intended. They should only reward exceptional performance with award fee. The base fee is earned by fulfilling the requirements of the contract. Under LOGCAP III, KBR received most of the award fee, while really failing to full fill all of the basic requirements of the contract, let alone provide the exceptional work which the award fee criteria called out. O course new guidance is not the total answer. There must be oversight to ensure the guidance is followed.

The DoD must issue direction that the Defense Contract Audit Agency is the only organization which should provide financial analysis of contractor proposals. This is an inherently governmental function and Agencies should be prohibited from hiring contractors to perform this function. Under LOGCAP III we found that contractors will produce

---

192 (Stanger 2009) p. 2
193 (Commission on Wartime Contracting 2011) p. 2

the finding which the customer desires, whether it is accurate or not. The support contract for LOGCAP IV with SERCO should be reformed to eliminate any financial analysis as a task. DCAA must be staffed to do this mission for contingency contracting. However, I believe more extensive reform in the area of audits would be advisable. I discuss this in some detail, below. James Risen quotes Representative Henry Waxman succinctly stating the issue here, "The Army can say that they are retaining the final say, but when they outsource this much work on contract management, they really are outsourcing oversight." [194]

While I believe the LOGCAP III contract contained sufficient guidance on electrical work, LOGCAP IV Task Orders should be very specific that the contractor should comply with NESC standards while performing operations and maintenance. Lessons learned from LOGCAP III require. All operations and maintenance scopes of work must emphasize the responsibility of the contractor for the safety of troops at the installation. The requirements should always state that only certified electricians perform electrical work.

DCMA government oversight capabilities must be significantly strengthened. Staff at an installation should include the ACO, a Quality Assurance staff capable of oversight of all work at the installation, a property accountability officer and designated Contracting Officer Technical Representatives (COTRS) who understand the various kinds of work which the contractor will perform. The COTRS will generally be supplied by the supported unit, which must have this capability.

As with the DCAA auditors and the DCMA administrative personnel, the contracting staff of the Army must be increased and improved. During the 1990s the military drastically increased the missions to be performed by contractors and significantly reduced the number of acquisition personnel. Laura Dickinson describes the situation, "thus at the very moment that the military was turning increasingly to contractors to provide support services to troops, the Pentagon, under pressure from Congress, cut back severely on the acquisition workforce that would become increasingly necessary to manage those contractors."[195] For 15 years my contracting organization did not hire any new personnel. Every retirement or other loss in a contracting employee resulted in the elimination of that position.

---

194 (Risen 2008) p. 1
195 (Dickinson 2011) p. 33

The general decline in acquisition personnel in the army has been re-versed, but more progress remains. I am concerned that once the wars in Iraq and Afghanistan end and LOGCAP contracting is reduced, there will be pressure to again reduce acquisition personnel. The consequenc-es will be a future conflict with limited resources. Allison Stanger noted, "Add it all up and it becomes quickly obvious that a rapid increase in Pentagon contracting, coupled with a decrease in resources devoted to oversight, have been a recipe for mismanagement and corruption."[196]

In addition to quantity, the quality of the workforce is important. Generally, you have to pay for quality. While many of us were willing to accept lower salaries in return for doing meaningful public service, that may not be the case at all times. This is especially important given the current attacks on civil servants. This is not a new problem. Over twenty years ago, Kenneth Adelman and Norman Augustine, two leaders at the Pentagon and in private industry wrote, "For some reason, the public has not concerned itself greatly with the quality of those individuals who will in the future carry out critically important roles in government, es-pecially in the civil service." [197] New contracting positions should have high educational requirements. Advancement should be based on accom-plishments. They must be paid accordingly.

Hiring quality people, even at a higher cost, would provide another benefit. Economist Murray Weidenbaum suggested, some time ago, that a higher quality procurement workforce would enable a reduction in the enormous amount of contracting regulations. He points out that many of the regulations are there specifically do deal with an accepted low level of quality in acquisition personnel.[198]

The Government must issue policy guidance for all Federal contract-ing activities prohibiting the use of contractors to provide oversight of other contractors. The guidance should emphasize that oversight of gov-ernment contractors is an inherently governmental activity which must be performed by government officials. Fortunately, the trend may now be to ins-source these functions. The GAO, in a report released in Janu-ary, 2011 describes the impact of new guidance:

Section 803 of the National Defense Authorization Act for Fiscal Year 2010 requires the Secretary of Defense to include information in DOD's annual budget justification materials related to the procurement of con-

---

196   (Stanger 2009) p.89

197   (Adelman 1990) p. 167

198   (Weidenbaum 1992) p. 163

tract services. Specifically, the legislation requires, for each budget account, to clearly and separately identify (1) the amount requested for the procurement of contract services for each DOD component, installation, or activity, and (2) the number of contractor FTEs projected and justified for each DOD component, installation, or activity based on the inventory and associated reviews.16

Collectively, these statutory requirements indicate that the inventory and the associated review process are to serve as a basis for identifying candidates for in-sourcing contracted services, supporting development of DOD's annual strategic workforce plan, and specifying the number of contractor FTEs included in DOD's annual budget justification materials.[199]

DoD contracting activities must be required to use internal government pricing personnel or DCAA for the audit and financial analysis of contractors. They must also be required to use internal resources or DCMA for the administration of contracts. Both DCAA and DCMA require additional resources and training for this function to be properly done. Doing so would eliminate the costs of contractors providing functions and improve performance and costs on the overseen contracts. This should more than offset the costs of improvements at DCAA and DCMA.

The concept of having a LOGCAP contracting officer forward, during contingency operations, should be re-evaluated. Certainly the LOGCAP Program office should have a significant presence in theater. However, my recommendation is to maintain the contracting officer, with authority to add new work and commit the government to prices, schedules and other contractual agreements at the CONUS location, which is now Rock Island. This will allow the development and maintenance of a permanent staff, skilled and knowledgeable in the LOGCAP contract. This will reduce the pressure both from the supported unit and the contractor which led to the disaster of Task Order 139 and the electrocution of SSG Maseth.

The Army Contracting Command, Rock Island Office must be reviewed to see if it can effectively manage the LOGCAP contract. This site was responsible for many of the problems associated with the management of LOGCAP III. The leadership is still the same. Lessons learned have not been acknowledged nor addressed. The new Assistant Secretary of the Army for Acquisition, Logistics and Technology should make this a priority along with the Commander of HQ, AMC.

---

199 (GAO 2011) p. 3

The authority of the Procuring Contracting Officer (PCO) to withhold payments to the contractor when business decisions make that essential, must be clarified and strengthened. While I believe the PCO has this authority, hearings before the Commission on Wartime Contracting indicated both the Army Contracting Command and DCMA were unsure of this authority. The Commission makes a similar recommendation.[200]

Congress must thoroughly investigate the management of LOGCAP IV. How were the task orders spread so evenly? Have there been any competitive consequences of poor performance? How did KBR receive the Iraq award? What influenced the Army's decision in 2004 to favor KBR over the troops? These are just a few of the questions which Congress must ask as the Army appears unwilling to consider them.

As I outlined in Chapter 11 the Congress and the Department of Defense need to seriously revisit the concept of contracting out combat service support. They must examine both the costs and the risks associated with using the LOGCAP Program rather than organic support. This would require Congress and the Administration to agree to adjust Army end-strength limits to reconstitute the support units. Limits on troops in theater would also have to be adjusted to accommodate the support units.

THE NEED FOR A FEDERAL CONTRACT AUDIT AGENCY

Last fiscal year, the United States Government awarded over $535 billion in contracts with private corporations, non-profits and other entities. A significant percentage of these contracts are awarded not as fixed-price contracts or they were awarded without adequate price competition, meaning auditing is the only real defense American taxpayers have against contractor overbilling. There is only one agency with the authority and the ability to audit contractor proposals, assist negotiations and audit incurred costs under cost-type contracts, such as the massive logistics contract awarded to Kellogg, Brown, and Root, better known as KBR, to support the occupation of Iraq. That agency, despite conducting work across most of the federal government, is located within the Defense Department, underneath several layers of senior officials. The Defense Contract Audit Agency, or DCAA, conducted 76 percent of contracts audits outside of the DoD, according to a Senate fact sheet recently published. But despite the existence of the DCAA as a de facto government wide contract audit agency, the U.S. government still does not have

---

200   (Commission on Wartime Contracting 2011) p. 5

the complete capability to use audits to help manage and provide over-sight on the hundreds of billions of taxpayer dollars that go out the door to contractors every year.

Senator Claire McCaskill (D-Missouri) held a hearing where she ex-plored this issue under the auspices of the Senate Homeland Security and Governmental Affairs Subcommittee on Contracting Oversight, which McCaskill chairs. She noted that the Defense Department utilized con-tract auditing far more than the rest of the federal government — while the DCAA conducts one audit for every $24.7 million, the rest of the U.S. Government conducted one audit per every $511 million spent.

The reason why the DoD had approximately 15,000 contract audits conducted in 2009, and the rest of our government had 1,800 audits con-ducted in the same period is due to DCAA's DoD-centric orientation, the way it is funded, and its lack of visibility to the rest of the federal gov-ernment. A proposed Federal Contract Audit Agency would remedy all of these problems, and bring numerous other benefits, such as greater independence.

Before offering a solution to improving federal contract audits, Let me describe the use of audits in federal contracting. Contract audits involve four main functions:

Prior to award audits examine the proposed price or cost of bidders on government contracts awarded through source selection procedures. These audits offer an opinion on whether the proposed price or cost is reasonable for the work expected to be performed. The Government cer-tainly does not wish to award a contract at too high a price. Also the Government also does not want to award at a price which is too low and will prohibit full performance of the contract. A price which is too low will generally result in some form of contract failure. The government wants to award at a fair price for both parties.

If the Government engages in price or cost negotiations with the con-tractor, the audit provides an analysis of the contractor's proposal and recommends the price or cost which should be achieved by the Govern-ment during negotiations. Within the DoD, the contracting officer must document any settlement which does not comply with the audit rec-ommendations. This is one of the many checks and balances in military contracting.

If the contract is a cost type contract, the Government audits the final costs incurred by the contractor. The audit examines these costs to de-termine if they were allocable to that contract, allowable under Federal Cost Accounting Standards, and whether they have been reasonably incurred by the contractor. The audit will recommend costs unreasonably incurred that should be recovered by the Government.

Auditors will audit contractor business systems such as cost accounting, purchasing, estimating and other business systems related to government contracting. The Federal Acquisition Regulation stipulates that, if contractor's business systems are inadequate, the contractor should not receive any contracts of a cost type.

The DCAA conducts all of these audits for the Department of Defense. Testimony given before Senator McCaskill indicates that other agencies use a variety of sources for their audits. Agencies, such as the Department of Education, Department of Energy, and the General Services Agency (GSA) testified that sometimes they use their agency Inspectors General, but more often pay the DCAA for audits, but are increasingly using outside contractors to perform audits. But as mentioned, the vast majority of the government outside of DoD heavily relies on DCAA.

Non-DoD agencies have trouble reimbursing DCAA for auditing services; the DCAA is only centrally funded to provide auditing for the DoD. Thomas Skelly, the acting chief financial officer at the Education Department, testified, "The department faces challenges regarding contract audits in deciding whether they take priority over other demands for limited administrative funds."

Furthermore, DCAA naturally gives the Defense Department priority on their services. DCAA has a large backlog of final cost incurred audits for DoD contracts, often taking years to perform this function. The massive contracting effort to support operations in Kuwait, Iraq and Afghanistan has exacerbated this problem. For this reason other agencies often find that DCAA cannot meet their expected timeframes for conduction an audit. So the other agencies often contract out audit functions to private vendors.

The use of agency inspectors general is also a problem for most agencies. Inspectors general are assigned multiple investigative and management oversight tasks. There experience and training is not always in financial accounting and auditing. The Education Department's Skelly added, "The department's inspector general has multiple priorities and DCAA cannot always accommodate non-DOD requests for audit support. Obtaining audit support from a nongovernmental firm can be costly and time consuming."

The use of private contractors for audits is especially troubling. The committee found that a DCAA audit costs approximately $114 per hour. A contractor audit costs approximately $150 per hour, which is a 36%

cost differential for using contractors. Even more important, contractor auditing involves the delegation of an inherently governmental function to contractors. Only governmental officials should be involved in reviewing the proprietary data of other contractors and making recommendations which lead to contract decisions. Also, contractors providing audit services often try to ascertain the results the agency wants, rather than the factual audit results. In other words, a contractor performing audits might view the government agency as their customer rather than the U.S. taxpayer. Additionally, there could be organizational conflict of interest concerns if a private sector auditor works for a prime contractor and also works separately for the government auditing a contract of the prime contractors. Such a situation would beg the question: who is that private sector auditor working for?

What is the resolution of this problem? I would propose that Congress should establish a Federal Contract Audit Agency (FCAA). This organization could be an independent agency which reports directly to the President, such as the Environmental Protection Agency. The organization could also be located in the Office of Management and Budget, reporting through the Director of OMB to the President; if this is a more efficient way of administratively achieving such a government wide agency..

The DCAA should be transferred to this agency and become the nucleus of the FCAA. Additional resources should be provided to this agency to preclude the use of agency contract personnel, agency IGs and contractors to perform contract audit functions. The agency's mandate should be to perform the contract audit functions described above. All agencies would identify their auditing needs and the FCAA would be resourced to the extent it can provide timely services to all of these agencies.

Agencies should be prohibited from using contractors for any of the audit functions described above.

There should be a formal adjudication rule for resolving differences between the findings of an FCAA audit and the agency contracting officers.

The FCAA should present a yearly public report to the President and to Congress on the results of their work. There must be transparency on how their recommendations are treated by the agencies.

The advantages of such an agency would be:

- A single agency could standardize audit approaches under government best practices and should eliminate the use of contractors for performing audits. This last is very important.

- A single, separate agency would enhance the independence of auditors for DoD work. Now, as part of DoD, they appear to sometimes react to departmental agendas rather than auditing data. For example the DoD is reducing their use of DCAA and transferring actions to the Defense Contract Management Agency (DCMA.)

- Budgeting and planning for audit support across the government would be strengthened. Today most agencies, including DoD, short change auditing resources since the recovery of funds does not always accord with the funding for audit resources. For example, in DoD audit resources are paid for by Operations and Maintenance funds. The money saved is often in procurement appropriation funds which do not provide money for the DCAA.

- The administrative costs would not be much, if any, greater than the costs of a robust DCAA. The GAO has estimated more significant costs of this transition; however, if these costs materialize they would be offset by not paying the differential between contractor auditors and Government auditors. The recovery of additional funds would also offset any increased administrative costs.

- The current arrangement of other agencies reimbursing DCAA for services would end — and an FCAA would be centrally-funded for audit work across the federal government. This would remove the budgetary disincentive to use contract auditing.

I am not the only advocate for a FCAA. Mr. Nick Schwellenbach of the Project on Government Oversight proposed this solution to the McCaskill subcommittee. While Senator McCaskill was somewhat apprehensive of creating a new government agency, I believe the currently available data suggest this agency would, in fact, pay for itself.

Mr. Schwellenbach stated, in his testimony:

> We need a contract audit agency that is not afraid of its own shadow. We need an independent and muscular audit agency that protects the taxpayers' interests. ... There are other possible benefits to pulling DCAA out from the DoD and transforming it into an FCAA, the most significant being the independence issue. Currently the DCAA reports to the DoD Comptroller, who is the Chief Financial Officer of DoD, and who in turn, reports to the Deputy Secretary of Defense. We have grave reservations whether this structure ensures adequate independence for DCAA, par-

ticularly as DCAA's work often establishes issues with how DOD works with contractors.

I have had great experience with the government auditors at DCAA during my career in military contracting. While the agency has had management problems in the recent past, the audit products which I received were accurate, comprehensive and indispensible for proper contract management and oversight. The entire Federal Government contracting community should have automatic access to this same level of support. Establishing an FCAA will provide that access.

As I mentioned, above, this agency must be robust, having the ability to manage the entire federal contract auditing requirements. Unfortunately, DCAA has not been maintained in this status. OMB Watch reported in January 2008 on this problem:

> Management of auditing resources at DCAA compounds another problem at the agency; an erosion of available resources. In Fiscal Year 2000, the Department of Defense spent over $160 billon (inflation adjusted for 2007 dollars) on private contracts. By 2007, that number had nearly doubled as DOD paid contractors $312 billion that fiscal year. And yet, as the Pentagon became more and more reliant on contracting to carry out its mission, employment at DCAA fell from the equivalent of 4,005 full-time employees (FTEs) in 2000 to 3,867 in 2007.[201]

This is another instance where acquisition management resources were allowed to decrease as acquisition management challenges increased. We have paid for this mistake with wasted resources which cost much more than the cost of adequate oversight.

CURING THE MILITARY/CORPORATE COMPLEX

A 2003 study by the Center for Public Integrity found that 60 percent of companies that received early contracts in Iraq and Afghanistan, "had employees or board members who either served in or had close ties to the executive branch for Republican and Democratic administrations, for members of Congress of both parties, or at the highest levels of the military."[202] This issue is so significant that I must devote some discussion to one of the main problems which besets military contracting. While the military industrial complex was identified in the work of the Truman Committee, President Dwight Eisenhower deserves credit for publicizing this in his farewell address. Since service contracting has come to play such a large role in military contracting, I believe the mili-

201 (OMB Watch 2008) p. 2
202 (Beelman 2003) p. 1

tary/corporate complex is now a more appropriate designation, though Eugene Jarecki would add Congress, making it the MICCC.[203]

Jarecki also points to one way of attacking the problem. He writes:

> The MICC is ultimately composed of human beings. And human nature being what it is, avaricious individuals surely exist and will seek to gain private benefit at public cost. But the idea that any such person or group of people could knowingly conspire to mastermind a system is harder — and unnecessary — to prove. It is more likely — and is indeed more troubling — that corruption among defense contractors, Representatives in Congress, and military brass is "standard operating procedure," in which these actors simply exploit the thick camouflage that an increasingly over tangled system provides. However challenging untangling system wide corruption is a far more useful task than holding any particular actor to account.[204]

While we cannot put the entire military and their corporate partners on the couch for therapy, there may be some ways to reduce the negative impact of this web of interests. Since this problem is in the Acquisition arena, I have looked back at my experience of acquisition reform efforts for some guidance. It is not the case that these efforts have been particularly effective. We are about to embark on another round of acquisition reform, led by some new proposals by DoD Secretary Gates. However, they do indicate a plan of action, which, if executed in a rigorous manner, might help.

The first step is to recognize the problem. In the 1980s Operation Ill wind exposed one of the most egregious situations where senior Navy leaders worked closely with contractors to advance the interests of those contractors. Outright bribery, the promise of future jobs and slush funds for entertaining leaders and politicians were utilized by the contractors. Andy Pastor describes these actions in detail in his book *When the Pentagon was for Sale*. He wrote "...the investigations markedly fell short in another arena. It failed to produce lasting, deep seated cultural change throughout the Pentagon. Although the opportunity to lock in authentic "reforms" may have been at an all time high, both Republican and Democratic administrations dropped the ball."[205]

---

203 (Jarecki 2008) p. 189 [I must say, I never saw any instance of Congressional action to benefit a contractor during my management of field support contracts. At this time, such a Congressional role may be found in major system acquisitions.

204 (Jarecki 2008) p. 193

205 (Pastor 1995) p. 366

The Iron Triangle of defense contractors, the military and some parts of Congress, identified by Gordon Adams in his 1981 book of the same name,[206] is operative with service contracts, in much the same way as system development programs and contracts. However, under LOGCAP it has generally been a bipolar relationship between the military and KBR. Congress has actually been a source of oversight and criticism of this relationship.

A recent study by the Boston Globe has found that this complex has been increasing in recent years. They state, "From 2004 through 2008, 80 percent of retiring three- and four-star officers went to work as consultants or defense executives, according to the Globe analysis. That compares with less than 50 percent who followed that path a decade earlier, from 1994 to 1998."[207]

Ernie Fitzgerald was the Pentagon whistleblower who was fired by President Richard Nixon for exposing cost overruns on the Lockheed C-130 airplane contract. After the courts ruled he should get his job back, he continued to argue diligently for better cost control and better quality products. He described the revolving door policy to Ken Silverstein in this way:

> Military officers for the most part are forced to retire when their family expenses are at their peak — they've got a couple of kids in college and they are still paying a mortgage. They won't starve on their retired pay. But at the same time, they can't keep up their lifestyle. What happens in our system is that the services see one of their management duties as placing retired officers, just as a good university will place its graduates. And the place the services have the most influence is with defense contractors. IF you are a good clean-living officer and you don't get drunk at lunch or get caught messing around with the opposite sex in the office and you don't raise too much of a fuss about horror stories you come across — when you retire, a nice man will come calling. Typically he'll be another retired officer. And he'll be driving a fancy car, a Mercedes or equivalent, and wearing a $2,000 suit and Gucci shoes and Rolex watch. He will offer to make a comfortable life for you by getting you a comfortable job at one of the contractors. Now, if you go around kicking people in the shins, raising hell about outrages committed by big contractors, no nice man comes calling. It's that simple.[208]

However, the web of retired generals and Army civilian leaders is capable of exerting great influence with current leadership. I have dis-

---

206 (Adams 1981) p. 11.Not much appears to have changed in the last 29 years.
207 (Bender 2010) p. 1
208 (Silverstein 2000) p. 190

cussed the role of LTG (RET) Paul Cerjan with KBR and Agility. MG (RET) Mongeon moved smoothly from the Government to Agility. In August of 2008, KBR hired LTG (RET) Richard Hack as a senior vice president. When I knew LTG Hack he was the Deputy Commanding General of Army Materiel Command, my command's senior organization. In his position he directly had influence on the LOGCAP contract in 2004 and 2005. KBR also hired LTG (RET) John Cusick to head their LOGCAP program in 2010. Just this year LTG (RET) Hack has moved from KBR to Fluor, a LOGCAP IV contractor.

In August, 2010 Honeywell announced that they would bid on the Army's new enhanced Army Global Logistics Enterprise (EAGLE).[209] The announcement goes on:

> "We have an important, long-term partnership with the Army's Materiel Command (AMC) and look forward to helping the Army Sustainment Command (ASC) meet their emerging logistics and readiness needs with the best team possible," said retired Army Maj. Gen. Jerome Johnson, vice president, Mission Logistics, HTSI. "Honeywell's employees deployed today bring faster, more flexible and more reliable logistics services to our troops fighting in the Middle East."

> Honeywell's key Army programs include the Theater Provided Equipment Refurbishment (TPER) program in Kuwait, the Army Prepositioned Stocks-3 (APS-3) program in Charleston, S.C., the Total Package Fielding program in Sterling, Mich., as well as myriad Sustainment Support Services under our Field and Installation Readiness Support Team (FIRST) and Global Property Management Support Services (GPMSS) contracts worldwide, including Iraq, Kuwait and Afghanistan.

> HTSI will respond to four major task areas that include a diverse range of logistics requirements across Plans and Operations, Maintenance, Supply and Transportation functions.

> "Honeywell's solution will offer the ASC efficiency and oversight," added Johnson. "Honeywell will partner with the best firms as a premier Army logistics support contractor."[210]

You remember MG (RET) Johnson, my former commander at Army Sustainment Commend (ASC). Here he will manage a contractor's bid for this critical Army program at a command where his old subordinates work. Some of them owe him their promotions and current positions. Think about his contacts at ASC and the parent command, Army Materiel Command (AMC.) I am not suggesting any wrong doing here, all I

---

209 As I said earlier, you have to have a catchy acronym for your program.
210 (Honeywell 2010) p.1

know is what I read in a press release. Does it pass the smell test for you? He was away for the required year and is now back to use every bit of influence he has for his current employer. Reforming this web of retired military, retired civilians, former Congressional staff and current officials is one of the major changes which need to happen in Army contracting.

There are numerous other examples I can site merely through my personal experience. The contractor I discussed earlier, Agility, who had the food prime vendor contract hired LTG (RET) Paul Cerjan and a former commander of the Defense Supply Center in Philadelphia, the organization which manages this contract. Though Agility received a bridge contract, a new prime vendor food contract was awarded to Supreme Food Service.

On January 4, 2011, the Defense Logistics Agency extended the Prime Vendor Food Contract with Supreme Food Service without competition. The contract is valued at over $4 billion dollars according to the Washington Post.[211] Supreme had hired a former Director of the Defense Logistics Agency, a retired Lieutenant General. Four months after Robert T. Dail retired from the Army he went to work for Supreme. His stance is that he did not participate directly in negotiations with the company.

Harry Truman identified the too close relationship between the Army and contractors as a major problem in World War II, at times responsible for poor quality, overpriced equipment which endangered the lives of soldiers and cost taxpayers money. President Eisenhower warned of the military industrial complex which now includes the major service providers. As long as these networks of current and retired leaders work both sides of the contracting relation, it will be difficult to achieve true reform.

This will be difficult to accomplish. As Mr. Fitzgerald noted above, General offices usually retire in their 50s and have not become wealthy as officers. They want to continue working and in some cases need to because of children in college or about to marry. Their experience and skill base is most valuable to defense contractors. Lower graded officers in acquisition may retire after twenty or twenty-five years of service. They have no financial incentive to stay in the military and may be pushed out when the next promotion does not come.

In 1988, J. Ronald Fox, former Assistant Secretary of the Army then teaching at the Harvard Business School, recommended that the Army offer additional pay incentives for acquisition officers to remain in the

---

211 (Pincus 2011) p. 1

military longer. This would keep them producing for the Government and out of the revolving door syndrome.[212] Unfortunately, the pay differential between business and the military has increased to the point that the Government would not be willing to pay enough for such an incentive to be effective.

Fortunately there are good examples of different post-retirement paths. LTG William G. Pagonis, who led the logistics effort in Desert Storm, took is skills and leadership ability to Sears. Here he worked to reform their supply chain and was not part of this web. I watched MG Wade Hampton McManus Jr., for whom I worked in the 2002-2004 period, pursue a post-retirement career. He was determined to find a position which did not involve his previous actions, was not based upon his influence and afforded him an opportunity to uses his abilities to continue to support troops on the contractor side. These are the paths we need to encourage for retired military, by additional regulations, if necessary.

The Boston Globe quotes Vice Adm. Lewis W. Crenshaw, who retired as the deputy chief of naval operations in the charge of the budget, and went to work for Grant Thornton, an international accounting firm where he is now a partner. "I wanted to be valued for something other than having a good rolodex," he said. "When I was in the Navy I was in charge of a $130 billion budget. Everybody laughed at my jokes and returned by calls. It wasn't because of my personality."[213]

Some people defend the revolving door between the Pentagon and contractors. Leslie Wayne reports:

> The steady march along the Potomac from the Pentagon to military contractors has its defenders. Steven Kelman, a professor at the Kennedy School of Government at Harvard, said the revolving door enabled hardworking government employees to accept low wages, if they knew there was a future benefit. Moreover, Mr. Kelman said, the large number of Pentagon officials working at military contractors infuses those companies with a Sense of public purpose.

> "Given the lower salaries in government for senior people," said Mr. Kelman, who also works for the Accenture Corporation as a lobbyist promoting closer links between business and government, "if you prevented them from having careers after they left government in the area where they worked, it would be harder to recruit and retain civil servants."[214]

---

212 (Fox, The Defense Management Challange 1988) p. 315
213 (Bender 2010) p. 2
214 (Wayne 2004) p. 3

Unfortunately, we will never increase government salaries to compete with the private sector. Other steps must be taken.

The first step in reform is changes in law and implementing regulations. What are the current rules? Basically:

A former employee may not represent anyone before a Federal agency or Federal court regarding: any specific-party matter on which the employee worked or for two years after leaving the Government, any specific-party matter on which a subordinate worked.

Senior employees (employees with base pay of $148,953 or more per year) are barred for one year from representing anyone before their former agency and from representing or advising a foreign government, procurement officials and project managers are barred for one year from receiving compensation from the winning bidder of a major procurement ($10,000,000 or more) on which they had significant responsibilities,

Why don't these restrictions work? The first problem is with the management of what is a "specific-party matter" on which the employee worked. While it is easy to tell that a GS-13 contracting officer worked on a specific program with one or more contractors, what about the Commanding General who was four levels above the contracting officer? Senior leaders almost always get a bye in these cases. A government attorney will sign a letter saying they did not work specifically on this contract, so they are free to go to work for the contractor who did significant business with their agency.

At best, if they were the Head of the Contracting Agency and thus a procurement official, they would have to wait one year before going to work for the winning contractor. This same logic appears to apply to most senior leaders, even though they may have had an opportunity to significantly influence contracting actions during their tenure. Only the little guy gets the two year restriction.

The timeframes seem also to be way too short. You can easily sit out a year, even two, working for a different firm before claiming your reward from a company you "helped" during your tenure. What is even more troubling is that after one or two years, there are still many employees of the organization you led who are still there. Some of the senior ones owe their promotions to you. Some are your good friends. All of them are subject to the pressure of a former Commander or Executive Director coming back to talk about her firm with you.

A colonel I worked for once asked me, "How do you address a retired general coming in to represent a company?" His answer was "Mister." Unfortunately, this is not common practice. Former general officers are usual referred to as "General." If you once worked for them, it is even harder not to use this accustomed title of respect. With that may come undue deference to their objective, which is to represent the company. Bryan Bender, in his Boston Globe study notes, "When a general-turned-businessman arrives at the Pentagon, he is often treated with extraordinary deference — as if still in uniform — which can greatly increase his effectiveness as a rainmaker for industry. The military even has name for it — the "bobblehead effect."[215]

How do you implement change within the organization? It is not easy. Organizational theorists demonstrate the role of "group norms" in obtaining desired outcomes. The problem is establishing the correct norms. One model is provided by John Cotter:

> 1. Establish a sense of urgency (from the top-down *and* the bottom-up).
>
> 2. Create a guiding coalition (to take the ball and run with it).
>
> 3. Develop a vision and strategy to integrate character and competence.
>
> 4. Communicate the change vision using senior leaders.
>
> 5. Empower broad-based action by removing barriers to change.
>
> 6. Generate short-term wins by integrating character education into our curriculums.
>
> 7. Consolidate gains and produce more change (by integrating character education into our training venues).
>
> 8. Anchor new approaches in the culture by challenging others in the organization to talk about the change.[216]

Training will play a major part in any change to the military culture concerning post retirement employment. In the 1990s the Army was doing one of its periodic attempts at acquisition reform. A training technique, known as "Road Show" was utilized. Groups of experts and leaders went to the major acquisition sites for a series of panel events to explain and reinforce the principles of reform. Such panels could be used, both to explain new laws and regulations and to emphasize the ethical considerations for senior leaders. In this the military would follow number 4 of Cotter's principles.

We must also reform the institutional setting for Government and Army contracting. The structure in which contracting officers work and the incentives which they see are crucial for making the process both

---

215   (Bender 2010) p. 2
216   (Kotter 1980)

efficient and effective. Following former Administrator of the Office of Federal Procurement Policy at the Office of Management and Budget Steven Kelman[217] we can outline the need for organizational reform:

The contracting community needs goals. These goals should reflect support to the troops and to the taxpayer, which are generally goals which match. The goal should not be supporting the leaders who wish to secure their future post-retirement careers.

The Army, and other government agencies, should have a way of determining the quality of contracting performance. There must be a standard for evaluating contracting performance, which should drive that performance. The DoD implemented a new performance evaluation system at the end of my career and is now dismantling it. Most of us recognized that the General Schedule, with step increases and performance bonus system based on the standard government evaluation did not work. Unfortunately, the new system was worse.

Inducements to good contracting practices must include pay and the possibility of promotion and assignments which provide responsibility for results. I would have been happy to continue with the LOGCAP management position without a promotion to a Senior Executive position, because the job was very rewarding as a means to support soldiers. My staff appeared to share this sense that the job was rewarding based upon its contribution to a national goal.

At the same time there should not be negative inducements to poor behavior. I firmly believe that my career is an object lesson for employees at the Army Contracting Command — Rock Island. Speak up, fight to support the troops when the actions are counter to leadership and you will effectively end your career. The fate of Bunnatine Greenhouse at the Corps of Engineers and April Stevenson at the Defense Contract Audit Agency are other negative examples.

The Army contracting community must see rewards (pay, recognition, a pat on the back) for supporting the goals of efficient and effective contracting. Supporting contractors over troops must be met with correction and reorientation of behavior.

Finally, contracting employees must be empowered to "call out" instances of undue influence when they see it. When a retired military or civilian leader comes to represent a company, which is acceptable if it is within law and regulation. However when closed door meetings with current leaders take place and lead to new, company favorable guidance,

---

217 (Kelman 1987) chapter 7

contracting officers should be able to object without damage to their careers.

It should be noted that this problem is not restricted to the military. We have come through a financial crisis from 2008–2011 which could have plunged us into another Great Depression. Actions to prevent this, however, seemed to benefit the banks and other corporate financial firms who generated the crisis. One problem identified way that the people who worked at these firms were the ones we counted on to get us out of this mess. As Nobel Prize winning economist Joseph Stiglitz wrote:

> Revolving doors in Washington and New York also stoked the movement to prevent new regulatory initiatives. A number of officials with direct or indirect ties to the financial industry were called on to frame the rules for their own industry. When the officials who have responsibility for designing the policies for the financial sector come from the financial sector, why would one expect them to advance perspectives that are markedly different from those the financial sector wants? In part it is a matter of narrow mindsets, but one can't totally dismiss the role of personal interests.[218]

The change from the Military Industrial Complex to a more complex web of interests and incentives has made the risk to the United States even greater. I noted, above, that Congress is a part of this web. Congress has operated mainly in the interest of major defense suppliers of equipment, who provide jobs in every state and most congressional districts in the country. While service providers do not usually provide these local jobs, they certainly can provide political contributions to members of Congress. With the *Citizens United* case offering even greater opportunities to acquire such influence, we can expect more congressional action in support of the service providers.

Another extension of this complex of interests is the web of think tanks, policy experts and political insiders who have influence on the actions of elected officials. We saw this web influence the Bush administration through the Heritage Foundation, the American Enterprise Institute, the Center for Security Policy, the Jewish Institute for National Security Affairs, the National Institute for Public Policy and the Project for the New American Century.[219] These organizations, and others, support an active military policy for the United States, strongly influencing the decision to invade Iraq. They also have some other targets, such as Iran, Yemen and North Korea.

---

218 (Stiglitz, Freefall 2010) p. 42
219 (Hartung 2003) Chapter 6, "Policy Profiteers"

These organizations are partially funded by the defense contractors who have a financial stake in military actions which will hire them to provide equipment and services. There is a self-reinforcing chemistry to this situation. The policy organizations provide advice to leaders, which is in the defense firm's interest. The defense firms provide financial support which makes that advice more accessible to the leaders. We see another instance of what defense analyst Chuck Spinney called "the self-licking ice cream cone." [220]

An especially disturbing aspect of this web of interests is the advent of the major service provider contracts, such as LOGCAP. When most of the defense acquisition budget went to equipment, there was ample funding for programs during peacetime. New equipment came on board on a regular basis. Old equipment was upgraded while research and development found the next solution. IT helped to have a national enemy such as the Soviet Union to keep the dollars flowing.

Now, half the procurements are for services. Many of these, such as base camp support in the United States and equipment maintenance continue in peacetime. However major services are dependent on the U.S. deploying significant troops in combat. LOGCAP II was worth several million per year without any combat operations. LOGCAP III was worth up to $6 billion per year in a combat environment. The combat environment requires much more maintenance of vehicles and more expensive costs for mechanics in a combat zone.

Perhaps this is a cynical view. As a student of economics I place some faith in the incentives people have as the motives for actions. The privatization of combat support and combat service support provides increased incentives for the nexus of private military contractors, think tanks, Congress and some in the military to support combat action as a viable policy decision. Decisions to go to war should not have this strong set of incentives for many of the key decision makers to choose war.

Conclusion

There remain significant shortcomings in the way the LOGCAP contract is managed which endanger performance under the new LOGCAP IV contract. Since we are quite likely to be involved in Afghanistan and Iraq for a significant period of time, additional work needs to be done to avoid wasting large amounts of taxpayer dollars and depriving soldiers of the effective support the deserve. LOGCAP shares many of the

---

220 (Hartung 2003) p. 23

same problems as other forms of military contracting. A thorough "lessons learned" approach to LOGCAP can provide many benefits to both taxpayers and to our troops.

It would be a good start if those in charge recognized the root cause of the problems described in the preceding pages, and that is the ability of the contractor, KBR, to influence the outcomes of the bidding process, performance audits, and so many other aspects of the program, in its favor. KBR did this through connections with the military. Retired officers worked their influence on current officers. Current officers looked out for their own future, rather than for the interests of the troops who had placed their trust in them.

Once again I return economist Joseph Stiglitz. In examining the financial crisis, he said:

> Much has been written about the foolishness of the risks the financial sector undertook, the devastation that the financial institutions have brought to the economy and the fiscal deficits that have resulted; too little has been written about the underlying "moral deficit" that has been exposed — a deficit that may be larger and harder to correct. The unrelenting pursuit of profits and the elevation of the pursuit of self-interest may not have created the prosperity that was hoped, but they did help create the moral deficit.[221]

The Army professes to have a set of values for all soldiers, enlisted and officers. The military contracting process must live up to these values, too, and avoid the moral deficit that is both costly and fatal.

---

221 (Stiglitz, Freefall 2010) p. 278

ACRONYM DEFINITIONS

ACO	Administrative Contracting Officer
A/DACG	Arrival/Departure Air Control Group
ADPE	Automatic Data Processing Equipment
AFSC	Army Field Support Command
AO	Area of Operations
ASCC	Army Service Component Commander
CEB	Clothing Exchange and Bath
CECOM	Communications and Electronics Command
COA	Course of Action
COCOM	Combatant Commander
CONUS	Continental United States
COR	Contracting Officer's Representative
CPAF	Cost Plus Award Fee
CPFF	Cost Plus Fixed Fee
CS/CSS	Combat Support/Combat Service Support
DA	Department of Army
DCAA	Defense Contract Audit Agency
DCMA	Defense Contract Management Agency
DoD	Department of Defense Directive
DOJ	Department of Justice
EUCOM	European Command
EVMS	Earned Value Management System
FAR	Federal Acquisition Regulation
FDO	Fee Determining Official
FFP	Firm Fixed Price
GS	General Support
HASC	House Armed Services Committee
HCN	Host Country Nationals
HNS	Host Nation Support
HQDA	Headquarters Department of Army
HUB-Zone	Historically Underutilized Business Zone
IDIQ	Indefinite Delivery, Indefinite Quantity
IGCE	Independent Government Cost Estimates
KBRS	Kellogg-Brown & Root Services (LOGCAP III Incumbent Contractor)
LMIT	Lockheed Martin Information Technology
LOGCAP	Logistics Civil Augmentation Program

MAC	Multiple Additional Contracts (Acquisition Strategy Option)
MACOM	Major Command
MEJA	Military Extraterritorial Judicial Act
MWR	Morale Welfare and Recreation
NAICS	North American Industrial Classification System
NEC	National Electric Code
MNC	Multiple New Contracts (Acquisition Strategy Option)
MSR	Major Supply Route
NORTHCOM	Northern Command
NTP	Notice to Proceed
OCONUS	Outside the Continental United States
OMA	Operations & Maintenance, Army
OMB	Office of Management and Budget
OPLANS	Operations Plans
PARC	Principal Assistant Responsible for Contracting
PCO	Procuring Contracting Officer
PMC	Private Military Contractor
QASP	Quality Assurance Surveillance Plan
RFP	Request for Proposal
ROM	Rough Order of Magnitude
SAC	Single Additional Contract (Acquisition Strategy Option)
SADBU	Small and Disadvantaged Business Utilization
SASC	Senate Armed Services Committee
SCAT	Special cost Analysis Team
SES	Senior Executive Service
SNAFU	Situation Normal, All Fouled Up (Clean Version)
SOFA	Status of Forces Agreement
SOUTHCOM	Southern Command
SOW	Scope of Work
T&M	Time and Materials
TCN	Third Country Nationals
TDA	Table of Distribution and Allowances
TO	Task Order
WMSP	Worldwide Management and Staffing Plan

BIBLIOGRAPHY

Aberbach, Joel D. *Keeping a Watchful Eye: The Politics of Congressional Oversight.* Washington: Brookings Institution Press, 1990.

Adams, Gordon. *The Iron Triangle.* New York, NY: Council on Economic Priorities, 1981.

Adelman, Kenneth L and Norman R. Augustine. *The Defense Revolution.* San Franciso, CA: Institute For Contemporary Studies, 1990.

AFP Washington. "Contractor served troops dirty food in dirty kitchens." *Taipei Times.* December 14, 2003. http://www.taipeitimes.com/News/world/archives/2003/12/14/2003079545 (accessed May 9, 2011).

Allen, T. Scott. "Testimony." *An Oversight Hearing on Accountability for Contracting Abuses in Iraq.* Washington: Senate Democratic Policy committee, 2006. 7.

Amey, Scott. *GSA Hired CACI to Process Suspension and Debarment Cases, Project on government Oversight, February 5, 2007.* February 5, 2007. http://www.pogo.org/pogo-files/alerts/contract-oversight/co-gp-20070205.html (accessed Jan 12, 2011).

Apogee Consulting Inc. "Shoddy Property Record-Keeping Leads to False Claims Allegations ." *apogeeconsulting.biz.* March 14, 2011. http://apogeeconsulting.biz/index.php?option=com_content&view=artic le&id=518:shoddy-property-record-keeping-leads-to-false-claims-allegations&catid=1:latest-news&Itemid=55 (accessed May 7, 2011).

Army Medical Directorate. *Environmental and Industrial Hazards Tier Two Assessment; Qarmat Ali Water Treatment Plant.* Internal Assessment, Washington DC: US Government, 2003.

Associated Press. "More examples of contractor headaches at a glance." *Washington Post,* December 19, 2010: 1.

Beelman, Maud et. al. "U.S. Contractors Reap the Windfalls of Post-War Reconstruction." *Center For Public Integrity.* October 30, 2003. http://www.commondreams.org/headlines03/1030-10.htm (accessed May 3, 2011).

Bender, Bryan. "From Pentagon to the Private Sector." *Boston Globe*, December 26, 2010.

Blair, Russell. *Contractor Confessions: Tales From Iraq*. Houston: Independent Texan Press, 2007.

Briody, Dan. *The Halliburton Agenda*. Hoboken, NJ: John Wiley & sons, 2004.

Brodsky, Robert. *Government Executive.com*. January 19, 2011. http://www.govexec.com/story_page.cfm?filepath=/dailyfed/0111/011911.htm&oref=search (accessed January 28, 2011).

Camm, Frank and Victoria Greenfield. *How Should the Army Use Contractors on the Battlefield?* Santa Monica: Rand, 2005.

Cancian, Mark. "Contractors, The New Element of Military Force Structure." *Parameters*, Autumn 2008: 61-77.

Capaccio, Tony. "U.S. Contractor DynCorp Cited By Pentagon For Deficiences at Afghan Bases." *Bloomberg.com*, March 27, 2011: 1.

Carter, Dr. Ashton B. "Testimony." *Armed Services Committee Panel on Acquisition Reform*. Washington: House of Representatives, 2010.

Censer, Majorie. "Army Puts Outsourcing on Hold." *Capital Business*, February 7, 2011.

Chandrasekaran, Rajiv. *Imperial Life in the Emerald City*. New York: Alfred A. Knopf, 2006.

Chatterjee, Pratap. *Halliburton's Army*. New York: Nation Books, 2009.

—. *Iraq, Inc.* New York: Seven Stories Press, 2004.

Cleland, Rick D. *Working for KBR in Iraq: An Exercise in Frustration*. Flower Mound, TX: Cleland, 2007.

Commission on Wartime Contracting. *At What Risk? Correcting over-reliance on contractors in contingency operations*. Second Interim Report to Congress, Washington: Commission on Wartime Contracting, 2011.

Congressional Budget Office. *Logistics Support for Deployed Military Forces*. CBO Study, Washington, D.C.: Government Printing Office, 2005.

Croft, Major Christopher D. *Contractors on the Battlefield: Has the Military accepted too much Risk?* Fort Leavenworth, KS: United States Army Command and General Staff College, 2001.

DCMA. "House Committee on Oversight and Investigations Hearings." *House Committee on Investigations and Oversight*. 2007. (accessed 2009).

Defendant's Amended Answer and Counterclaims. Case 1:09-cv-00351-CCM Document 47 (United States Court Of Federal Claims, March 15, 2011).

Dickinson, Laura A. *Outsourcing War & Peace*. New Haven: Yale University Press, 2011.

DoD Inspector General. *Audit of Potable and Nonpotable Water in Iraq*. Washington, D.C.: Government Printing Office, 2008.

DoD Inspector General. *Contracting for Tactical Vehicle Field Maintenance at Joint Base Balad, Iraq*. Investigation, Washington: Us Government, 2010.

DoD Inspector General. *Logistics Civil Augmentation Program Support Contract Needs to Comply With Acquisition Rules*. Washington: Department of Defense, 2011.

DoD Inspector General. *Report No. D-2010-046, Contracting for Tactical Vehicle Field Maintenance at Joint Base Balad, Iraq.* DoD IG Investigation, Washington: US Government, 2010.

DoD Inspector General. *Report on Review of Army Decision Not to Withhold Funds on the Logistics Civil Augmentation Program III Contract.* IG Investigation, Washington: US Government, 2010.

DoD Inspector General. *Review of Army Decision Not to Withhold Funds on the Logistics Civil Augmentation Program III Contract; Report No. D-2010-6-001.* Washington: Department of Defense, 2010.

DoD Inspector General. *Review of Electrocution Deaths in Iraq: Part I — Electrocution of Staff Sergeant Ryan D. Maseth, U.S. Army.* IG Report, Washington, DC: US Government Printing Office, 2009.

DoD Inspector General. *Review of Electrocution Deaths in Iraq: Part II — Seventeen Incidents Apart.* Investigation, Washington, DC: US Government Printing Office, 2009.

Donahue, John D. *The Privatization Decision.* New York: Basic Books, 1989.

Dorgan, Byron and Henry Waxman. *Halliburton's Questioned And Unsupported Costs in Iraq Exceed $1.4 Billion.* Investigation Results, Washington: US Congress, 2005.

Dorgan, Byron L. *Reckless!* New York: St. Martin's Press, 2009.

Eccles, Henry E. Rear Admiral Retired. *Logistics in the National Defense.* Harrisburg, PA: The Stackpole Company, 1959.

Engels, Ronald W. *Alexander the Great and the Logistics of the Macedonian Army.* Berkeley, CA: University of California Press, 1980.

Erwin, Sandra I. "More Services, Less Hardware Define Current Military Buildup ." *NDIA.* June 2007. http://www.nationaldefensemagazine.org/archive/2007/June/Pages/MoreServLess2623.aspx (accessed May 3, 2011).

Fleischer, Ari. "Press Briefing by Ari Fleischer." *The White House.* October 30, 2002. www.whitehouse.gov (accessed September 13, 2010).

Foreman, Christopher H.Jr. *Signals From the Hill.* New Haven: Yale, 1988.

Fox, J. Ronald. *Arming America.* Cambridge, MA: Harvard University Press, 1974.

—. *The Defense Management Challange.* Boston, MA: The Harvard Business School Press, 1988.

Gansler, Jacques S. *Affording Defense.* Cambridge, MA: The MIT Press, 1989.

—. *Defense Conversion.* Cambridge, MA: The MIT Press, 1995.

—. *The Defense Industry.* Cambridge, MA: The MIT Press, 1980.

GAO. *DEFENSE ACQUISITIONS Further Action Needed to Better Implement Requirements for Conducting Inventory of Service Contract Activities.* Report to Congressional Committees, Washington: Government Printing Office, 2011.

GAO. *DEFENSE CONTRACTING: Army Case Study Delineates Concerns with Use of Contractors as Contract Specialists.* Washington: US Government, 2008.

GAO. *DoD Force Mix Issues: Greater Reliance on Civilians in Support Roles Could Provide Significnt Benefits.* Washington, D.C.: Government Printing Office, 1994.

GAO. *WARFIGHTER SUPPORT Continued Actions Needed by DOD to Improve and Institutionalize Contractor Support in Contingency Operations.* Testimony befor the House Appropriations Committee, Washington: Government Accountability Office, 2010.

Glanz, James. "Senators Accuse Pentagon of Delay in Recovering Millions." *New York Times*, May 3, 2009: 2.

Granger, Will. *Report of Findings & Root Cause Water Mission B4 Ar Ramadi.* Internal Report, Houston, TX: KBR, 2005.

Grasso, Valarie. *Defense Contracting in Iraq: Issues and Options for Congress.* Congressional Research Service Report For Congress, Washington, DC: Government Printing Office, 2007.

Gregory, William H. *The Defense Procurement Mess.* Lexington, MA: Lexington Books, 1989.

Halliburton Watch. *Army will withhold payment to Halliburton due to suspicious bills.* August 17, 2004. http://www.halliburtonwatch.org/news/withhold_payment.html (accessed Feb 1, 2010).

Hamill, Thomas. *Escape in Iraq.* Accokeek, MD: Stoeger Publishing, 2004.

Hamilton, James. *The Power to Probe.* New York: Random House, 1976.

Hanania, Ray. *MidEast Youth.* April 28, 2008. http://www.mideastyouth.com/2008/04/18/truth-comes-out-in-iraq-war-related-corruption-case-finally/ (accessed March 18, 2010).

Harris, Joseph P. *Congressional Contraol of Administration.* Washington: Brookings Institution Press, 1964.

Hart, Albert G. and E. Cary Brown. *Financing Defense.* New York: Twentieth Century Fund, 1951.

Hartung, William D. *How Much are YOu Making on the War, Daddy?* New York: Nation Books, 2003.

Hastings, Michael. *The Operators.* New York: Blue Rider Press, 2010.

Honeywell. *Honeywell.com.* August 17, 2010. http://www51.honeywell.com/honeywell/news-events/press-releases-details/8.17.10HTSIEagle.html (accessed December 21, 2010).

HQ, AFSC. *Implementation of the Limitation on Reimbursements in FAR 52.216-26 – Payments of Allowable Cost Before Definitization, Logistics Civil Augmentation Program (LOGCAP) III, Contract DAAA09-02-D-0007, Kellogg Brown & Root Services Inc. (KBRSI).* Position Paper, Rock Island: Army, 2004.

Ivanovich, David. "Pentagon Makes Deal with Halliburton on Billing Dispute." *Houston Chronicle*, April 6, 2005: 2.

Jarecki, Eugene. *The American Way of War.* New York: Free Press, 2008.

Kapstein, Ethan B. *Downsizing Defense.* Washington, DC: Congressional Quarterly, Inc, 1993.

Kaufmann, William W. *1985 Defense Budget, The.* Washington, DC: Brookings Institute, 1984.

KBR. *Electrocution Deaths in Iraq.* 2010. http://www.kbr.com/Newsroom/Fact-Sheets/Electrocution-Deaths-in-Iraq/ (accessed December 22, 2010).

Kelman, Steven. *Making Public Policy.* New York: Basic Books, 1987.

Kidwell, Deborah C. *Public War, Private Fight?* Ft. Leavenworth: Combat Studies Insitute Press, 2009.

Knight, Paul. *Houston Press.* December 15, 2010. http://www.houston-press.com/2010-12-16/news/american-grocers/ (accessed December 17, 2010).

Kotter, John. *A Force for Change: How Leadership Differs from Management.* New York: Free Press, 1980.

L. A. Times. News Report, Los Angeles: Los Angeles Times, 2007.

Lendman, Stephen. "Outsourcing War: The Rise of Private Military Contractors (PMCs)." *The Peoples Voice.* Jan 19, 2010. www.thepeoples-voice.org/TPV3/Voices.php/2010/01/19/outsourcing-war-the-rise-of-private-military-contractors (accessed Jan 29, 2010).

Light, Paul C. *The True Size of Government.* Washington, D.C.: Brookings Institute, 1999.

Lipowicz, Alice. "Waxman suggests SBI-Net contractor Booz Allen has conflict." *GCN (Government Computer News).* February 8, 2008. http://gcn.com/articles/2007/02/08/waxman-suggests-sbinet-contractor-booz-allen-has-conflict.aspx (accessed January 13, 2011).

Lukas, J. R. *Responsibility.* Oxford: Oxford University Press, 1993.

Lynn, John A. *Feeding Mars.* Boulder, CO: Westview Press, 1993.

Machaivelli, Niccolo. *Art of War.* Chicago: University of Chicago Press, 2003.

Machiavelli, Niccolo. *The Prince and the Discourses.* New York: Random House, 1950.

MacIver, R. M. *The Web of government.* New York: The Free Press, 1965.

Mayer, Kenneth R. *The Political Economy of Defense Contracting.* New Have, CT: Yale University Press, 1991.

McNaugher, Thomas L. *New Weapons, Old Politics.* Washington, DC: The Brookings Institution, 1989.

Metheny, A. G. *Baghdad F. T. U.* Omaha, NE: Concierge Publishing, 2009.

Miller, John Perry. *Pricing of Military Procurements.* New Haven, CT: Yale University Press, 1949.

Miller, T. Christian. *Blood Money.* New York: Little, Brown & Company, 2006.

Morgan, Cynthia I. *Cindy in Iraq.* New York: Free Press, 2006.

Nordland, Rod. "U.S. Military Faults Leaders in Deadly Attack on Base ." *New York Times*, February 5, 2010: 1.

Office of Senator Ron Wyden. "Dorgan, Wyden, Waxman, Dingell Call to End Outsourcing of Oversight for Iraq Reconstruction." *Press Release.* Washington, DC: US Government, September 19, 2006.

O'Harrow Jr., Robert. "Army to Pay Halliburton, For Now." *Washington Post.* August 17, 2004. http://www.washingtonpost.com/wp-dyn/articles/A8013-2004Aug17.html (accessed Feb 1, 2010).

OMB Watch. *Defense Contract Oversight Faces Multiple Challenges.* August 19, 2008. wwww.ombwatch.org/print/3759 (accessed January 11, 2011).

Pagonis, Lt. General William G. *Moving Mountains.* Boston, MA: The Harvard Business School Press, 1992.

Parsons, Jeffery P. "Statement before Panel on Defense Acquisition Reform." *House Armed Services Committee.* Washington: House of Representatives, 2008. 12.

Pastor, Andy. *When the Pentagon was for Sale.* New York: Scribner, 1995.

Peck, Meron J. and Fredrick M. Scherer. *The Weapons Acquisition Process: An Economic Analysis.* Boston, MA: The Harvard Business School Press, 1962.

Phinney, David. *CorpWatch.* March 29, 2005. http://www.corpwatch.org/article.php?id=12011 (accessed March 18, 2010).

Pincus, Walter. "Agency extends Afghan food-supply contract for firm that hired former director." *Washington Post,* January 4, 2011: 1.

Pittsburg Tribune-Review. *Electrocuted soldier's mom drops lawsuit against KBR.* Jul7 29, 2009. http://www.pittsburghlive.com/x/pittsburghtrib/news/s_635741.html (accessed December 22, 2010).

Pois, Joseph. *Watchdog on the Potomac: A Stud of the Comptroller General of the United States.* Washington: University Press of America, 1979.

Project on Government Oversight. *The Art of Congressional Oversight.* Washington, DC: Project on Government Oversight, 2009.

Quirk, Paula J. and Sarah A. Binder. *The Legislative Branch.* New York: Oxford University Press, 2005.

Rasor, Dina and Robert Bauman. *Betraying Our Troops.* New York: Palgrave MacMillan, 2007.

Rasor, Dina. "Bush Fears that the New Truman Commission Could Be a Threat to National Security." *Huffington Post.* January 30, 2008. http://www.huffingtonpost.com/dina-rasor/bush-fears-that-the-new-t_b_84022.html (accessed March 16, 2010).

—. *More Bucks Less Bang.* Washington, DC: Fund For Constitutional Government, 1983.

—. *The Pentagon Underground.* New York: Times Books, 1985.

Reed, William H. "Statement befor the House Committee on Oversight and Government Reform." *Hearing on Costs for Projects in Iraq.* Washington: House of Representatives, 2007. 4.

Reuters. "Halliburton Lands $72 Million in Bonuses." *Reuters,* May 10, 2005: 1.

Riddle, Donald A. *The Truman Committee: A Study in Congressional Responsibility.* New Brunswick, NJ: Rutgers University Press, 1964.

Risen, James. "Controversial Contractor's Iraq Work Is Split Up." *New York Times,* May 24, 2008: 1.

Ross, Stephen. "Thhe Economic Theory of Agency: the Principal's Problem." *American Economic Review,* 1973: 134-139.

Sandler, Todd Hartley, Keith. *The Economics of Defense.* Cambridge, UK: Cambridge University Press, 1995.

Scherer, Fredrick M. *The Weapons Acquisition Process: Economic Incentives.* Boston, MA: The Harvard Business School Press, 1964.

Schlesinger, Arthur M. Jr. and Roger Burns eds. *Congress Investigates 1792-1974.* New York: R. R. Bowker Co., 1975.

Scholes, David. *Without Prejudice.* Leicester, UK: Matador, 2008.

Senate Armed Services Committee. *The Department of Defense's Management of Costs Under the Logistics Civil Augmentation Program (LOGCAP) Contract in Iraq.* Hearings Transcript for April 19, 2007, Washington, DC: Government Printing Office, 2007.

Sherman, Stanley N. *Government Procurement Management.* Gaithersburg: Woodcrafters Publications, 1985.

Silverstein, Ken. *Private Warriors.* New York: Verso, 2000.

Singer, Peter W. *Corporate Warriors.* Ithaca, NY: Cornell University Press, 2003.

Singer, Peter W. "War, Profits, and the Vaccum of Law: Privatazed Military Firms and International Law." *Columbia Journal of Transnational Law, vol24, no. 2,* 2004: 537.

Stanger, Allison. *One Nation Under Contract.* New Haven : Yale University Press, 2009.

Stiglitz, Joseph E. *Freefall.* New York: Norton, 2010.

—. *Globalization and Its Discontents.* New York: Norton, 2003.

Tappan, Sheryl Elam. *Shock and Awe in Fort Worth.* San Mateo, CA: Pourquio Press, 2004.

Uesseler, Rolf. *Servants of War.* Berkeley, CA: Soft Skull Press, 2008.

United States Army. *The Army Values.* May 19, 2011. http://www.army.mil/values/ (accessed May 19, 2011).

US Army. *Contract DAAA09-D-0007 Task Order 59.* Contract, Rock Island, IL: US Army, 2003.

US Government. *Federal Acquisition Regulations.* Washington: Government Printing Office, 2011.

Van Buren, Peter. *We Meant Well.* New York: Metro[politan Press, 2011.

Van Creveld, Martin. *Supplying War.* Cambridge, UK: Cambridge University Press, 1977.

Vann, John W. "The Tooth to Tail Ratio." *United States Army Logistics 1775-1992: An Anthology, ed by Charles R Schrader,* 1997: vol 3, 773-789.

Verkuil, Paul R. *Outsourcing Sovereignty.* Cambridge: Cambridge University Press, 2007.

Waxman, Henry. "Letter to Acting Secretary of the Army Les Brownlee." *Committee on Oversight and Reform.* May 29, 2003. http://webharvest.gov/congress110th/20081125183239/http://oversight.house.gov/documents/20040625112555-72751.pdf (accessed June 15, 2008).

—. *The Waxman Report.* New York: Twelve, 2009.

Wayne, Leslie. "Pentagon Brass and Military Contractors' Gold." *New York Times.* April 29, 2004. http://www.nytimes.com/2004/06/29/business/pentagon-brass-and-military-contractors-gold.html (accessed May 3, 2011).

Webb, James. "Remarks on PResidential Signing Statement." *Congressional Record,* January 29, 2008.

Wedel, Janine R. "The Shadow Army." In *Lessons From Iraq,* by Miriam and William D. Hartung Pemberton, 116-123. Boulder: Paradigm Publishers, 2008.

Weidenbaum, Murray. *Small Wars, Big Defense.* New York: Oxford University Press, 1992.

Weston, Jana L. "ACO Change Letter (ACL) 07-139-D9-005; Operation and Maintenance for Radwaniyah Palace." Rock Island, IL: US Army, January 23, 2007.

Williams, Charlie E. Jr. "Statement." *Commission on Wartime Contracting.* Washington: Commission on wartime Contracting, 2008. 8.

Wilson, David. "Statement of David Wilson Former KBR Convoy Commander in Iraq." *Committee on Oversight and Government Reform Chronology of Committee Work.* June 13, 2004. http://webharvest.gov/congress110th/20081125182334/http://oversight.house.gov/documents/20040623112742-66875.pdf (accessed May 13, 2011).

Wilson, Woodrow. *Congressional Government.* New York, 1913.

Zamparelli, Colonel Stephen J. USAF. *Contractors on the Battlefield: What Have We Signed Up For?* Maxwell Air Force Base, AL: Air War College, 1999.

INDEX